Workfare
or Fair Work

Nancy E. Rose

— Workfare
or Fair Work

women, welfare,
and government work programs

RUTGERS UNIVERSITY PRESS

New Brunswick, New Jersey

Library of Congress Cataloging-in-Publication Data

Rose, Nancy Ellen.
    Workfare or fair work : women, welfare, and government work
programs / Nancy E. Rose.
      p.   cm.
    Includes bibliographical references and index.
    ISBN 0-8135-2232-3 (cloth : alk. paper)
    ISBN 0-8135-2233-1 (pbk. : alk. paper)
    1. Women—Employment—United States—History—20th century.
2. Welfare recipients—Employment—United States—History—20th
century.   3. Public service employment—United States—History—20th
century.   4. Job creation—United States—History—20th century.
5. Occupational training for women—United States—History—20th
century.   6. Welfare recipients—Employment—Law and legislation—
—United States.   I. Title.
HD6095.R73   1995
331.4'0973—dc20   95-8589
                                              CIP

British Cataloging-in-Publication information available

Published by Rutgers University Press, New Brunswick, New Jersey
Manufactured in the United States of America

Dedicated to my extended family web,
especially the memory of my brother-in-law,
Bruce Priebe (1951–1994),
who died long before
it was time for him to go

Contents

Preface and Acknowledgments

This book had its genesis in the 1970s when I lived in Durham, North Carolina. Working for a few years as a social worker, I became convinced that the welfare system needed to be redesigned in ways that accorded people more dignity. Becoming involved in political work through the women's movement, I began to understand how women's work is trivialized in our society. And, later, finding out about the massive government work programs in the 1930s led to the realization that there was an alternative to mandatory workfare.

My thinking on this subject has been influenced by many people. The women's groups I was involved in were critical to my political development. The examples set by Sara Evans and Sandra Morgen, as well as their encouragement that I study political economy, was very important at that time. Sara's review of an article several years ago that dealt with some of the ideas in this book was a great delight, allowing us to work together again. And Samuel Bowles's influence on my ideas during formative years in graduate school will always stay with me.

Discussions over the past seven years with Mimi Abramovitz have been especially critical in helping shape the theory and clarify important issues. Her enthusiasm for my work will always be appreciated. Discussions with Mary Jo Hetzel, especially during the past two years, helped strengthen political points and more clearly explain the programs of the 1970s. Nancy Naples shared her knowledge and interviews on the community action agencies and New Careers program in the 1960s, as well as detailed readings of congressional testimony on the 1988 welfare reform legislation. And discussions with Patty Domingues were extremely helpful in clarifying issues in the introductory and concluding portions of the book.

Several people supplied me with information. William R. Gulley, Jr., archivist at the Walter Reuther Library at Wayne State University, sent memos from the Association of Federal, State, County, and Municipal Employees (AFSCME) regarding their concerns about the Comprehensive Employment and Training Act (CETA) program. Jacqueline Finkel, research fellow at the Center for Law and Social Policy (CLASP) in Washington, D.C., got together a range of materials, from current unpublished data on welfare to information about various proposals. Memoranda from Casey McKeever at the Western Center on Law and Poverty provided an invaluable source of information about social welfare policy in California. And Beth Stroud, from Monthly Review Press, found the evocative cover photo.

Research at the National Archives was facilitated by grants from the National Endowment for the Humanities and from California State University, San Bernardino. These grants allowed me several weeks to pour over materials collected during the 1930s work programs.

The people at Rutgers University Press have been helpful and encouraging. Marlie Wasserman's suggestions when I first proposed the book several years ago were important in making it more historically balanced. Karen Reeds provided ongoing support and guidance after she became editor. And Willa Speiser's careful editing helped clarify issues and concepts while remaining true to the spirit of the book.

Others have had ongoing influence on my work. Discussions about theory and ideology over the past decade with Mayo Toruño have been stimulating and enlightening. Several people were kind enough to share their stories with me: Chani Beeman, Sue Hamlin, Portia Craven, Lori Richard, Nora Farabaugh, Lupe Rosas, and Elizabeth Briano all participated in one of the programs and talked avidly about their experiences. The women I've worked with in the welfare rights movement have also been influential—from the Massachusetts Coalition for Basic Human Needs, who I first met in 1979 on a trip to Cuba, to the Women's Economic Agenda Project in California. My students at California State University, San Bernardino, especially the welfare mothers returning to school, have been a continual source of inspiration. And thanks to Patty for her love, support, and back rubs.

My family has been encouraging and supportive, eagerly anticipating the book's completion. The book is dedicated to them—to my entire, very nontraditional, extended family web—mother, father, sister, brother, several sisters-in-law, significant others, and the children: Joshua, Aarin, Sam; my sons, Jesse and Zachary; and those yet to come.

Programs, Agencies, Acts, and Organizations

The following initials are used in the text to refer to various programs, agencies, acts, and organizations. The dates of enactment are indicated in parentheses.

AAA Agricultural Adjustment Act (1933)

ABE adult basic education

ADC Aid to Dependent Children (1935)

AFDC Aid to Families with Dependent Children (1962)

AFDC-UP Aid to Families with Dependent Children—Unemployed Parent

AFSCME American Federation of State, County, and Municipal Employees

AOP Apprenticeship Outreach Program (1964)

ARA Area Redevelopment Act (1961)

ASU area of substantial unemployment

BPA Bureau of Public Assistance

CAP Community Action Program (1964)

CCC Civilian Conservation Corps (1933)

CEP Concentrated Employment Program (1967)

CETA Comprehensive Employment and Training Administration (1973)

CT classroom training

CWA Civil Works Administration (1933)

CWEP Community Work Experience Program (1972)

CWT Community Work and Training program (1962)

DH displaced homemaker

DPSS Department of Public Social Services (California)

E&T Employment and Training

EITC Earned Income Tax Credit

ESL English as a second language

ET Choices Employment and Training Choices (Massachusetts) (1983)

FAP Family Assistance Plan (proposed 1969)

FERA Federal Emergency Relief Administration (1933)

FRED Fraud Early Detection Program (1988)

FSA Family Support Act (1988)

GA General Assistance

GAIN Greater Avenues for Independence (California) (1985)

GED General Equivalency Degree (high school)

HIRE Help through Industry Retraining and Employment (1977)

JOBS Job Opportunities in the Business Sector (1968)

JOBS Job Opportunities and Basic Skills Training (1988)

JTPA Job Training Partnership Act (1982)

MDRC Manpower Demonstration Research Corporation

MDTA Manpower Development and Training Administration (1962)

MFY Mobilization for Youth (1961)

NAB National Alliance for Business

NIRA National Industrial Recovery Act (1933)

NRA National Recovery Administration (1933)

NRPB National Resources Planning Board (1933)

NTO   nontraditional occupation

NWRO   National Welfare Rights Organization (1966)

NYA   National Youth Administration (1935)

NYC   Neighborhood Youth Corps (1964)

OEO   Office of Economic Opportunity (1964)

OIC   Opportunities Industrialization Centers (1964)

OJT   on-the-job training

PBJI   Program for Better Jobs and Income (proposed 1977)

PEP   Public Employment Program (1971)

PIC   Private Industry Council

PRA   Personal Responsibility Act (proposed 1995)

PREP   Pre-Employment Program

PS   Performance Standard

PSC   Public Service Careers (1970, based on New Careers, which existed 1966–1970)

PSE   Public Service Employment (1973)

PSIP   Private Sector Initiative Program (1978)

PWA   Public Works Administration (1933)

SDA   Service Delivery Area

SIP   Self-Initiated Program

SSI   Supplemental Security Income (1972)

SSP   Supplemental Security Program

STIP   Skills Training Improvement Program (1977)

SWD   Supported Work Demonstration program (1977)

TJTC   Targeted Jobs Tax Credit

UI   unemployment insurance (also called unemployment compensation)

WET   Work Experience and Training program (1964)

WIC   Nutritional supplements for women, infants, and children

WIN   Work Incentive Program (1967)

WNW   Work Not Welfare (Wisconsin) (1994)

WPA   Works Progress Administration (1935, in 1939 the name was changed to Work Projects Administration)

WRE   work-related expense

WSP   Work Supplementation Program (1983)

YEDPA   Youth Employment and Demonstration Projects Act (1977)

Workfare
or Fair Work

Introduction

"California GAIN Program Requires Welfare Mothers to Work." "ET Choices in Massachusetts Provides Work and Training for AFDC Recipients." "President Clinton Vows to 'End Welfare as We Know It' by Terminating AFDC Payments after Two Years on the Rolls." "Newt Gingrich Proposes Personal Responsibility Act to End 'Welfare Dependency' as Part of His Contract With America." Headlines such as these were common in the 1980s and early 1990s as an array of programs forced poor women to work outside their homes. Drawing on negative stereotypes of recipients of Aid to Families with Dependent Children (AFDC), commonly known as welfare, and justified by arguments that "welfare dependency" should be replaced by the "independence" that comes from working for wages, the federal government gave individual states wide discretion in setting up welfare-to-work programs. Ignoring the value of their caretaking work in the home, Work Incentive (WIN) demonstration programs in the 1980s and Job Opportunities and Basic Skills (JOBS) programs in the 1990s required welfare recipients considered employable to perform additional work in order to remain eligible for welfare.

These mandatory work programs exacerbated the growing impoverishment of women. Providing little education and training that would prepare women for jobs paying high enough wages to get them not only off welfare but also out of poverty, welfare recipients were channeled instead into low-wage labor markets. And if they failed to find a job they were usually required to work off their welfare payments in Community Work Experience Programs (CWEPs), more commonly known as workfare. Although the term "workfare" technically applies only to programs in which recipients work outside the home in exchange for welfare payments, it will be used in this study as it is in common parlance, to refer to the range of mandatory, punitive work programs.

Attacks on poor women intensified further during the late 1980s and early 1990s. Recipients of AFDC, as well as other assistance programs, who received overpayments were targets of well-publicized prosecutions for "welfare fraud." State budget deficits served as a rationale for cutting welfare payments, which were also justified as a "work incentive." And, viewing "welfare dependency" as a disease that could be cured by learning to make responsible decisions, many states implemented programs designed to modify behaviors. These included "learnfare," which docks a family's welfare check if students have too many unexcused absences from school, "healthfare," which cuts payments for recipients who fail to immunize their children properly, "family caps," which do not increase payments for children born to women already receiving AFDC, and "wedfare," which disregards the income of stepparents and thereby provides bonuses to women who marry a man other than the father of their child(ren). As those involved in welfare rights organizing explained, the War on Poverty of the 1960s became the "war on the poor" in the 1980s and 1990s.

How did we get to the point where poor women are punished for the economic and social ills of the United States? Where false stereotypes of "undeserving" welfare mothers serve as a lightning rod for sexist and racist ideology? Where women are arrested for the "crime" of trying to supplement their insufficient welfare payments in order to provide food, clothing, and shelter for their family? Where paternalistic policies ignore the structural causes of poverty and treat adults like misbehaving children? And where women face the possibility of removal from the rolls if they have received welfare for two years?

The current historical juncture, in early 1995, is a difficult and despairing time to finish writing a book about welfare and government work programs. Welfare reform is in a state of flux, as the punitive policies initiated in 1981 under President Reagan and augmented during the late 1980s and early 1990s have been followed by draconian proposals that would have been unimaginable to most people a few years ago. The Personal Responsibility Act, introduced in Congress in February 1995, aims to turn back the clock to an era before the advent of federal support for welfare and end the entitlement status of AFDC and other social welfare programs. They would be dramatically shrunk through severe restrictions on eligibility, deep cuts in appropriations, and by collapsing most programs into a few block grants to be turned over to the states. Although the precise outcome is not known at this time, the evisceration of welfare along these lines seems likely in the near future.

This makes it even more important to remember that the U.S. has another tradition as well. In contrast to punitive policies that blame the poor for their poverty and abdicate societal responsibility for protecting children, there are measures rooted in an understanding of the structural causes of poverty and the value of unpaid labor in the home. And in contrast to mandatory workfare there are fair work programs—public employment job creation and related education and training programs—that respect the dignity of the individual, have voluntary participation, base payments on labor market wages, and often develop innovative projects.

In fact, fair work programs have a long history in the U.S. Beginning with public works projects set up by cities during recessions and depressions from the late 1700s through the early 1930s, they reached their peak in the massive programs of the Great Depression—the Federal Emergency Relief Administration (FERA), Civil Works Administration (CWA), and Works Progress Administration (WPA). Although they ended as World War II brought the nation out of the depression, a large-scale, permanent job creation program was advocated in the early 1940s by an executive-level federal commission, the National Resources Planning Board. Through the 1950s the focus of fair work shifted to training programs, which were recommended by manpower institutes such as the National Manpower Council. The 1960s saw their return—in the 1962 Manpower Development and Training Administration (MDTA) and, after 1964, in the War on Poverty programs, which provided education, training, work experience, and support services on a voluntary basis. Job creation programs similar to those of the 1930s returned in the 1970s through the Public Employment Program (PEP) and the Public Service Employment (PSE); the latter was part of the Comprehensive Employment and Training Act (CETA). It was not until 1981 that public sector job creation programs disappeared from the policy mix.

There are fundamental differences between workfare and fair work programs. Workfare is mandatory for some relief recipients, fair work is voluntary. Workfare is developed for those considered undeserving, who are required to work in order to prove that they are not lazy; fair work is designed primarily for people seen as deserving, disproportionately white men who are normally expected to have jobs. Workfare is highly stigmatized, based on the view that relief recipients must be forced to work; fair work is founded on the assumption that its participants want to work. Workfare ignores the value of work in the home and requires participants to work for low pay or no pay, that is, for only their welfare payments; fair work programs base payments in some manner on local wages. Historically, workfare programs have been an almost continual component of the relief system; job creation programs have been developed during recessions and depressions, often spurred by protest accompanying increased unemployment. Although through the 1930s workfare targeted both women and men, since that time women have been the main focus of the programs; fair work programs have predominantly been aimed at men. And, most fundamentally, workfare supports the logic of production-for-profit, lowering wages by channeling the poor into low-wage labor markets. However, the very existence of job creation programs exposes a basic inequity in capitalist economic systems: that production based on capitalists' profits rarely corresponds to production based on people's needs, since jobs are not usually created for everyone who wants one.

As a result, the programs have been viewed very differently. Workfare has been politically popular and widely supported; in contrast, fair work has typically been castigated as inefficient and unnecessary make-work, a criticism captured during the 1930s in the epithet "boondoggle." It is telling that although workfare is rarely attacked as make-work, these negative assessments continue to characterize the job creation programs. In fact, jobs are also created through Community Work Experience Programs (CWEPs), as welfare recipients are required to work in community service positions. Yet although the business sector applauds CWEPs, it is highly critical of similar jobs created as part of fair work programs.

In fact, much of value has been done in job creation programs: millions of people have been put to work in a range of projects, including sewing clothing and mattresses, staffing education and health care programs, performing plays and creating public works of art, and building and repairing tens of thousands of public facilities and hundreds of thousands of miles of roads. These accomplishments are typically glossed over, however, and the programs are dismissed as impractical and unrealistic.

Yet fair work programs have been so constrained that in a sense they have been set up to "fail." In order to limit interference with the logic of production-for-profit, they have been subjected to contradictory regulations that left them vulnerable to criticism as inefficient and unnecessary make-work. Most important have been mandates to create as many jobs as possible with the allocated funds—but at the same time not to replace "normal government operations" or compete with private enterprise. However, restrictions on "normal government operations" mean that work done through the programs is easily construed as unnecessary and make-work. And using a maximum of labor and minimum of machinery means that construction projects are clearly inefficient by industry standards.

These often repeated criticisms have been reflected in the temporary status of most of the programs. In fact, attempts were made to establish a permanent job creation program, but they never came to fruition. While Employment Assurance, which would have provided a government-created job after people exhausted their unemployment compensation, was included in the initial draft of the 1935 Social Security Act, it was killed during committee deliberations. Although the National Resources Planning Board proposed a permanent Work Administration to continue the 1930s programs as part of a "new bill of rights," its ideas were never even developed into legislation. And the proposed 1945 Full Employment Bill, which could have provided an opening for a federal job-creation program, was transformed into the watered down Employment Act of 1946. A similar fate was met by the Humphrey-Hawkins Bill in the 1970s, as the original mandate that everyone had the right to a decent job was diluted into a call for "balanced growth" in which low inflation took precedence over full employment. In light of these restrictions in both regulations and status, it is even more telling that to this day job creation programs are characterized by negative evaluations, while their accomplishments are often forgotten. Thus, a reevaluation is sorely needed.

It is important to be clear, however, that although the fair work programs have much to commend them, they have had serious limitations. There are two main types of problems. First, the programs have never created enough jobs. Even during the 1930s they provided work for no more than one-third of the unemployed. Viewed from another angle, at their height in January 1934, they put 4.4 million people to work—more than at any other time in U.S. history—showing that the government has the *capacity* to create jobs for millions of people.

The other major problem with fair work programs has been their incorporation of discrimination based on gender, race, and class. Whereas since the 1930s the workfare programs have focused mainly on women, the fair work programs have been intended primarily for men. Furthermore, women of color have been overrepresented (in relation to their proportion of the total population) in the workfare programs and underrepresented in fair work. These inequities were particularly blatant in the 1930s, when approximately three-fourths of the participants were white males. Class-based discrimination was also clear, as so-called white-collar workers received special treatment.

The focus on men in fair work programs has been bolstered by the historical view of work as fundamentally men's responsibility. Thus the 1960s title, "manpower programs," was no aberration: these programs were rooted in policies intended to provide work experience and training primarily for men. By the early 1970s, the women's movement led to an increased awareness of the need to address issues concerning women. One result was a change in the name to the gender-neutral "employment and training programs." Although the focus remained primarily on men, women's participation (as a percentage of those in the programs) increased throughout the 1970s and experimental training programs for women were implemented, illustrating the potential of these programs in meeting women's needs vis-à-vis education, training, and employment. And while it seems obvious that women would be the primary target of workfare programs since the 1930s because they have been the main recipients of welfare, steadily increasing numbers of women in the labor force belie the traditional rationale justifying the focus on men in the fair work programs. Furthermore, although men have been overrepresented in the workfare programs in the 1980s and 1990s in relation to their small percentage of the AFDC population, women have been the focus of the debate. In fact, the rhetoric has consistently stressed the supposed unworthiness of welfare mothers, while scant attention has been paid to AFDC fathers. Instead, discussions of fathers focus on "deadbeat dads" who should be paying child support.

Even more fundamentally, neither fair work nor workfare programs have thus far taken into consideration unpaid labor in the home. Women's caretaking work—for children and, increasingly, for elder parents—represents a tremendous amount of socially necessary labor. If this work were recognized as "real work," it would be clear that AFDC recipients are already working, and the rationale for forcing them into wage-labor would evaporate.

Workfare or Fair Work explores the history of women in welfare and government work programs, paying special attention throughout to the situation of women of color. Chapter 1 develops the conceptual framework that underlies the examination of women, welfare, and government work programs, incorporating analyses of gender, race, and the logic of capitalist production-for-profit that illuminate the nature and contradictions of welfare and government work programs. In the second half of the chapter, relief and government work programs before the 1930s are described in order to provide a background for the historical study.

The remaining chapters examine welfare and government work programs in each of the decades from the 1930s through the 1990s, with the 1940s and 1950s discussed in a single chapter. This division is not always precise; most importantly, there is a break between the World War II years of the early 1940s and the postwar period. Yet, with this exception, it actually is relatively easy to characterize each decade: the most innovative and extensive fair work programs in U.S. history during the 1930s; punitive welfare and workfare policies in the years following World War II through the 1950s; an explosion of welfare and fair work programs in the 1960s; the return of job creation programs in the 1970s; another era of reaction and workfare in the 1980s; and even more intense workfare and the revival of moralistic policies in the 1990s.

Each of these chapters begins with a description of the economy, the general social and political climate, and the social and economic status of women and people of color in order to provide the foundation for examining welfare policies and government work programs, and their impact on women and people of color. Segments on the job creation programs in the 1930s and the 1970s include discussions of policies regarding eligibility and target populations, how payments were determined, and content of the projects, as well as a reassessment of the programs. Finally, the Conclusion builds on progressive components of past programs to develop a set of policies designed to reverse the impoverishment of women.

Several lessons emerge from this history of women, welfare, and government work programs. First, the punitive nature of the 1980s and 1990s workfare programs is even more clearly exposed when they are juxtaposed with earlier fair work programs. This can help counter the generally accepted view that welfare recipients will work outside the home only if they are forced to do so, a perspective that helped justify programs forcing poor women into low-wage jobs without the necessary supports. Who can have peace of mind if her children are not in a safe child-care situation? Does it make sense to work for wages and thereby give up health insurance in the form of Medicaid? In fact, the economically irrational situation often occurs in which women are left with less money from wage-labor—after paying taxes, health insurance, and child-care costs—than they receive on welfare.

Second, this history shows the impetus for changes in policies. Protest by the unemployed in the 1930s and the poor in the 1960s and 1970s shows that political pressure can bring about more progressive policies. It also becomes clear that these programs and policies were implemented through active intervention by the federal government. In contrast, periods of reaction were marked by a return to "state's rights" and increased control of welfare and work program policy by individual states.

Finally, this history can be used to help advocate for the reinstatement of large-scale fair work programs. The job creation and employment and training programs of the 1930s, 1960s, and 1970s offer important alternatives to the onslaught of mandatory and punitive programs in the 1940s and 1950s, and again in the 1980s and 1990s. The range of projects and sheer size of the 1930s programs shows that government is indeed capable of creating socially useful work for millions of people, and the 1960s and 1970s provide examples of education and training programs that did a better job of meeting people's needs, especially for women and people of color, than did the limited programs of this nature in the 1980s and 1990s.

Critically evaluating the entire spectrum of work programs can inform responses to charges of inefficiency and make-work that inevitably surface whenever job creation is mentioned. It becomes clear that constraints imposed on the programs followed from the logic of production-for-profit, and that the often contradictory regulations led to projects that were both inefficient when compared to private industry and easily construed as unnecessary make-work. In addition, the history shows the importance of job creation programs in both putting people to work and providing needed services and other projects. And the 1930s programs illustrate the percolator effect of getting money into the hands of people who will quickly spend it, thereby stimulating the economy through increased demand for goods and services. This offers a different path from the supply-side policies of the 1980s and 1990s that increased income and wealth for the rich at the expense of everyone else, and exacerbated economic hard times. It becomes clear that fair work is a real alternative to workfare.

1

Women, Welfare, and Government Work Programs

Government work programs have been a basic part of the U.S. welfare state since the 1600s. Workfare, which ignores unpaid caretaking work in the home and requires additional labor in order to maintain eligibility for relief, has been most common, regularly complementing punitive relief policies. In contrast, recessions and depressions since at least the late 1700s have triggered the development of fair work programs, as the government created jobs for some of the unemployed. Although most government work programs through the 1960s were tied to relief, all programs are characterized by this fundamental difference between workfare as punishment for the "undeserving" poor and fair work as job creation and training for the "deserving" unemployed who would normally have jobs. In large part because work for wages has traditionally been seen as men's responsibility, the voluntary job creation programs focused on men, primarily white men. On the other hand, although workfare programs through the 1930s included both women and men, since that time women, disproportionately women of color, have made up the majority of welfare recipients and consequently been the main target of the programs.[1]

The Conceptual Framework

The conceptual framework of this book has three main components. Reflecting the importance of gender, race, and class, it incorporates a feminist analysis of social welfare policy, an analysis of race in social welfare policy, and an analysis grounded in radical political economy in order to examine social welfare policy in terms of the logic of capitalism. These components function as "lenses"—overlapping sets of dynamics that need to be looked through simultaneously in order to understand the treatment of women and people of color vis-à-vis welfare and work programs.[2] Since cogent analyses of gender and race have been developed by others and consequently are only briefly described here, most of the discussion involves how the logic of capitalist production-for-profit has affected welfare, and, especially, government work programs. Particularly important are the contradictions manifested in fair work programs and the resultant policies that have seriously constrained them.

Gender

A feminist analysis of social welfare policy has been developed most articulately by Mimi Abramovitz.[3] This helps explain the "impoverishment of women," a more accurate term than the "feminization of poverty," since women have always been relatively poorer than men.[4] Abramovitz posits that welfare policy has been shaped by both a work ethic and a family ethic. The work ethic, which concerns capitalism and affects both women and men, leads to setting welfare payments below the amount that could be earned through wage labor in order both to avoid interfering with low-wage labor markets and to maintain a rational economic incentive to choose wage labor instead of relief.

The family ethic, on the other hand, concerns only women and deals with the maintenance of patriarchy. Compliance involves adhering to the societal norm of marrying men who earn enough money so that women can remain in the home performing unpaid labor. Women who conform to the family ethic and become poor "through no fault of their own" are considered deserving poor and have been treated relatively well by the social welfare system. Through the early 1900s they were primarily white, native-born, middle-class gilt-edged widows who received relief while continuing to live in their communities. The fact that this relief was seen as a replacement for their deceased husband's wages became even clearer in 1939 when widows became eligible for social security survivor's benefits.[5]

Although the amounts received by the "deserving poor" have been low, and indeed usually left them in poverty, this segment of the population has been accorded better treatment than "undeserving poor" women who have not conformed to societal norms and whose poverty has been caused by divorce, desertion, single motherhood, or failure of their husbands to provide sufficient income. Through the early 1900s these women were often required to perform some type of work to prove they were not "lazy" and were worthy of aid. Since the Social Security Act was passed in 1935, "undeserving poor" women with dependent children have been eligible for Aid to Families with Dependent Children (AFDC), originally enacted as Aid to Dependent Children (ADC).[6] Required to continually certify and recertify their eligibility for welfare by showing that they have insufficient income and resources, they have often been forced into workfare programs. It is important to note that although men have also been subjected to mandatory work programs, in the past few decades women have been the main focus of the debates and discussions.

Even though "deserving poor" women have generally received higher payments in a less stigmatized manner than "undeserving poor" women, relief has never been designed to end poverty for women. Instead, it has been based on a male pauper model, as a job has been seen as the only real cure for poverty. And the job is assumed to pay "breadwinner"—that is, male—wages. However, a sizable female/male wage gap has persisted throughout the 1900s, as women's median wages have ranged between 58 and 72 percent of men's median wage. Thus, Women have a better chance of gaining access to sufficient wage-income by living with a man. Since the 1960s, these ideas have provided the basis for claims that the cure for poverty among African-Americans lies in men's employment, as this would not only allow men to earn money but would also encourage "family formation" and help stem the rise of poor black female-headed families.[7]

Race

The second component of the conceptual framework concerns race and the importance of racial discrimination for the economy and for social welfare policy. Ever since slaves were brought to colonial America in the 1600s, people of color have performed the most strenuous and least desirable work under the most hazardous conditions.[8] Institutionalized violence, rationalized by a paternalistic ideology, supported the slave system in which African-Americans were forced to work for their owners in exchange for minimal food, clothing, and shelter.[9] Government relief programs were contraindicated by slavery, and virtually no such programs existed in the antebellum South, although a private, community-based system of care was developed.[10] After the Civil War, sharecropping kept many African-Americans tied to the land, while some blacks joined other people of color, primarily Mexican-Americans and Native American Indians, in predominantly low-wage jobs at the bottom of the economic ladder. In order to maintain a sufficient supply of people of color in low-wage labor markets, racial discrimination has been incorporated into social welfare policy as people of color have typically been treated as "undeserving poor" and consequently received the most meager and stigmatized relief.

Class, Capitalism, and the Logic of Production-For-Profit

The third component of the analysis concerns class, reflecting the dynamics of capitalism. At issue is the logic of production-for-profit and the support or contradictions engendered by social welfare and government work programs. This is important because in capitalist economic systems, production and investment are determined primarily by the rates of profit that capitalists (owners of the means of production) expect to accrue from these activities. If expected rates of profit are less than alternative uses of their money, most importantly financial speculation, then production and investment will be cut and the economy will stagnate. In essence, since capitalists own the marbles they can choose what to do with them.

As a result, government policies are developed in ways that try to entice capitalists to expand investment and production—or at least not interfere with it. A critical issue is maintaining a sufficient supply of workers. However, a sufficient supply actually means more workers than jobs available. Low unemployment can be a problem for capitalists not only because of their immediate needs for workers to fill positions but also because it can lead to higher wages for those who are already employed. When unemployment is low, workers cannot readily be replaced and jobs are more secure, making it easier to demand higher wages and better working conditions. The opposite holds as well. When unemployment is high, jobs are less secure; workers can more easily be replaced, making them more susceptible to attempts to cut wages and increase the intensity of work.

This dynamic underlies three types of policies designed to ensure that private-sector jobs remain preferable to relief. First, payments are generally set at levels lower than the amount that could be earned through wage labor, both for work relief (relief in exchange for work outside the home) and for direct relief (relief without additional work required). Second, relief for the "undeserving poor" is so stigmatized that most people try to avoid it, depending instead on wage labor, and, for women, marriage. Third, workfare programs are developed to channel the poor into low-wage labor markets, thereby increasing the supply of low-wage labor and helping keep wages down.

However, protest sometimes leads government officials to liberalize relief, increasing the level of payments and adding people to the rolls, as well as developing less stigmatizing work programs. This expansionary dynamic was described by Frances Fox Piven and Richard A. Cloward in their classic book, *Regulating the Poor: The Functions of Public Welfare,* in which they argued that welfare is broadened in response to protest by the unemployed, and then restricted when the pressure dies down.[11] This can clearly be seen in welfare and government work programs since the 1930s: organizing in the 1930s and in the 1960s and 1970s led federal officials to expand the welfare system and develop fair work programs, while the decline of protest in the 1940s and 1950s and in the 1980s and 1990s paved the way for restrictions in welfare and the resurgence of workfare.

Another impetus for fair work programs has been concern about the effects of prolonged unemployment on male heads of household. Government officials and social pundits have sometimes worried that widespread unemployment could undermine men's role as the family breadwinner, leading to social dysfunction. It could also erode people's faith in the system, contributing to an increase in protest. As a result, during recessions and depressions from the late 1700s through the early 1930s, many local governments created jobs in public works and government services for some of the unemployed, mostly white men. By the 1960s, urban ghetto riots extended this concern to African-American men, and they became the focus of the War on Poverty programs.

Fair work programs have either been connected to relief, and therefore also work relief, or separated from it. Work relief as fair work includes the public works projects set up by local governments through the early 1930s, as well as the New Deal programs—the Federal Emergency Relief Administration (FERA), the Civil Works Administration (CWA), and the Works Progress Administration (WPA); relief eligibility was required for most people before they were given work through these programs. However, an important exception was made in the CWA, which was quickly set up during the winter of 1933–1934, as two million people were added to the work program rolls without first qualifying for relief.

By the 1960s fair work was separated from relief, which was then called welfare. The Manpower Development and Training Administration (MDTA) was passed in 1962 to provide training for primarily white, industrial workers, who lost their jobs as a result of automation. While the urban poor were the main focus of the War on Poverty programs, as well as the MDTA by the mid-1960s, certification for welfare was not a prerequisite for participation. And although welfare recipients were sometimes targeted in the job creation programs revived in the 1970s, the Public Employment Program (PEP) from 1971 through 1973, and the Public Service Employment (PSE) program that was part of the Comprehensive Employment and Training Act (CETA) from 1974 through 1981, welfare eligibility was not a general requirement.

In contrast, workfare programs have always been connected to relief, and include both formal and informal mechanisms. Informal work requirements involve setting such low levels of relief that the poor are forced into low-wage labor markets to either supplement relief or provide their sole income. In addition, when large supplies of low-wage labor are needed, the relief rolls are sometimes closed altogether. This was common as late as the 1960s in rural areas during planting and harvesting times; the primary targets of exclusion were people of color, especially African-Americans in the South after the Civil War and Mexican-Americans in the Southwest.[12] The practice of setting low relief payments to force the poor into low-wage work reappeared in the 1980s, as cuts in inflation-adjusted welfare payments helped channel poor women into low-wage labor markets.

Formal workfare programs also have a long history. Beginning with workhouses and poor farms in the 1600s and extending through the Work Incentive (WIN) Program in the late 1960s and 1970s, they proliferated during the 1980s in WIN demonstration programs (alternatives to WIN), Community Work Experience Programs (CWEPs), and, after 1988, Job Opportunities and Basic Skills (JOBS) programs. All of the formal programs require recipients to work in order to continue receiving relief. The only work considered valid in this context is paid labor outside the home; unpaid labor in the home is disregarded. Although some of the workfare programs since the 1960s also provided education and training, especially since the early 1980s training has usually been limited and aimed at immediate placement in low-wage jobs, primarily in services, rather than at developing skills leading to jobs paying wages above the poverty line.[13]

Workfare programs are congruent with the logic of production-for-profit. In fact, they lower wage costs and boost profits in the short run by channeling the poor into low-wage labor markets, where the increased supply of labor makes it more difficult for workers to demand higher wages and better working conditions. Expanding the numbers of people available for low-wage jobs has been done directly since the 1960s through WIN, WIN demonstration, and JOBS programs. There has also been an indirect effect since the beginning of the work-test in the 1600s, as workfare programs discourage eligible people from applying for relief, causing them to depend instead on wage labor and/or marriage.

The Contradictions of Job Creation Programs

In contrast, fair work programs, especially public employment job creation, have proven problematic. Most fundamentally, job creation programs bring to light the failure of capitalist economic systems to provide enough jobs, thereby demonstrating that basing production on capitalists' profits results in fewer jobs than if it were based on people's needs. Furthermore, since the programs draw in participants by offering sufficiently high wages and often interesting work, they can provide alternatives to jobs obtained through the labor market, and the projects themselves can pose alternatives to capitalist logic.

As a result, three types of regulations have been developed to differentiate job creation from work available through the labor market. The first involves the level of payments, which have been determined by often complex methods intended to keep them below market wages, but high enough to entice participation. The second ensures that the jobs are temporary, and therefore insecure, to be used only until a "regular" job is obtained, and involves limitations on the length of time in the program as well as requirements to accept private-sector jobs. The third set of policies has proven most problematic, dealing with the actual work allowed in the programs. Most important have been prohibitions against the work programs engaging in "normal government operations" or competing with the private sector, as well as mandates to create as many jobs as possible by using a maximum amount of labor and a minimum amount of capital goods (plant and equipment). These regulations have their own logic, but they have left the programs open to criticisms of inefficient and unnecessary make-work.

It is reasonable to require projects to be useful. The antithesis is the make-work of the pre-1930s work-tests in which people dug ditches or moved piles of rocks simply to prove they were not lazy. Part of the problem concerns the interpretation of what is considered useful; many of the complaints about make-work have been directed at services. Among the primary targets, especially in the 1930s, were maintenance projects, such as raking leaves in parks and collecting garbage. Yet maintenance is analogous to housework—very necessary and only noticed when it is not done. Even though maintenance was prohibited after April 1934, these charges continued, and, in fact, the programs are still sometimes characterized as "leaf-raking." Other service projects, from conducting surveys of community needs to staging musical performances, were also criticized as unnecessary. Indeed, because the 1970s programs were restricted to services, they were even more vulnerable to these criticisms.

However, these charges reflect a narrow view of what is deemed appropriate government activity. Why are programs that enhance people's lives—from the arts projects of the 1930s to the recreation projects of the 1970s—so easily construed as unnecessary, while building prisons and bailing out failed financial institutions is rarely questioned?

The requirement to devise work that would not be carried out as part of normal government operations is also sensible, since the object of the programs is to create jobs for the unemployed. Obviously, if the work would be done by someone hired through the labor market, it should not be carried out through the work programs. Despite this mandate, the depletion of tax revenues at the local and state levels during the 1930s meant that a great deal of work that would normally be done by the government—from operating schools in rural areas to repairing roads to building public facilities—was done instead through the work programs. And although PEP and CETA programs were routinely criticized for substituting their workers for "normal government workers," a careful multiyear study of PSE found that rates of substitution were only 11 to 18 percent.[14] Yet the mere fact that the work is required to be outside the usual scope of government activity means that it is easily perceived as unnecessary and therefore readily categorized as make-work.

Job creation programs have also been plagued by charges of inefficiency. In the 1930s these followed naturally from mandates to use maximum amounts of labor and minimum amounts of machinery—that is, to *make* work by creating as many jobs as possible. For example, roads were built using mostly hand tools, such as picks and shovels, and relatively little grading and paving equipment. Consequently, these projects were clearly inefficient when compared to the more capital-intensive methods normally used in the private sector. Efficiency could have been increased if some project workers made machinery that was then used in other projects, but this would have elicited even more intense objections and was never tried.

In addition to a relative lack of machinery, criticisms of inefficiency were exacerbated by policies that led to frequent turnover of workers and short work shifts. Short work shifts were a problem in the 1930s for many skilled laborers whose higher wage rates meant that they worked relatively few hours, often two or three days a week, causing a lack of continuity on the projects as different people worked on different days. And frequent turnover, which characterized both the 1930s and 1970s programs, followed from limits on the amount of time people could spend in the programs. The temporary and insecure nature of job creation positions was intended to push workers into private sector jobs, but meant that much time was spent adjusting to new workers.

Yet the whole concept of efficiency warrants closer examination. Those embedded in the logic of capitalism tend to believe that production can be efficient only if it is based on competition for profits. If not, unwise—that is, unprofitable—decisions are made. Since work program projects are not based on profits, but on people's needs, then by definition they cannot possibly be efficient.

Further, the definition of efficiency is often misunderstood. In economists' terms, a production process is more efficient if the same quantity of goods and services can be produced using fewer inputs of capital goods, labor, and/or materials. Capital goods can be reduced by developing machines that are less expensive and/or do the job faster (for example, replacing mainframe computers with desktop models that have the same capacity). Materials can be reduced by eliminating waste in production processes.

Most important for evaluating the work programs, labor can be reduced either by replacing people with machines or by increasing the intensity of work (for example, using incentives such as pay raises and promotions, or threats of unemployment, to prod people into doing more work in the same amount of time). Neither method is appropriate for work programs, however. The first option, replacing workers with machines, is antithetical to the goal of creating as many jobs as possible with the allocated funds. This was especially clear in the 1930s mandate to use a maximum amount of labor and a minimum amount of capital goods. The second method could not be used either. It was not possible to increase the intensity of work, since this requires incentives such as the promise of higher wages or sanctions such as the threat of unemployment. Higher wages could not be offered, since payments were constrained to try to keep them below market wage rates in order to help ensure that people would accept private-sector jobs. Indeed, during both the 1930s and the 1970s, payments were determined by formulas based sometimes on need and more often on a person's skill level, as well as prevailing wages in the area. Furthermore, firing workers from job creation programs lacked the import that this has with regular jobs. Most fundamentally, job creation is designed to be temporary and insecure. This is evident in the time limitation regulations as well as the increases and decreases in the programs that resulted from economic and political pressures.

In the 1930s, one response to criticisms of inefficiency was to expand projects in which consumer goods were produced and then distributed to other people on relief or used in other relief projects or in public institutions. Yet these projects, known as production-for-use or production-for-use-and-distribution, were lambasted for competing with the private sector. Even though the goods remained outside normal market channels and were distributed only to people who had minimal resources after several years of the Depression, business owners complained that they detracted from sales of their products. However, the underlying problem was that production-for-use fundamentally contradicted production-for-profit, since it was clearly based on people's needs instead of capitalists' profits. As a result, some of these projects became targets of intense criticism and were severely restricted.

Relief and Government Work Programs Before the 1930s

Poverty has been endemic in colonial America and the United States since the 1600s.[15] Many immigrants, especially from the 1830s on, arrived destitute, with only their ability to work. Many others came as indentured servants, and African-Americans were brought to America against their will as slaves. As capitalism took hold in the early 1800s and mass-produced goods increasingly replaced goods produced by craftsmen, wage labor became more widespread. Periodic depressions and seasonal work in agriculture and construction generated high rates of unemployment, and illness and old age contributed to destitution. Private charity was limited, forcing many people to turn to public poor relief.

Principles of Early Relief

The system of relief set up in colonial America and continued in the United States after the American Revolution was modeled on British poor laws. These policies began to be developed as early as 1642 by officials in the Plymouth Colony, with Virginia following in 1646, Connecticut in 1673, and Massachusetts in 1692.[16] Although far less severe in the United States than in England, similar principles formed the basis of American relief.[17] All the principles were connected to formal and informal workfare programs, and were fundamentally designed to deter the "able-bodied poor" from going on relief and lead them to depend instead on wage labor. The first of these, local responsibility for relief, was eroded in the 1930s when the federal government took over some of the provision of relief, but the others continue to provide the basis for our welfare system to this day. Other principles include deterrence of the "able-bodied poor;" differentiating between the "deserving poor" and the "undeserving poor"; "less eligibility"; the "ideology of the dole"; the means test and the work-test. As they were developed into policies, these principles incorporated the family ethic, racial discrimination, and the logic of production-for-profit.

Settlement and Local Responsibility for Relief. A basic poor-law principle until the 1930s was local responsibility for relief. This meant that towns, cities, and counties provided relief for their own poor, and that nonresidents, sometimes called transients, received nothing. During colonial times nonresidents were usually "warned out"—told to leave town and return to their former place of residence in order to receive relief. In order to prevent potential paupers from becoming a charge on the resources of a town, newcomers were sometimes required to post a bond or otherwise prove that they would be economically productive.[18]

Women were not exempt from warning out. For instance, during 1657, Mary Percie, a destitute widow with a child, was warned out of Warwick, Rhode Island, and told to return to Providence. Another woman, Mrs. Hayman, who was then "great with child" and whose husband had left six months earlier to go to sea, was told to leave Providence and return to Boston in order to receive relief.[19] Married women could be warned out even though they were living with their families. From 1670 through 1672 selectmen of the town of Melton, Massachusetts, told several families that their married daughters, even one who was "neere the time of her deliuery," had to leave.[20]

As the eighteenth century progressed and industrial capitalism took hold, settlement laws became more complex and comprehensive. Establishing settlement typically involved living in a place for a specified period of time (ranging from less than six months to ten years) without needing relief, earning a certain amount of income or owning property above a minimum value, and establishing a record of paying taxes.[21] Consequently, a great deal of time and expense went into proving residency.[22] Local settlement laws were in effect during the Great Depression of the 1930s, compounding the problems of people who left their homes to search for work, and were finally declared unconstitutional in the 1960s.

Deterrence of the "Able-Bodied Poor." All the other principles of American relief have been designed to deter the "able-bodied" poor, that is, those considered able to work, from receiving relief. This has followed from the logic of the labor market—to try to ensure that wage labor would always remain preferable to relief. Especially as the United States was industrializing in the early nineteenth century, it was critical for capitalists to make certain that they had a sufficient supply of people willing to work for low wages under often hazardous working conditions.

Ensuring a sufficient supply of workers meant that relief should not become a realistic alternative to wage labor. Indeed, relief itself was periodically denounced for promoting "idleness," as some believed that providing any relief to the able-bodied would undercut the incentive to work for wages. This concern was expressed in the early 1800s by the overseers of the poor in Beverly, Massachusetts, who worried about the "industrious poor" who would be "discouraged by observing that bounty bestowed upon the idle, which they can only obtain by the sweat of their brow."[23] Underlying this belief was the assumption that jobs existed for everyone willing and able to work, a view that persisted in spite of the massive unemployment generated by severe periodic depressions and by the seasonal nature of agricultural and construction work, which greatly increased unemployment during the winter months.

The "Deserving Poor" and the "Undeserving Poor." While the able-bodied poor received only meager and stigmatized relief, or none at all, others were considered deserving. Although they were given very little and remained in poverty, they received more relief, and in a less humiliating manner, than those believed to be undeserving. Thus a great deal of effort went into differentiating between the able-bodied "undeserving poor," who were considered "idle and vicious," and the "deserving poor," who were seen as subjects of "misfortune, sickness, and adversity."[24] The latter category included widows, the aged, those who were infirm or sick, and children. As an influential 1821 Massachusetts report on the poor made clear, no one would hesitate to help these "impotent poor."[25]

Reflecting historical racial discrimination in social welfare policy, the "deserving poor" were almost exclusively white and native-born. Recent immigrants were usually considered undeserving, as were free blacks in the North.[26] Reflecting gender discrimination, the family ethic was manifested in the classification of women. Those who abided by the family ethic and became poor "through no fault of their own"—mostly white, native-born widows—were considered deserving. On the other hand, those who did not abide by societal norms—and were abandoned or never married—were classified as undeserving.

In reality, however, the lines between the "deserving poor" and the "undeserving poor" often became blurred. Particularly problematic was illness and temporary disability among the able-bodied. A person could be considered employable and undeserving one week, and disabled and therefore unemployable and deserving the next week. Furthermore, during periods of economic expansion, when the demand for labor increased, people who had previously been considered unemployable easily became employable. This was most clearly evidenced during World War II, when large numbers of married women with children and the disabled were brought into factories to produce war materiel and consumer goods.

"Less Eligibility." One way of keeping the able-bodied poor from receiving relief ways to implement policies that made relief less desirable than wage labor. This was most clearly articulated in England's 1834 Poor Law as the principle of "less eligibility": "The first and most essential of all conditions . . . is, that [the relief recipient's] situation on the whole shall not be made really or apparently so eligible [that is,

desirable] as the situation of the independent laborer of the lowest class."[27]

This principle was carried out, in part, by setting relief payments below the amount that could be earned through wage labor. Clearly, this made sense from the perspective of employers—who would want to work for wages if they could do better on relief?

"Ideology of the Dole." The principle of "less eligibility" was also reflected in policies designed to degrade relief recipients. Captured in the phrase "ideology of the dole," this involved making the poor feel so ashamed to receive relief that being on the dole became something to avoid if at all possible. Although the "deserving poor" were supposed to be distinguished from the "undeserving poor," and consequently receive better treatment, they often became targets as well. Thus, as Frances Fox Piven and Richard A. Cloward point out, the poor have been periodically subjected to "public rituals of degradation as 'paupers.' "[28] In the colonial era, relief recipients were sometimes required to wear a badge with the letter *P* on it, clearly identifying them as paupers.[29] In some colonies they were denied civil rights, such as the right to marry, and could be jailed, sold at auction, or indentured.[30] Continuing beyond colonial times was the practice of denying paupers the right to vote or hold office. Reflecting the ongoing punitive nature of relief, this practice persisted through the 1930s in fourteen states.[31]

Policies designed to humiliate the poor have also included requiring them to wait in public places in order to receive relief. Soup kitchens and bread lines have historically forced the poor to stand in the street waiting for often meager servings of food. Food stamps make their users quite visible as well. Indeed, the rationale for in-kind relief reflects both public degradation and a distrust of poor people's ability to make wise choices about cash expenditures.

The Means Test. Establishing eligibility for relief, a process known as the means-test, has rarely been easy. It requires applicants, both "deserving" and "undeserving" poor, to prove that they lack sufficient income and assets. Before the 1930s applicants also had to show that their relatives could not provide for them, as the family was always the first line of defense against poverty.

Means tests have changed over time. Pauper's oaths were required in some areas from colonial times through the 1930s. As Charity Organization Societies developed in the 1870s, "friendly visitors" went to the homes of the poor to determine their worthiness for relief. By the turn of the century the scientific charity movement had evolved into social casework and the early professionalization of social work. Means tests have also been performed by people in other institutions. From the 1600s through the 1930s, relief investigations were sometimes carried out by churches, and during depressions in the early 1900s unions often determined their members' eligibility for relief.[32] Although proving themselves destitute usually was a sufficient means test for the "deserving poor," the "undeserving" often faced another hurdle—the work-test.

The Work-test and Workfare. Work-tests are simply workfare programs: relief recipients are required to perform some type of work, other than taking care of their family in the home, to prove that they are not lazy and, indeed, deserve to receive relief. The importance of work-tests was explained at the 1892 National Conference of Charities and Corrections: "the only righteous and practical check on adult pauperism, the only check at once just and efficient [was] the compulsory imposition of labor on every pauper to whom God has given, in even the slightest degree, the laboring ability."[33] According to the New York Association for Improving the Condition of the Poor, those who would not work were believed to be "impoverished by their indolence and vices, for which they are responsible."[34] They were widely considered to deserve little or nothing.

Outdoor Relief, Indoor Relief, and Poorhouses

Until the 1930s, work-tests were often carried out through poorhouses, which the poor had to enter to receive food (in meager amounts) as well as shelter. Poorhouses were initially built during the 1700s in the larger towns such as Boston and New York.[35] As industrial capitalism took hold in the early 1800s and more and more goods were produced outside the home (as opposed to being produced in the home by women), unemployment increased, sometimes dramatically. In order to help discipline the unemployed to accept employment, additional poorhouses were built, especially in and near the emerging industrial cities.[36]

The early poorhouses were not as punitive as their 1800s counterparts. Thus both "deserving" and "undeserving" poor made use of the poorhouse, and one could often find the insane, the elderly, the infirm, and pauper children residing in them. In fact, many able-bodied people also used poorhouses on a short-term basis, particularly during the winter months, to tide them over during periods of unemployment.[37]

Workhouses and houses of industry were often attached to poorhouses or established as separate entities. They were designed to set "such poor to work as are able to labour and to prevent their being a Charge and Burthen to the Publick by sloth and Idleness and for Carrying on Trades, Occupation and Manufactures."[38] While some reformers saw the workhouse as a "bettering house," in which the poor would build their character by learning the virtues of the work ethic and temperance, during the course of the 1800s its punitive qualities overwhelmed attempts at education and reform, and conditions often became deplorable.[39] By the late 1800s, dread of the poorhouse had become universal, and that fear was crucial in sustaining the work ethic.[40]

Many people avoided the poorhouse by working, usually for very low wages. In order both to aid developing industries, especially textiles, and provide work for the poor, societies "for encouraging manufactures" opened spinning schools and developed manufactories. Often set up with public as well as private funds, they employed women and girls who would otherwise be on relief. In 1751, the Boston Society for Encouraging Industry and Employing the Poor was established to promote industry and employ "our own women and children who are now in a great measure idle."[41] The following decade, the New York Society for the Promotion of Arts, Agriculture and Economy was commended for its linen manufactory, which employed "above three hundred poor and necessitous persons," and by 1787 the Pennsylvania Society for the Encouragement of Manufactures and the useful Arts provided work for two to three hundred women spinning linen yarn.[42]

Other forms of workfare were used as well. One common type was auctioning off the poor to the lowest bidder, who then used their labor as he or she saw fit. Another involved contracting for the maintenance of the poor with an individual, a method most frequently used in smaller communities where fewer numbers of poor people made it impractical to build a poorhouse. In addition, poor children were often indentured as apprentices, sometimes until age eighteen.[43]

Poorhouses, workhouses, and houses of industry were all considered indoor relief, as the poor had to enter these institutions to receive aid. In contrast, there was outdoor relief, through which the "deserving poor" could receive relief while continuing to live in the community, either in their own home or in the home of a neighbor.[44] From the 1600s through the 1930s, outdoor relief was provided in the form of wood or coal in the winter, clothing, food (often grocery orders), and medical care year-round, and sometimes a small cash allowance.[45] In addition, beginning in 1911 with Missouri and Illinois, "deserving poor" women could receive Mothers' Pensions. Designed to allow native-born white widows to remain in their homes taking care of their children, Mothers' Pensions spread rapidly after 1915 so that by 1921, forty states had adopted them in some form.[46]

Attacks on Outdoor Relief. Campaigns to substantially cut or terminate outdoor relief and leave only indoor relief occurred periodically throughout the 1700s and 1800s. Just as the early relief principles continue to provide the foundation of our current welfare system, the gist of the arguments made as part of these early attacks on relief were repeated in the 1950s, 1980s, and 1990s.[47] Although most recipients of outdoor relief were widows, children, aged, and sick and therefore not able to work; the attacks were fueled by the belief that the rolls were filled with able-bodied poor. Even more important than terminating outdoor relief for people perceived as able to work was the lesson that would be learned by those who had jobs: wage labor, at almost any wage, would become preferable to relief.

Central to these campaigns against outdoor relief was the argument that relief itself caused poverty. Opponents claimed that relief eroded people's independence, promoting idleness and undermining the incentive to work. One such critic described the supposed effect of outdoor relief on the poor in New York City during the 1820s:

> More than twenty thousand persons were degraded to the condition of public paupers, deprived of their feelings of honourable independence and self-respect, and, together with many others who were rejected applicants for relief, were exposed to a powerful temptation to practice deception and fraud, had their fears of the consequences of idleness, improvidence, and vice, at least greatly lessened.[48]

Anticipating George Bush's "thousand points of light," opponents further claimed that most people did not really need relief and that those who did could be adequately aided by private charity.[49] Furthermore, although outdoor relief actually cost less than indoor relief, it was criticized as too expensive.[50] Underlying all of these criticisms was the fear that relief would become a viable alternative to wage labor.

Campaigns against outdoor relief were especially strident and successful in the 1820s and 1870s. During the 1820s industrial capitalism was taking hold in the United States, and the demand for wage workers increased. Partly to help push people into wage labor, relief policy became more restrictive. In his widely influential *Essay on the Principle of Population,* which appeared in 1798, British economist Thomas Malthus advocated abolishing outdoor relief entirely, arguing that it worsened the condition of the poor by allowing them to survive and have children, thereby increasing the poverty population and preventing starvation from naturally ridding England of some of its "surplus poor."[51] Although not as blatant in the United States as in England, some social welfare critics insisted that poorhouses would check the spread of pauperism through both cheaper care and deterrence.[52]

The attack on outdoor relief in the 1870s came during a particularly turbulent time in United States history, as the great railroad strike of

1877 and the rise of socialist and communist ideas in Europe, which were brought to the United States by immigrants entering the country in increased numbers, engendered in capitalists an increased wariness of workers. Arguments similar to those of Malthus further rationalized the assault on outdoor relief, as social Darwinism and the eugenics movement supported the idea that the poor were inferior and should be restrained from reproducing and passing on the "biological defect" of poverty.[53] During both periods, cities from New York to New Orleans to San Francisco terminated outdoor relief for several years, leaving the poorhouse as people's only recourse.[54]

The Expansion of Work Programs during Depressions

Primary reliance on workfare programs became problematic during the severe depressions and crises that periodically ravaged the economy. Widespread agreement among relief officials that work was preferable to "charity," combined with protest by the unemployed, led municipalities to provide jobs. For example, when unemployed seamen in New York-City held a mass meeting to protest the suspension of shipping caused by the Embargo of 1807, the municipal government responded by paying for the U.S. naval yard to hire unemployed seamen and also provided additional jobs on public projects, including building the new City Hall and cleaning and repairing streets.[55] Indeed, most of the jobs were developed by expanding public works and other government services.[56] Prefiguring the massive work relief programs of the New Deal, road repair and construction of public facilities, from buildings to culverts and sewers, were the most common types of work provided. Other projects included whitewashing tenements, laying water mains, improving parks, repairing public buildings, clearing trees from land about to be flooded by dams, and maintenance tasks such as shoveling snow or collecting garbage.[57]

The expansion of work programs during depressions was intended almost exclusively to benefit white men. In part this was because it was easier to increase public works and thereby create jobs in construction deemed appropriate only for men than it was to set up workrooms for women. But the family ethic was also critical in these decisions: men were the ones who were *supposed to* work in order to support their families. In fact, married women were given work relief only if their husbands could not find either work or work relief of their own.

However, since it was recognized that some women were indeed responsible for supporting dependents, projects were developed in which they were put to work in workrooms doing "women's work"— primarily spinning cloth, making rag rugs, and sewing garments. During the severe depression of 1873–1879, the Industrial Aid Society of Boston opened a workroom in which women sewed and knit garments. Twenty years later, during the similarly devastating 1893–1897 depression, sewing rooms were again set up in Chicago, New York, Boston, Philadelphia, and other cities. In addition, laundries, representing another form of "women's work," were established.[58]

Work relief was also undertaken outside workrooms. Reflecting the family ethic and the importance of allowing "deserving poor" women to remain in their homes in order to take care of their families, some projects were developed in which women could work at home. In New York City and Philadelphia during the 1893–1897 depression and in Cleveland during the depression of 1914–1915, relief committees allowed women to work in their homes sewing, knitting, and making mats and quilts.[59]

Projects involving work other than manufacturing were also developed. During the depression of 1857–1858, associations in New York and Philadelphia sent single women to the country to work in the homes of other women. Similar "housekeeper services" projects were again established during the 1893–1897 depression. And during the depression of 1914–1915, projects involving training in salesmanship and office work were set up.[60]

Gender-based discrimination was clearly apparent in the depression-generated projects. In addition to the general lack of work for women, women were paid less than men for the same types of work. Leah Hannah Feder, who wrote a book surveying relief during depressions from 1857 through 1922, noted that these wage rate differentials were accepted as the norm. For example, in the Boston workrooms during the depression of 1893–1897, women received 80 cents per day while men were paid one dollar.[61] Racial discrimination was similarly evidenced in lower payments and the dearth of projects for people of color, especially for women of color, compared to whites. Furthermore, when projects were established for African-American women, they were usually segregated.[62]

The Contradictions of Early Work Programs

Work programs before the 1930s were marked by two interrelated contradictions that also characterized the later programs: the disparity between providing "real work" and training on one hand and deterrence on the other; and the contradiction between the production of useful goods and its suppression by capitalists (mostly small business owners) who objected to competition from work relief labor and the consequent predominance of make-work.

The deterrent elements of most work relief were spelled out at the 1895 National Conference of Charities and Corrections:

The work given must be adequate in amount to prevent families from suffering either hunger or cold; but at the same time it must be really hard work in order to prevent dabbling, and it must be decidedly underpaid in order not to attract those who already have work at half-time, or who have otherwise disagreeable work. The whole must be so unattractive as to guarantee that, when other work can be had, the laborer will seek it.[63]

This was most clearly seen in hard-labor work-tests that were obvious make-work; the most common tests involved breaking stones or moving piles of rocks from one site to another. A telling example can be found in the 1820s, when managers of the poorhouses in both Philadelphia and New York purchased clearly inefficient tread wheels (in which human labor is used to move grindstones), instead of steam-driven machinery, in order to make the work more onerous and discourage the able-bodied poor from seeking relief.[64]

More useful work (although also obvious work-tests) was developed in woodyards, set up both to put able-bodied poor men to work in exchange for relief and to provide fuel as in-kind relief for the poor. These proliferated during depressions in cities and towns throughout the country, along with other work that more clearly resembled "real work," primarily public works and maintenance for men who were physically able, as well as workrooms for women and for men unable to labor outdoors.[65] And on an ongoing basis, farming was perhaps the most important form of "real work."[66]

The work-test nature of most work relief was strengthened by business opposition to the production of useful goods. This was clearly seen in the poorhouse. Reformers periodically advocated that poorhouse inmates (as they were called at the time) should produce useful goods in order to earn some of the cost of their support. In fact, inmates performed much of the routine work, including cooking, cleaning, gardening, and nursing other inmates, as well as making clothing, shoes, and coffins.[67] With the exception of oakum, however, business owners prevented goods produced in workhouses and on other work projects from being sold on the open market.[68] As a result, they could be used only by others on relief or in public institutions, severely limiting both the amount and types of goods produced. As Piven and Cloward explain, "[C]osts aside, manufacturers were always wary of the possibility that the workhouse, or any organized work-relief program, would nurture nascent forms of social production to compete with the market."[69]

A telling example of the limits of useful work projects was seen in a plan proposed in 1803 by New York City Mayor Edward Livingston to provide training and jobs for the urban poor. Livingston suggested that skilled craftsmen (identified and provided through the Mechanics Society), in conjuction with the municipal government, would establish and supervise public workshops in trades such as shoe-/ and hat making, and would also hire the poor when they needed additional helpers. The Mechanics rejected the plan outright, however, claiming that it would undermine the system of apprenticeship by making skills widely available and that the lower wages paid to those given work under the plan "would strike at the very vitals of mechanic interest" by creating "ruinous competition." The plan was defeated, and Livingston resigned as mayor shortly thereafter amid charges of corruption.[70]

An additional factor constrained workhouse production and encouraged projects that were seen as inefficient make-work. Although incentives such as tea, sugar, and even money were sometimes given to those who produced more than the quota, most inmates received nothing more than the usual food and shelter for their labor.[71] Since they had little inducement to work very intensively, fewer goods were produced with the same hours of labor compared to production in private sector firms. In other words, inefficiency was endemic to most workhouse production.

However, both reliance on the work-test and exclusion of useful production became problematic during the severe depressions and crises. As unemployment soared and emergency work relief was expanded, the distinction between "real work" and work relief sometimes became blurred. Furthermore, since it was not possible to force people to accept jobs that did not exist, a work-test to prove that they wanted to work often seemed absurd.

In addition, liberal reformers wanted the depression-generated work projects to seem as much like "real work" as possible in order to maintain the morale of the mostly white male workers. This perception was bolstered by the fact that the work done in the projects would otherwise have been carried out as part of normal government operations by workers employed by local governments. However, most of these projects were characterized by five traits that marked them as work relief. First, private contributions, which were associated with charity, were sometimes used by municipalities to finance the public works. Second, a means test was usually used to choose the project workers. Indeed, the work was often restricted to men with dependents. For example, in Boston during the 1893–1897 depression, only "respectable men with dependent families who were out of work through no fault of their own" were given work on the projects.[72] Third, inefficient methods of work, typically using more people with simple tools instead of machines, were the norm.[73] Yet, as discussed earlier, this "work program efficiency" has its own logic as it creates more jobs. Fourth, the work was performed for short periods of time, as men worked only enough hours to earn their allotted relief.

Finally, in order to help ensure that people would accept private-sector jobs, relief payments were kept below the amount that could be earned through labor market work. This was facilitated by providing most relief in kind instead of in cash. When cash was used, relief payments were usually based on market wage rates with fewer hours of work allowed each week in order to keep the total payment below the amount that could be earned through wage labor. Over time, debates about the level of work relief wage rates became increasingly intense. Representatives of organized labor argued for higher work relief rates, claiming that low rates depressed industry wages, and some social welfare officials worried that low rates demoralized workers.[74] Employers, on the other hand, continued to press for low rates.

Competition with the private sector presented few problems in the public works projects. Two factors account for this. First, since inefficient production methods, usually the replacement of machines with hand labor, were the norm, public works projects operated on a different basis than most private-sector production. Second, the work done on the projects was often confined to repair and maintenance, work that was normally carried out by municipal governments.

Competition did become an issue, however, in the workrooms, which were also expanded during depressions; there, useful garments and other goods were produced. These goods were either kept by the people who made them or distributed to others on relief or to public institutions. Nothing produced in the workrooms was sold on the open market.

In at least one case, however, goods produced in work projects were sold for a profit. This happened with garden projects established in Detroit during the 1893–1897 depression. Although the surplus produce was sold by the individual gardeners to private consumers, business complaints seemed to have been averted by the project's small size.[75]

Conclusion

Welfare and government work programs have been shaped by often contradictory forces. While punitive pressures were engendered by the logic of capitalist production-for-profit and the dynamics of discrimination based on gender and race, liberalizing pressures came primarily from protests by the poor. Until the 1930s the work programs were primarily punitive and mandatory, as the poor—both men and women—were forced to work in exchange for meager relief. Programs that were less coercive were developed during the depressions that raised unemployment rates to over one-quarter of the labor force. These relatively small-scale emergency work programs proved to be precursors of the massive work relief programs of the 1930s, both in terms of how the programs were set up as well as the debates—work relief versus. "real" jobs, production methods on the projects, levels of work relief wage rates, and competition with the private sector. And as was true in the earlier programs, most of the work in the 1930s was created for white males, while women and people of color remained marginalized.

2

The 1930s: Job Creation Programs in the Great Depression

The 1930s were marked by economic depression, social protest, and the development of new federal government policies, including the most innovative and extensive fair work programs in United States history. The New Deal administration of Franklin D. Roosevelt established three job creation programs for adults. The Federal Emergency Relief Administration (FERA), from May 1933 through December 1935, was the first federal program to provide unemployment relief.[1] The Civil Works Administration (CWA), from November 1933 through March 1934, was quickly set up to head off another depression winter of increased need and increased protest. The Works Progress Administration (WPA), perhaps the best known of all the 1930s work programs, lasted from September 1935 through June 1943, when mobilization for World War II substantially increased production and employment and finally brought the Great Depression to an end.[2] Even though the programs came under unremitting attack from the business sector, they provided work each month for 1.4 to 4.4 million people, primarily white men; based payments on local wage rates; and put people to work in a variety of projects, including construction and repair of roads and public facilities, the arts, research and surveys, and production of consumer goods for others on relief. In direct contrast to the punitive workfare programs developed in the 1980s and 1990s, these programs provide models for alternative government policies during economic hard times.

The Crisis of the Great Depression

The Great Depression of the 1930s surprised most people by its depth and severity.[3] Herbert Hoover, who became President in 1929 a few months before the Depression began, followed the conventional economic doctrine of laissez faire, keeping the government out of the economy so that the "natural" functioning of the market would allow it to "bottom out" and wages and prices would again begin to rise. By the time Roosevelt became President in March 1933, however, the bottom was still nowhere to be seen. Measured unemployment had risen to 25 percent of the total labor force—and 38 percent of the nonfarm labor force.[4] Yet even this figure understates the true amount of unemployment, since it excludes "discouraged workers" who stopped looking for work and dropped out of the labor force. The high unemployment pushed down hours of work, so that approximately two-thirds of those with jobs were only working part-time.[5] By 1933, average weekly income in manufacturing had fallen 33 percent from its 1929 level, while prices fell 25 percent.[6]

Women in the Depression

Women's increased responsibility for their families was met with increasing unemployment and lower wages. Although these problems were common to women of all races, the situation was especially desperate for women of color.

The mounting economic dislocation led to an increase in desertion—the "poor man's divorce"—often leaving women as the mainstay of the family. This was reflected in a nationwide census taken in the late 1930s, which showed that one-tenth of all families were headed by women. However, Mary Elizabeth Pidgeon, who wrote about women's economic situation during the 1930s, noted that this was a conservative estimate, since census enumerators "normally report a man as the family head wherever possible to do so"; she believed that women were the sole wage-earners in approximately one-sixth of all urban families.[7] This figure was even higher for African-Americans: approximately 30 percent of all black families were headed by women in the 1930s.[8]

Women's concentration in the service sector of the economy (as opposed to goods production) was relatively helpful during the early years of the Depression, since the steeper decline in goods production often allowed them to keep their jobs longer than men.[9] Some jobs held by women in both services and manufacturing were protected by sex-role stereotyping; they were seen as "women's work" and were simply not considered suitable for men. Women's jobs were also safeguarded by their lower wages compared to men. Women's wages in manufacturing employment remained between 60 and 70 percent of men's wages throughout the 1930s, leading many employers to retain their lower-cost women workers.[10] When considering all jobs held by women and therefore incorporating lower wages resulting from sex-role stereotyping as well as fewer hours of work per week compared to men, the differential is even greater. A 1937 Social Security Administration study, for example, found that women's average yearly pay was only 51 percent of men's pay.[11]

As the Depression worsened, however, so did unemployment among women. Surveys taken in 1934 by state relief administrations and the Bureau of Labor Statistics found unemployment rates for women ranging from 18 to 31 percent.[12] The U.S. Bureau of the Census estimated that by 1937 approximately three million of the eleven million women in the labor force were unemployed.[13] Yet these statistics continued to omit "discouraged workers." As economist Margaret H. Hogg noted in 1931, women more readily than men stopped looking for labor market work in order to avoid seeing themselves as unemployed, returning instead to their traditional role in the home.[14] Women's work in the home did indeed become increasingly important, as more and more women produced goods such as clothing and bread, and preserved fruits and vegetables instead of purchasing them.[15]

Women's employment situation was further weakened by campaigns to fire married women in order to make their jobs available for men. The Federal Economy Act, passed in June 1932, mandated that only one member of a family could have a job in the civil service. Within one year, approximately sixteen hundred people were fired, three-fourths of them women.[16] Similar "economy measures" were introduced, although not always enacted, in almost every state, and many cities conducted similar campaigns to rid their work forces of married women. Some of the support for these moves to fire married women came from the idea that women were only working for "pin money" which was used for unnecessary purchases. Even Frances Perkins, the first women cabinet member (she became secretary of labor under FDR), criticized the "pin money worker" as a "menace to society, [and] a selfish shortsighted creature who ought to be ashamed of herself."[17] However, defenders of working women pointed out that their earnings were necessary for survival and that women's "so-called pin money [was] often the family coupling pin, the only means of holding the family together."[18]

The economic situation of women of color was even more precarious than that of white women. Concentrated in marginal jobs of domestic service, low-wage manufacturing (including industrial homework), and, for black women, sharecropping, they bore a disproportionate share of the economic hard times. Although most unemployment statistics were too low, the relative rates are telling. A 1934 survey conducted by the Pennsylvania relief administration, for example, found unemployment rates for African-American men and women of 45 percent, compared to 31 percent for white women and 27 percent for white men.[19] The difficulty black women encountered in finding jobs was also reflected in the decline of their labor force participation rate (that is, the percentage of black women in the labor force compared to their total in the population), which fell from 42 percent in 1930 to 37.8 percent in 1940.[20]

In spite of this decline, labor force participation rates for African-American women remained higher than those for white women throughout the 1930s. It is important to note, however, as Jacqueline Jones does, that higher labor force participation rates for black women obscure the nature of their work, which tended to be degrading and temporary.[21] Even these jobs were not secure. As the Depression wore on, many African-American women were fired from their domestic service jobs, which had long been a mainstay of their employment. Although the immediate cause was declining white family incomes, black workers were sometimes replaced by whites.[22] Not content to accept their displacement from domestic service work, black women in some cities organized "slave markets" where they waited on street corners for white women to drive up and offer them a day's work.[23] And, not surprisingly, illegal means of earning money, primarily prostitution, also increased among women of all races.[24]

Mexican-American women, as well as men, endured another hardship. As the Depression deepened, "foreign" workers were accused of taking increasingly scarce jobs. In response, more than four hundred thousand people of Mexican origin, including many who were U.S. citizens, were deported to Mexico.[25] In an action indicative of the anti-alien mood, Colorado Governor Johnson in April 1936 declared martial law on the state's southern border (with New Mexico) and called out the National Guard to prevent Mexicans and Mexican-Americans from entering Colorado.[26]

A few women did have a little to fall back on during the hard times, however. The Mothers' Pensions that had been enacted in most states during the preceding two decades provided relief payments for some single women considered "worthy." This aid was given, sparingly, primarily to white native-born widows. A 1931 survey of half of the approximately one hundred thousand recipients of Mothers' Aid pensions throughout the country found that 96 percent were white, 3 percent were black, and 1 percent were other women of color.[27]

The Need for Federal Action

The worsening economic depression took its toll on people's lives. Suicides increased as pessimism grew. The numbers of transients rose as people left their homes in search of work elsewhere. Although the majority were single men, single women and families also swelled their ranks. Some of the families, known as Okies, were driven from their communities by the severe drought that turned much of the Midwest into a dustbowl. Although always difficult to measure accurately, estimates of transiency in the early 1930s ranged from five hundred thousand to five million, the higher number reflecting the fear of veritable armies of homeless on the road or living in areas of makeshift housing erected on the outskirts of major cities throughout the country, commonly called Hoovervilles in honor of the President.[28]

Protests began rather quickly. March 1930 saw the first hunger march called by Unemployed Councils groups of unemployed people and supporters organized by the Communist Party to demand relief and jobs. In addition to demonstrations and sit-ins at government offices, the councils organized "rent riots," returning the belongings of evicted families to their homes, and reconnected gas and electricity after it had been shut off.[29] Others protested as well. Hog and dairy farmers in the Midwest, the backbone of America, developed "penny auctions" to prevent foreclosures, and dumped milk on highways to demand government price supports for agricultural products.[30]

Some of the unemployed developed alternative means of support outside normal economic channels. Women, organizing as housewives, were central to the establishment of self-help cooperatives, elaborate systems of barter through which people traded hours of labor to farmers in exchange for the opportunity to harvest crops that otherwise would have rotted in the fields.[31] And bootlegged coal, dug out by miners in narrow and dangerous shafts they built themselves on company property, kept the economy of western Pennsylvania from total collapse.[32]

One of the most often cited protests in the early years of the Depression was the Bonus Expeditionary Force, or Bonus Army, of World War I veterans who went to Washington, D.C., in June 1932 to demand early payment of their veterans' bonuses. Erecting a Hooverville near the Capitol, veterans and their families continued to pour into the city after the measure was defeated, reaching a total of approximately twenty thousand by the end of July. The presence of women and children did not prevent the federal government from sending cavalry, infantry, and tanks under the command of General Douglas MacArthur to set the entire encampment on fire.[33]

This attack on women and children in the Bonus Army epitomized the Hoover administration's tenacity in clinging to principles of repression rather than accommodation. Yet while its conservative laissez-faire philosophy prevented the federal government from dispensing relief, existing arrangements were increasingly inadequate to cope with the continually growing unemployment and destitution.[34] Lower tax revenues resulting from the economic decline meant that local government funds for relief, as well as for other functions, continued to decrease.[35] And contributions from private charity did not come close to compensating for the shortfall in public funds. A survey by the American Association of Social Workers showed that by 1932 only one-fourth of the unemployed received any relief, and those who did were given food, a little clothing, and medical care.[36]

As in earlier depressions, cities throughout the country used some of their scarce funds for public works projects. These were expanded during the winters when people's needs for fuel and shelter increased, so that in March 1933, before the New Deal relief programs began, approximately two million people were on local work relief.[37] As in the past, most of the projects were for white men and involved construction and repair of roads, sewers, parks, and recreation buildings, as well as chopping wood in woodyards.[38] Women were given a small amount of work in nonprofit agencies or distributing food, fuel, and clothing in relief commissaries.

When women were given work relief they were paid less than men, as dual wage rate scales were adopted unapologetically by cities such as New York, Philadelphia, and Pittsburgh.[39] Reflecting women's lower wages throughout the economy, relief authorities were simply abiding by the policy of setting work relief payments below the amount that could be earned in the private sector in order to make sure that women continued to fill available lower-wage jobs.

The New Deal

By the time Roosevelt became President in March 1933, the worsening economic situation, along with mounting and visible protests, had created a policy vacuum that allowed a great deal of room for experimentation with social and economic programs. The New Dealers proved up to the task, as the "alphabet soup" of acts passed during Roosevelt's first hundred days attempted to quell protests and deal with problems in manufacturing, agriculture, and finance, in addition to relief.

Restoring a sound basis to the financial system, most importantly banks and securities trading, was dealt with through a series of legislation over the first few years of the New Deal. Farmers' demands were addressed through the 1933 Agricultural Adjustment Act, which set up the Agricultural Adjustment Administration (AAA) to try to raise prices of agricultural commodities by reducing their supply, and by the Farm Credit Act, which refinanced one-fifth of all farm mortgages.[40] Some of the surplus agricultural commodities were collected by the Federal Surplus Relief Corporation (FSRC), which distributed them to relief recipients.[41] Most ambitious of all the early pieces of legislation was the National Industrial Recovery Act, which set up the National Recovery Administration (NRA) to bring together capitalists and workers under the aegis of the government to negotiate wages and prices through "codes of fair competition." This act contained the infamous Section 7(a), which recognized the right of workers to organize unions of their own choosing and led to a surge of union activity.[42]

Several measures were designed to provide jobs for unemployed men. The Public Works Administration (PWA), implemented as part of the National Industrial Recovery Act, was given an initial appropriation of $3.3 billion for public works construction. Designed to stimulate the construction industry and thereby help prime the pump of economic recovery, the PWA functioned solely through normal market channels, as work was contracted out to private-sector firms, which hired workers through the labor market. Thus, issues of need were of no concern.[43] An ambitious public works project was also planned through the Tennessee Valley Authority (TVA), which set up a public corporation to build dams to aid flood control efforts, provide fertilizer, and generate electric power.[44] The "wild boys of the road" and young unemployed men of the cities were provided for through the Civilian Conservation Corps (CCC), which put them to work at conservation projects in the national forests. Over its ten-year history, the CCC provided work for 2.5 million young men, who were paid thirty dollars a month and housed in camps run by the army.[45]

These work programs were not only designed for men, but for white men, as African-Americans were marginalized or excluded outright. In the CCC, enrollment of African-American men was limited to 10 percent of the total, and they were placed in segregated camps.[46] Blacks were similarly restricted from participation in the TVA and were barred from living in the TVA's model town of Norris.[47] Other New Deal measures also harmed African-Americans. The AAA's crop-reduction program pushed tenant farmers and sharecroppers off their land, while white landowners kept the government subsidy payments, sometimes using the money to purchase farm equipment, which further reduced the demand for black labor. Furthermore, a disproportionate number of African-Americans lost their jobs as the National Recovery Administration codes led to many small business failures, causing some black leaders to call the program the Negro Removal Act.[48]

Fair Work Programs: The FERA, CWA, and WPA

Relief was a major focus of the New Deal. Responding to the protests by the unemployed and to the fear of increasing turmoil, the federal government for the first time in U.S. history took responsibility for unemployment relief. All the programs were temporary, set up to meet the emergency of depression-generated unemployment. And they were fundamentally work relief, designed for people who were considered employable.

The relief programs were surrounded by contention and debate, especially during the first two years. There was little protest over eligibility policies, since aside from the short-lived CWA, a means test was used to evaluate a family's income and need. However, policies concerning the level of wage rates and the types of projects often provoked strident criticisms and were sometimes substantially changed.

The barrage of criticisms limited the size and scope of the programs. While much of value was done and millions of people were put to work, millions more who were in need never received relief, and payments were generally too low. Even Harry Hopkins, chief administrator of all three programs, admitted, "We have never given adequate relief."[49] Not surprisingly, women, especially women of color, received the least adequate work relief.

The Three Programs

The initial New Deal response to the crisis of relief was the Federal Emergency Relief Act (FERA), passed on May 12, 1933, to provide grants-in-aid to states for relief. In order to receive federal funds, state relief administrations were required to follow rules and regulations developed by federal relief officials.[50] Policies were quickly developed concerning eligibility and determination of wage rates, and projects and special programs were set up for target populations, notably transients and teachers. Everyone was means-tested; most projects were in construction and some in production-for-use (production of consumer goods for relief recipients); and wage rates were based on the prevailing wage for similar work in the community. Some wage rates were extremely low, however, and concern that use of the prevailing wage would do nothing to raise these low rates led federal relief officials, in July 1933, to set a thirty cents per hour minimum. This policy provoked strident complaints from employers that continued unabated until it was rescinded in November 1934.

The FERA was interrupted for a few months by the Civil Works Administration (CWA). Established on November 9, 1933, by executive order from the same authorizing legislation as the PWA, it was intended to counteract another winter of increased need and heightened protests by creating jobs for an additional 2 million people, mostly white male heads-of-household. In order to accomplish this goal quickly and to counteract the "ideology of the dole" for these new workers, PWA regulations were followed: the 2 million new participants were exempted from the means test; the higher PWA wage scale was adopted; and money was used only for construction projects. But white males were not the sole concern. In order to operate construction projects that paid lower wages for some men, mostly African-Americans, as well as nonconstruction projects for women, the Civil Works Service (CWS) was developed. The CWA rapidly lived up to its promises, as 4.3 million people were put to work by the following January (and an additional 100,000 on other work relief projects). Not surprisingly, the business sector bitterly complained that it was too large, too expensive, and wages were too high.[51] In response it was cut back in mid-January, only two months after it began, and the entire program was ended two months later.

The FERA was resumed in April 1934, with the urban unemployed targeted through the Emergency Work Relief Program (EWRP) and those in rural areas coming under the Rural Rehabilitation Program (RRP). Relief administrators tried to develop policies and projects to meet the needs of diverse populations, including unemployed professionals, women, and students, as 1.4 to 2.4 million people were put to work each month. Responding to criticisms of the early FERA and the CWA for creating make-work and boondoggles, federal relief officials expanded production-for-use. Projects to process cattle dying from the drought, sew mattresses with surplus cotton collected by the AAA, and put idle workers to work in idle factories evoked charges of unfair competition from employers. Giving in to business complaints about policies they saw as interfering with labor markets and with the logic of production-for-profit, federal relief officials in the fall of 1934 rescinded the thirty cents per hour minimum work relief wage rate, withdrew federal support for providing relief to strikers, condoned the policy of dismissing workers from the rolls when their labor was needed, and ended the most controversial production-for-use projects.

By the time the WPA began in September 1935, the most contentious issues had been settled. Although debates continued about specific policies, especially determination of payments, most of the criticisms concerned the nature of the projects. Another round of reactionary changes occurred in 1939 and included economic policies that made WPA jobs less secure and less remunerative, as well as political regulations that excluded communists and gave preference to veterans. The WPA lasted for eight years, providing work for more people on a regular basis, 1.4 to 3.3 million each month throughout the 1930s, than had been the case on the FERA. It tapered off in the early 1940s as unemployment fell below 2 percent of the labor force, for the time being ending the need for job creation programs.[52]

Eligibility for Relief

The FERA and WPA were clearly relief programs. Eligibility was based on need, which called for a means test; local relief agencies investigated applicants. The procedure, spelled out early in the FERA, was supposed to include "a prompt visit to the home; inquiry as to real property, bank accounts, and other financial resources of the family; an interview with at least one recent employer; and determination of the ability and agreement of family, relatives, friends, and churches and other organizations to assist." In addition, there were to be visits to the home at least once a month "in order to establish the continued need of those who are receiving relief."[53] In practice, however, there were wide variations in the application of these standards, depending primarily on the level of protest, availability of funds, numbers on the rolls, and local traditions and attitudes regarding relief.[54]

Women faced particular difficulties getting on the work programs. Only heads of households could be declared eligible for the FERA, CWA, and WPA, and when a man was present he was usually the one chosen. This policy was clearly stated in the Louisiana WPA manual: "As a general rule, a woman with an employable husband is not eligible for referral, as her husband is the logical head of the family."[55] Indeed, relief administrators considered it important to protect the husband's positions as family head. According to Donald S. Howard, whose history of the WPA remains the most comprehensive, this involved putting "some brake upon women's eagerness to be the family breadwinner, wage recipient, and controller of the family pocketbook."[56] By the late 1930s it also led relief administrators to abandon a practice sometimes used earlier of bypassing the husband in favor of a younger and stronger worker, since this would "weaken the responsibility and authority of the family head and injure the family structure."[57]

In addition to trying to preserve men's authority in families, WPA administrators wanted to "protect the WPA program against possible public criticisms for employing 'too many women.' "[58] Thus, while women made up almost one-quarter of the national labor force in 1940, their numbers in the FERA and the WPA were kept to one-sixth of the total, and they represented only 5 percent of the rolls on the massive CWA and CWS.[59] Women's share of work relief did not increase above one-sixth of the rolls until the early 1940s, when the need for relief and total numbers on the programs declined as mobilization for World War II led to expanded job opportunities for both women and men in the private sector.[60]

The policy of restricting women's participation in the programs led to at least one instance of unwarranted dismissals. In 1936, WPA chief administrator Harry Hopkins ordered the Colorado WPA to remove almost half of the women from its program when it was discovered that women made up 27 percent of the rolls in that state compared to a national average of only 16 percent.[61]

The importance of providing work for men was also demonstrated by the exception made to the "one member per family" rule for those in the CCC, as young men could enroll in the CCC while an adult family member worked for the FERA, CWA, or WPA. Women were not totally forgotten in the camp category, as educational camps were set up for their use. Also known as "she-she-she" camps (a play on Cee-Cee-Cee), they provided work relief for single women age sixteen through thirty-five. Yet the "she-she-she" camps paled in comparison to the CCC camps. Whereas men received one dollar per day in the CCC, women were paid only fifty cents per week in the "she-she-she" camps. While men received vocational training, women's camps provided only education and recreation. The size of the programs further attested to women's marginalization. Through May 1, 1936, a total of only 6,400 women had participated in the "she-she-she" camps.[62] Yet at that time 348,000 men were enrolled in the CCC, a reduction from the high point of 483,000 the previous fall.[63]

Charges of racial discrimination were routinely made against the work programs. Chronicled by Alfred Edgar Smith, Labor Relations Staff Advisor in the WPA, the main complaints were that skilled black workers were routinely put in unskilled jobs; very few African-Americans were assigned to administrative positions; black women were placed in "gang work" (outdoor manual labor); blacks were forced off the rolls and into agricultural work at wages that were too low to support themselves and their families; and African-Americans were dismissed more readily than whites when reductions were ordered in the rolls.

The first step in getting on the work programs involved establishing eligibility. Although regulations forbade racial discrimination, it was clearly evidenced. As with women, the number of people of color on the rolls was sometimes restricted to a specified proportion of the total. Most fundamentally, lower standards of need were applied. As Donald S. Howard explained: "Negro workers, accustomed to relatively low standards of living, may be denied WPA employment on the grounds that they are not in need whereas workers accustomed to relatively higher standards of living may be declared eligible for such employment even though they have as large and possibly larger resources than the former."[64]

Thus it was more difficult to be certified as eligible for relief, and once on the rolls people of color received lower payments than whites. In addition, they were required to accept lower-wage jobs in the private sector compared to whites, again since lower pay was the norm, and could be denied jobs on the work programs if they failed to do so. Administrative methods also limited their enrollment, as their applications were handled more slowly than those of whites.[65]

Even when people of color were admitted to the relief rolls, there was no guarantee that they would obtain work placements. Most of the projects were segregated, limiting the amount of work available. This was particularly true for African-Americans. Black men usually worked in segregated construction gangs, the main type of work provided, and separate transient camps were set up for them.[66]

Women of color confronted both racial and gender-based discrimination. This is borne out in statistics on participation by both gender and race. It is telling that these statistics were not gathered until February 1939, reflecting federal officials' reluctance to acknowledge the extensiveness of racial discrimination.[67] Yet the numbers are clear: only 2.1 percent of WPA workers were black women. In comparison, 12.1 percent were black men, 11.0 percent were white women, 74.4 percent were white men, and 0.4 percent of those on the rolls were classified as "other."[68]

Relief administrators complained that appropriate work was difficult to find for women of color, especially African-Americans, since they were trained primarily as domestic service workers. Yet the real problem seemed to be the reduced supply of domestics if a sizable number of black women were given work on the programs. In fact, even though women working in domestic service usually earned less than half of what they could make on the work programs, they were often forced off the rolls and "frankly told they must accept proffered employment [in domestic service] or be stricken forever from all relief rolls."[69] And, as will be discussed further under the following section, potential agricultural workers, primarily blacks in the South and Mexican-Americans in the

Southwest, were routinely dismissed from the relief programs when their labor was needed in the fields.

Not only were women of color usually placed in segregated projects, as were men of color, but the work was often differentiated according to race. This was particularly clear in the housekeeping projects developed in the WPA. Housekeeping Aide projects involved manual labor, including cleaning, laundering, and cooking—that is, domestic service work. In contrast, Home Demonstration projects involved teaching others housekeeping skills. While most of the women in the Housekeeping Aide projects were black, those in the Home Demonstration projects were almost exclusively white.[70] And while Mexican-American women were sometimes assigned to Housekeeping Aide projects, in cities with a large Hispanic population they could be found instead in the Home Demonstration projects.[71]

Class-based differences were also apparent in the work programs, as Caucasian white-collar workers, including women, were targeted for special treatment. Concern about unemployment among professionals and other white-collar workers led relief administrators to develop rules and regulations designed to entice them onto the rolls. These included establishing separate relief offices, using a less onerous eligibility investigation, granting higher payments, and setting up special work relief projects.

Relief administrator and historian Josephine C. Brown explained that separate offices were set up so that white-collar workers "might avoid incurring the stigma of mingling with 'ordinary' relief applicants."[72] And, beginning in the CWA, less humiliating relief investigations were also important in cajoling white-collar workers into the programs. Federal relief officials clearly spelled out this policy in a July 1934 directive: "Eligibility for employment [of white-collar workers in work-relief programs] will be established by means of a questionnaire filled by the applicant and verified by a professional or technical organization or by a case worker."[73] This constituted a far more congenial approach than the rigorous investigation used for all other relief applicants.

African-American white-collar workers received little of this special treatment. Indeed, some forms of discrimination were particularly galling. Although a small number of blacks were put to work conducting surveys, they were often kept from these positions because "whites do not like to be interviewed by Negroes."[74] In Oakland, California, skilled black workers were sent to a project where they were told that they could only work in the cafeteria.[75] And although projects for blacks were often supervised by other African-Americans and a few were given administrative jobs in the relief program, the relief agencies themselves frequently allowed African-American relief workers to investigate only other blacks, thereby reducing their numbers as social workers.[76] Gains were especially limited in the South. For example, in May 1940 in fourteen southern states, there were only 11 black supervisors compared to 10,333 whites in supervisory positions.[77]

Special Divisions and Programs

Throughout the FERA, CWA, and WPA, special divisions and programs were established to meet the needs of target populations. These included a Transient Program, Emergency Education Program, Rural School Continuation Program, Women's Division, and College Student Aid and National Youth Administration. Women received relief through all these programs.

Widespread concern about millions of transients on the road and living in Hoovervilles led federal relief officials to create a Transient Program soon after the FERA began. This program set up shelters (usually renovated factories or warehouses) in cities and camps outside cities in which people could receive food, clothing, and a place to sleep. Most of those given aid were single men; better treatment was accorded to the single women and families who also received assistance.[78]

Up to forty-four thousand people a month, many of them women, were given work through the FERA's Emergency Education Program. Set up in August 1933, this program developed adult education classes in areas such as vocational rehabilitation, worker's education, and Home Demonstration projects, as well as nursery schools for preschool children from needy families. And although federal administrators believed that urban cities should pay for their own public education system, the situation in rural areas had become so desperate that the Rural School Continuation Program was created to reopen some of the hundreds of schools that were running only part of the year or had been shut down entirely due to lack of tax revenues.[79]

Responding to prodding from women interested in relief policy, FERA administrators established a Women's Division in October 1933. Gearing up as the CWA began, a Conference on the Emergency Needs of Women was held in November 1933 to discuss projects that would be appropriate for the estimated three hundred thousand to four hundred thousand women who needed work.[80] Although little headway was made in the CWA, one of the reasons for the expansion of production-for-use and white-collar projects when the FERA was resumed in April 1934 was to provide more work for women.

Concern about unemployed youths quickly led Congress to establish the CCC. It also led the FERA to develop the College Student Aid program, which provided students with part-time work. Under the WPA this program was expanded into the National Youth Administration (NYA) and provided work for up to six hundred thousand young women and men each month.[81]

Wage Rate Policies

Work relief wage rate policies proved a source of contention throughout the 1930s, especially during the FERA and the CWA. Employers persistently argued that rates were too high, attracting workers away from private-sector jobs. If this continued, they asserted, they would be forced to increase wages, which would discourage them from expanding production and would prolong the Depression. Most vocal were southerners, who objected to any policies that might threaten their supply of low-wage African-American agricultural and domestic service workers. In fact, since millions of the jobless did not get on the work programs, workers could always be found. The issue was to ensure that there would be many more unemployed workers than there were jobs available so that people would be willing to work for low wages, often under oppressive conditions.[82]

Workers countered with arguments that low work relief wage rates would further depress private-sector rates. Representatives of organized labor were particularly vocal about the need to set work relief wage rates at prevailing private-sector levels in order to maintain labor market wage rates.

New Deal relief officials tried to steer a middle course. In theory, work relief wage rates were supposed to be set at levels higher than direct relief payments in order to provide an incentive to work for relief instead of receiving an outright dole, but lower than private-sector wage rates for similar work in order to prevent work relief from becoming more attractive than private-sector employment. Furthermore, work program participants were always required to accept private-sector employment if it became available.[83] In practice, however, relief officials were predisposed to setting rates at levels similar to or higher than those in private industry in order both to increase the "purchasing power of the masses" who would quickly spend the money and help spark a recovery and to differentiate the work programs from the old "work-for-relief" work tests.[84] Again, they were primarily concerned about white males, as industry differentials according to gender and race were carried into the programs; work relief wage rates for most women and people of color were usually near the bottom of the scale.

In the FERA a family's total payment was based on its "budgetary deficiency," that is, the difference between its income and the amount needed as determined by the local relief agency. Hours of work were then calculated by dividing the budgetary deficiency by the relevant wage rate.[85] Initially, the rate used was the prevailing market wage for similar work.[86] However, worries that private-sector wage rates as low as 10 to 12.5 cents per hour throughout the South would lead to correspondingly low work relief wage rates quickly led federal relief officials to set a minimum work relief wage rate of thirty cents per hour, a policy that provoked ceaseless criticism until it was ended.[87]

Business-sector complaints were intensified by the CWA wage rate policy. Budgetary deficiency was abandoned and people worked according to the PWA scale: thirty hours per week at rates determined by the area of the country in which they lived and by their level of skill. And the already controversial thirty cents per hour minimum was replaced by a new minimum of forty cents per hour.[88] The higher rate was intended primarily for white men, however. The old thirty cent minimum was retained in two types of projects: road projects, which provided work for unskilled blue-collar workers, many of whom were African-American; and the Civil Works Service program, which provided almost all of the work relief for women.[89]

Employer protests against CWA wage rates provoked a rapid response. In January, two months after the program began, hours for workers on the CWA were cut.[90] By March 2, a means test was again used to determine eligibility, and payments were again based on budgetary deficiency with the thirty cents per hour minimum.[91] Yet the minimum rate, too, fell victim to endless complaints and was rescinded shortly after the Democrats' resounding triumph in the November 1934 midterm elections. As the *New York Times* explained, the FERA "capitulated."[92] Without the minimum, work relief wage rates throughout the South quickly fell below thirty cents per hour, plummeting by January 1935 to between ten and twenty cents per hour throughout Alabama, Georgia, South Carolina, and Tennessee, and making it even easier to maintain low wages for people of color.[93]

Wage rate policies caused fewer problems on the WPA than they had on the FERA and CWA. Total monthly payments were determined by a scale based on the region of the country, the degree of urbanization, and the degree of skill. Although the amounts in the categories were sometimes changed—most importantly, the low rates for unskilled workers in the southern region were raised—this basic method was maintained.[94]

Removing Low-Wage Workers from the Work Programs. Employers of low-wage labor were always concerned about having more than enough available workers in order to keep wages low.[95] As early as the fall of 1934 relief officials in some areas resumed the pre-FERA practice of removing groups of people, usually people of color and often women, from the rolls when their labor was needed, primarily in agriculture and domestic service work. This practice was common in cotton and tobacco regions, where crops depended on large supplies of African-American workers, and in sugar beet areas of the Southwest that relied on Mexican-American labor.[96] As anticipated, this policy helped maintain a large pool of people desperate for work. In Colorado, people with Mexican and Spanish surnames were dropped from the rolls in early spring, several weeks before the work was even available.[97] Thad Holt, director of the Alabama Relief Administration, described the situation in Alabama in September 1934, writing to Harry Hopkins that at least nine thousand day laborers, many of whom would not be able to find work, had been dropped from the relief rolls and that consequently "anybody applying for cotton-pickers can have ten of them for the job."[98] Federal relief officials condoned this policy, stating that "[the FERA] not only approves this procedure, but insists upon its being followed by those States in which conditions of seasonal employment warrant such action.[99]

Women of color were also dismissed from the rolls in response to complaints of shortages of domestic service workers. The Birmingham News reported that 150 African-American women were dropped from the WPA rolls in January 1937 in Birmingham, Alabama, "because of sharply increased demand for servants."[100] And a North Carolina work program policy was unapologetically described by an official:

In April, 1936, all sewing rooms, both white and colored, in the strawberry section of this county were closed because of the fact that labor was available to these women both in picking and packing of strawberries. Since employment was available in the tobacco fields, these rooms were not re-opened until after the tobacco season, which was sometime during the month of November, 1936.[101]

White women were soon readmitted to the rolls, but the same was not true for black women:

Since the colored case load was so low in the county and business conditions in general were much improved, it was felt both by WPA authorities and also by local sponsors and the Department of Public Welfare that to re-open the colored sewing rooms would tend to increase the shortage of domestic labor in this county.[102]

A woman who was taken off the rolls in Brewton, Alabama, described her situation and pleaded for help:

They cut me off [the WPA rolls] and I have nothing to go upon. When they cut me off the first time they sent me to the blueberry farm and promise to put me back after the berries was over. But they didn't they told me to go to the cotton patch for 60¢ a hundred. And I really cant support myself and little girl at that rates for it is school time now and she hasnt got her books nor clothes [sic].[103]

Wage Rate Differentials. Additional methods were used to maintain wage rate differentials based on race, gender, and class in the work programs and therefore in the private sector as well. Regardless of the skill and occupation of people of color, they were usually classified as unskilled and consequently paid the lowest rates. And when payment of one rate for people of all races would have contradicted existing differentials, dual wage scales were sometimes adopted outright. For example, in Houston, Texas, white teachers on the CWA received one dollar per hour while African-American teachers were paid sixty cents per hour, and in Jackson, Mississippi, black men were paid thirty cents per hour while whites were paid forty cents.[104] Evangelist John R. Perkins captured their reaction:

> We received our work cards marked 40 cents per hour
> And went to work without any regret
> On Saturday two hundred colored men was deceived
> And 30 cents was all we could get . . .
>
> We only want Uncle Sam to know
> They did not treat us right
> They cut our wages to 30 cents per hour
> Yet 40 cents was paid to the white.[105]

Dual wage scales for women and men were also common in other New Deal programs. In addition to the work programs, they were adopted in the "codes of fair competition" developed by the National Industrial Recovery Administration, the cornerstone of New Deal economic policy.[106] This government-condoned wage gap was apologetically explained by a NRA official: "Numerous differentials of various kinds can be found in the codes which it may be difficult to defend on purely logical grounds, but they represent long established customs."[107]

For all whites, however, class-based differentials proved more important than those based on gender, as white-collar workers consistently received among the highest rates of pay. During the WPA those on white-collar service projects, slightly over half of whom were women, were paid an average of fifty-seven cents per hour, while blue-collar workers received an average of thirty-nine cents per hour.[108] This differential was rationalized early in the programs, as an August 1934 FERA directive mandated that budgets for nonmanual and professional workers should provide for health, decency, and comfort "commensurate with the previous standard of living."[109]

The Variety of Projects

The projects developed in the FERA, CWA, and WPA were targets of criticism, and often contradictory regulations were developed to try to prevent interference with the logic of production-for-profit. Although it was reasonable to require that a maximum number of jobs should be developed in ways that did not replace normal government workers or compete with the private sector, this left the programs vulnerable to charges of inefficiency, make-work, and all-around boondoggles. Indeed, the programs are still commonly characterized by these criticisms, obscuring the fact that a wide variety of useful work was done.

The main category of work was construction, which absorbed approximately three-fourths of the funds throughout the 1930s.[110] The results are indeed impressive. They include construction and repair of more than one million miles of roads; approximately two hundred thousand buildings (including my schools, libraries, courthouses, firehouses, and armories); tens of thousands of recreational facilities (such as parks, stadiums, and swimming and wading pools); several thousand public utility plants; miles of sewers, drainage ditches, and electric power lines; thousands of flood and erosion control projects (for example, firebreaks, retaining walls, levees); and several hundred airports.[111]

The construction projects were designed for men. Only a very small number of white-collar women were placed on them, conducting surveys and doing clerical work.[112] Although manual labor was not considered suitable for white women, the same assessment did not hold for women of color. In 1936 some African-American women on the WPA were given work in "beautification" projects in which they worked in groups using picks and shovels to clean up roads and parks. The obvious racism of allowing what was seen as "gang labor" for black women but not for white women led to protests, and the projects were quickly curtailed.[113]

The second major category of work was white-collar projects, which grew in importance through the 1930s. In addition to the Emergency Education Program and the Rural School Continuation Program, which provided work for teachers and schooling for children and adults, projects were established in public health, recreation, libraries, museums, conducting research and surveys, and the arts. In fact, the WPA Federal Arts project for artists, writers, musicians, and actors and actresses is still one of the best known of all the 1930s projects, with the posters, paintings, murals, guidebooks, and plays remaining as examples of federal support of the arts.[114] These, too, were routinely criticized as boondoggles.

White women were relatively well represented on the white-collar projects. Reflecting the common perception of much white-collar work as "women's work," from one-third to one-half of those on the projects throughout the 1930s were women, and approximately one-third of all women on the programs were involved in white-collar work.[115] People of color, however, were seriously underrepresented. A FERA survey found that they made up only 5 percent of the white-collar project rolls, a figure that was probably not much higher in the WPA.[116]

The Controversy over Production-for-Use

While professional and clerical women were given work on the white-collar projects, most of the blue-collar women, including women of color, were put to work on projects in which consumer goods were produced. Commonly known as production-for-use or production-for-use and distribution, their early existence was turbulent. They were significantly expanded after the CWA ended, providing work for only 5.4 percent of relief workers in May 1934 and growing to encompass more than 15 percent by the following October, as some very innovative projects were developed. The primary impetus for these stemmed from criticisms of the early FERA and CWA for unnecessary make-work. A secondary motivation was to provide more work for women, and from one-half to two-thirds of all women on the programs worked in production-for-use.[117]

The expansion of production-for-use was countered by vociferous complaints that the projects competed unfairly with private enterprise.[118] This happened even though the goods were not sold through normal market channels but were either given only to relief recipients, who had minimal resources after several years of the Depression, or used in other relief projects or public institutions such as hospitals. However, production-for-use contradicted the logic of production-for-profit, since the government was producing needed consumer goods, and the offending projects were quickly curtailed.

Most of the initial production-for-use under the FERA was expanded from pre-FERA projects and elicited relatively little criticism. Labor-intensive workrooms in which women sewed and mended garments, rag rugs, and bedding provided one-third or more of the total production-for-use in the FERA.[119] Although most of the work was initially done by hand, the sewing rooms became increasingly mechanized throughout the 1930s, as cutting rooms were often centralized and foot treadle and electric machines replaced some of the hand sewing.[120]

Subsistence gardens were expanded from their limited use before the FERA to encompass both community gardens and home gardens and were complemented by projects in which the produce was canned. Also continued from pre-FERA work relief was fuel procurement, primarily chopping wood in woodyards. These projects, designed to provide work for men, were a critical source of in-kind relief for others on the rolls.[121]

The production-for-use projects begun under the FERA also created work for women. The FERA provided aid to the self-help cooperatives that were set up by the unemployed during the Hoover years of the Depression, since the AAA's program had increased prices of agricultural commodities and made farmers unwilling to continue the earlier barter arrangements.[122] The mattress-making project expanded the work in labor-intensive sewing rooms, as women sewed mattresses and comforters by hand using some of the surplus cotton the AAA had taken off the market.[123] The projects for canning garden produce were extended into centers to process (slaughter and preserve) animals that were dying from the severe drought and to produce and repair goods, primarily shoes and wearing apparel, from the hides, pelts, and wool.[124]

The most contentious of all the new projects were those in which relief recipients were put to work in factories that had been partially or entirely shut down and then rented from their owners by state or local relief administrations. This was commonly known as the Ohio Plan, since the practice was most extensive in that state. Relief workers produced clothing (for example, long underwear, coats, knitted goods), furniture (primarily wooden beds and kitchen-type chairs), metal ware (stoves, heaters, and skillets), china, and blankets.[125] The Ohio Plan most vividly revealed the contradictions of production-for-profit: the government was combining idle workers with idle factories to produce consumer goods because capitalists were failing to do so.

The new production-for-use projects quickly came under fire. The business sector complained that the projects were inefficient and, most importantly, that they competed unfairly with private enterprise.[126] Production-for-use was condemned in the *Report* from a December 1934 conference of ninety business leaders, who indignantly declared that "[g]overnment competition with private business leads toward socialism."[127] This was simply their worst fear—that production based on capitalist's profits would be replaced by production based on people's needs.[128]

Throughout the rest of the 1930s most production-for-use was carried out in the sewing rooms. These absorbed almost two-thirds of the funds spent on the more broadly construed health and welfare activities, and a full 93.5 percent of actual consumer goods production in the WPA, as 383 million garments and 118 million other articles were produced.[129] In spite of the earlier fight against it, mattress-making was brought back briefly in 1939 and 1940, this time clearly as part of the sewing rooms for women instead of as a separate project.[130] However, as in the FERA, employer objections led to their demise.[131]

Most of the remaining health and welfare activities involved gardening and canning. These were also extended into food preparation and distribution. Particularly important was the school lunch program, with more than 1.2 billion meals served using surplus agricultural commodities and food grown in relief gardens.[132] And many women of color worked on the Housekeeping Aide projects described earlier.[133]

With mobilization for World War II in the early 1940s, the WPA developed a variety of national defense projects, most notably airport construction. In-plant training in defense industries also became an increasingly important WPA project. Although white women were actively recruited into these programs, there was a marked reluctance to accept African-Americans.[134]

The Social Security Act:
A Permanent Federal Relief Program

Formulation of the Social Security Act began in June 1934 with Roosevelt's appointment of the Committee on Economic Security. Subcommittees were set up to develop programs for unemployment compensation, old age insurance, medical care, public employment, and supplementary assistance. Originally entitled the Economic Security Act to reflect its comprehensive nature, the more progressive elements were deleted during congressional deliberations in the winter and spring of 1935.

The Economic Security Act was introduced with a great deal of fanfare. It began with Roosevelt's speech to Congress on January 4, 1935, which was often quoted in later years. Condemning relief as "a narcotic, a subtle destroyer of the human spirit," the President vowed that "the Federal Government must and shall quit this business of relief"; he went on to explain that there were "some 3,500,000 employables" on relief for whom "it is a duty . . . to give employment . . . pending their absorption in a rising tide of private employment."[135] In other words, the government would provide fair work, instead of cash relief, for these primarily white men who would normally have a job. Roosevelt did not intend to deny federal subsidies of relief for poor mothers. In fact, two weeks later in his message to Congress introducing the Social Security Act, Roosevelt advocated "Federal aid to dependent children through grants to states."[136] Decades later, critics wanting to replace welfare with workfare periodically reiterated the first part of Roosevelt's statements but conveniently ignored the rest.

A critical component of the early plans was Employment Assurance.[137] This would have established a work program as part of the permanent system of relief by providing public employment to recipients of unemployment compensation after their payments were exhausted, as well as to "able-bodied workers" not covered by unemployment compensation soon after the loss of their jobs. Although there were debates about whether it should be included in the Economic Security Act itself or established as a separate program, its importance was clearly acknowledged by the Committee on Economic Security in its *Final Report*: "While it will not always be necessary to have public-employment projects to give employment assurance, it should be recognized as a permanent policy of the Government and not merely as an emergency measure."[138]

The Social Security Act that became law on August 15, 1935, and has continued to provide the foundation for relief was far narrower than the original Economic Security Act. Controversial proposals for Employment Assurance and for a national health care program were entirely absent.[139] Only the following remained: social insurance programs (social security and unemployment compensation); categorical assistance programs (Old Age Assistance [OAA] for those failing to qualify for social security, Aid to the Blind [AB], and Aid to Dependent Children [ADC]); and limited funds for public health. Social insurance was limited. Although social security, which provided pensions to people who were no longer in the labor market, was a federal system, this was not the case for unemployment compensation, which supplied payments to current workers. Southern congressmen, who effectively stymied most progressive legislation through the 1960s, insisted on a system in which individual states retained most of the control.[140]

Discrimination based on race and gender was incorporated into the Social Security Act. Fundamentally, the social insurance programs were designed as income replacement for lost wages, primarily for white men, while the socially stigmatized categorical assistance programs, based on the poor law, were intended mainly for white women and people of color. Clarifying this basic dichotomy, the act specified that those who worked in agriculture, domestic service, the government, and nonprofit organizations—jobs typically held by women and people of color—were specifically excluded from the social insurance programs.

Racism was further manifested in the OAA program. The requirement that it provide "a reasonable subsistence compatible with decency and health" and that it could not be denied if criteria of age and need were met, provisions that would have helped prohibit racial discrimination, were replaced by the toothless phrase that general assistance payments would be furnished "as far as practicable under the conditions in such State." University of Chicago economist Paul H. Douglas explained that the original phrase was changed because southern congressmen worried that it "might be used by authorities in Washington to compel the southern states to pay higher pensions to aged Negroes than the dominant white groups believed to be desirable."[141] Indeed, as these provisions began taking effect, many aged African-Americans experienced difficulties in obtaining payments because they were unable to prove their age, and those who managed to get on the rolls usually received less than whites.[142]

Direct Relief and the Return of the Work Test

The work programs were intended for people who were considered employable; those deemed unemployable were supposed to be cared for through state and local resources. Not surprisingly, these supposedly unemployable individuals were mostly women and people of color. However, the turmoil that preceded the New Deal, as well as the pleas for help from local government officials throughout the country, led the FERA to provide direct relief along with work relief.[143] It was this turmoil that also led the FERA to provide relief for transients, many of whom were considered unemployable. As the FERA and CWA brought the crisis of relief under control, however, and the business sector continued to demand the return of all relief to state and local authorities, Roosevelt decided to terminate federal provision of the hated "dole"—that is, direct relief. Thus when the FERA ended in December 1935 so did the Transient Program and federal responsibility for "unemployables."

The results were predictable. State and local revenues had not appreciably increased, and immediate reductions were seen in both the number of cases receiving direct relief and the level of payments. In many areas pre-FERA practices designed to discourage relief were reinstated. These included investigation of cases by police and firemen, forcing people to stand in line in public places in order to receive surplus commodities, sending single people to almshouses and county poorhouses instead of providing outdoor relief in communities, and providing an increasing portion of relief payments in kind instead of in cash.[144] This led, in turn, to a resumption of many of the practices that characterized relief before the FERA, as soup lines and organized begging increased and jungles of the unemployed flourished by freight yards throughout the country.[145]

It also led to the return of the work-test, labeled "work-or-starve" or "work-for-relief" by some commentators. Paid starvation wages that

were again based on budgetary deficiency, participants primarily performed maintenance work such as cutting grass, collecting garbage, and
cleaning sewage-disposal plants. By 1940 local relief administrations in
forty states used a work-test, and the use of such tests was authorized in
nine more. Approximately 180,000 people, including less than 2 percent
of the families on relief in Virginia and more than 25 percent in Kansas,
were subjected to these workfare programs by the end of the decade.[146]

The FERA, CWA, and WPA: Success or Failure?

Much that was of value resulted from the FERA, CWA, and WPA.[147]
Millions of people were put to work, they were paid decent wages, and
innovative projects were developed. Throughout the country, roads and
public facilities were built and repaired, theatrical productions and paintings were created for the public, surveys were conducted, adult education was broadened, garments were sewn, and lunches were served to
needy children.

Yet there were two very different problems. First, women and people of color were marginalized, never receiving their fair share of the
work or fair level of payments. Second was the perception, continuing to
the present time, that the work programs were failures. In conjunction
with a similar assessment of CETA in the 1970s, this view has stifled
consideration of government job creation programs as part of the policy
mix. A reevaluation is in order.

The most common charges made against the work programs during
the 1930s were that they were too costly, local administrations were
prone to graft and corruption, participants were paid too much, the
work was unnecessary and inefficient, and some of the projects competed unfairly with private enterprise. The first two complaints—of excessive expenditures and graft and corruption—are frequently made
about government programs. In fact, the military and high-level federal
departments periodically face these often justifiable accusations. The
most telling objections, however, are those involving interference with
the logic of the market—in other words, when programs appear to or
actually do hinder the profitable production of goods and services in the
private sector. This is the nature of the remaining complaints.

The work programs, especially the CWA, were often criticized for
providing high payments that allegedly attracted potential workers away
from private-sector jobs. These charges continued even though one-
sixth to one-fourth of the labor force remained unemployed throughout
the 1930s, assuring employers an ample supply of labor. Furthermore,
relief workers were required to accept private-sector jobs when they

became available, and potential shortages of agricultural and domestic service workers were routinely dealt with by removing people from the rolls. The real issue was the very existence of decent government jobs, especially for low-wage workers.

The remaining objections dealt with the logic of production-for-profit itself. Charges that the projects were inefficient and unnecessary boondoggles haunted the programs throughout the 1930s. While the charges had some validity, that validity resulted from requirements to create as many jobs as possible with the allocated funds and to avoid replacing normal government operations. Thus, projects were mandated to use a maximum amount of labor and a minimum amount of machinery, to use production methods that were clearly inefficient compared to private-sector standards. Requirements to avoid replacing normal government operations made sense, since workers for those jobs should have been hired through the labor market, not provided by the relief programs, but they left the programs open to charges that the work was not really necessary.

Yet it was the charges of unfair competition from the production-for-use projects that most clearly revealed the contradictions of production-for-profit. New and innovative projects were lambasted even though several years of depression had left relief recipients with so little money that their purchases were not curtailed by the distribution of relief goods, although the composition of what they bought might change. As J. C. Lindsey, a regional engineer for the FERA, wrote in response to complaints that FERA shoe repair shops would take business away from private merchants: "If these shoes were not repaired or furnished by us, the men and women for whom we are doing this work would simply be without shoes."[148] The underlying problem was that relief production exposed the inability of an economic system based on profit to provide goods that people needed. In essence, since production-for-profit was not a sufficient motive to induce capitalists to produce basic consumer goods, and the government was producing them instead, why depend on private enterprise at all?

Some federal relief officials in the 1930s responded to these criticisms by challenging their appropriateness for judging the work programs. Nels Anderson, director of labor relations in the WPA, asserted that the government differed from private industry because it was "guided by social rather than profit motivations."[149] Following this line of reasoning, it becomes clear that the criteria used to evaluate job creation programs need to be challenged. Measures founded on the logic of production-for-profit should be replaced by more fitting assessments based on people's needs. Instead of having to defend the programs against charges of being inefficient and unnecessary, which follow from their mandates, they can be seen as successes. In the midst of the most severe depression in the twentieth century, a variety of useful work was created for millions of people. Although nothing since then has approached the achievements of the FERA, CWA, and WPA, they remain as models of what is possible, programs that could now be brought back in ways that meet the needs of women and people of color as well as white men.

3

The 1940s and 1950s: Return to the Dark Ages

The post–World War II period was one of economic prosperity accompanied by social and political reaction. This reaction, mobilized through anticommunist witch hunts and exhortations about defending freedom and democracy, was mirrored in relief policy. Similar to early attacks on relief in the 1820s and 1870s and to the "war on the poor" in the 1980s and 1990s, age-old arguments blaming relief itself for poverty were dredged up and repeated in the media as punitive policies were implemented. Fair work programs were absent, buried when the Works Progress Administration (WPA) ended in 1943.

Not only were they gone, but by the end of World War II job creation programs were clearly separated from relief. Thereafter, only workfare remained connected to relief, while fair work programs evolved into what was called "manpower policy." This label was not a misnomer, and the separation of the programs made it even easier to aim fair work at men, while workfare dealt primarily with women. Although they lay dormant from 1943 to 1962, interest in fair work programs broadened to incorporate training, and received boosts from the periodic sharp recessions that marked the postwar era.

Postwar Prosperity

The period after World War II was one of economic expansion and prosperity.[1] Emerging as the most powerful country in the world, the United States was able to structure the postwar system much to its liking and to protect its interests through periodic invasions of developing countries.[2] Central to U.S. economic policy was anticommunism: the 1947 Truman Doctrine decreed that communism must be stopped anywhere in the world. This included stopping it domestically; the anticommunist witch hunts of the 1950s effectively removed most progressives from the labor movement and the struggles for workers' rights, as well as from Hollywood and its influence on public opinion through movies, and a period of political reaction set in.[3]

Workers shared in the postwar prosperity. Average weekly earnings (adjusted for inflation) increased 33 percent between 1947 and 1960, lending credence to the idea that hardworking (white) families could have "a chicken in every pot and two cars in the garage."[4] Rising wages were bolstered by institutions set up in the 1930s. The social insurance programs of social security and unemployment compensation replaced a portion of income lost through retirement or unemployment for people, mostly white males, who had worked long enough in jobs covered by the programs. Unemployment compensation provided a cushion against job loss for these workers, allowing them to more easily risk losing their jobs to demand higher wages and better working conditions. Also enacted in 1935 along with the Social Security Act, the National Labor Relations Act, or Wagner Act, established the National Labor Relations Board (NLRB) to protect the right of workers to organize unions of their own choosing and ensure that employers bargain in good faith. Although it was partially counteracted by the 1947 Taft-Hartley Act, which prohibited secondary boycotts and allowed individual states to enact antiunion right-to-work laws, the Wagner Act was a hard-won protection of workers' rights.

The Social Security Act and the National Labor Relations Act formed the basis of what is sometimes referred to as the "capital-labor accord." Workers received these government protections, such as they were, in exchange for labor "peace," primarily tempering strikes and consenting to labor-saving changes in production processes, terms that were aided by the removal of most communists from labor unions.[5] Yet it was the labor-saving—actually labor-replacing—technological changes, along with periodic recessions, that helped keep alive interest in fair work programs.

The postwar economic growth was far from steady, however. Sharp recessions in 1948–1949, 1953–1954, and 1957–1958 sent overall unemployment rates from lows of around 3 percent to as high as 7.6 percent of the labor force.[6] Furthermore, everyone did not share equally in the postwar prosperity. Not surprisingly, the main beneficiaries were white males. This was particularly apparent in contrast to the gains made by women and people of color during World War II. Although employers were initially reluctant to hire women of all races, as well as African-American men, during the war their opposition was tempered by the Japanese attack on Pearl Harbor.[7] As stories spread about women's productivity, symbolized by "Rosie the Riveter," nineteen million women obtained jobs, often at high wages, in war industries and other manufacturing and service work.[8] While some companies and communities helped facilitate wage labor for married women by providing child care, it was always seriously insufficient.[9] Racial discrimination remained strong during the war. Although people of color obtained well-paying war jobs, their wages were lower than whites and they were typically given the most dangerous work. Since segregation remained largely intact during the war, many small firms that did not have separate facilities for blacks simply refused to hire them at all.[10]

Most of the gains made by women during the war were lost when it ended. Many women, especially women of color, struggled in vain to retain their high-paying war jobs, eventually returning to lower-wage jobs in services and sweatshop manufacturing.[11] Other, primarily white, women returned to the home, a movement facilitated by an ideological barrage that insisted women's true roles were as wives and mothers. Magazines were filled with stories of "latchkey" children becoming juvenile delinquents when deprived of their mother's care, and stories extolling "Rosie the Riveter" were replaced by recipes. The ensuing baby boom, along with constricted economic choices, was testimony to the effectiveness of this media blitz. Contrary to popular belief, however, women's return to the home was far from universal, as their labor force participation rate climbed steadily in the postwar years, from 32.7 percent in 1948 to 37.7 percent by 1960.[12] Low wages for black men and the difficulty they had in obtaining jobs made it necessary for many African-American women to seek wage labor, keeping their labor force participation rates 12 to 13 percentage points above those for white women throughout this period.[13]

The lives of many people of color were disrupted by economic displacement and migration during these decades. As southern agriculture became increasingly mechanized, especially with the mechanical cotton picker, many African-Americans who had been subsisting as sharecroppers and tenant farmers became superfluous to the rural economy, leaving for cities in the North and the South.[14] Mexicans, primarily men, were drawn into the U.S. as seasonal low-wage labor through the Bracero Program, described as "legalized slavery" by a Department of Labor official.[15] And as citizens of a U.S. commonwealth, Puerto Ricans were displaced by Operation Bootstrap, which pushed them out of agriculture and led many to migrate to the U.S.[16] All of these factors helped maintain a large pool of people of color who were unemployed. When they did find work it was typically at the bottom of the economic ladder, with lower wages and more hazardous working conditions compared to whites, and their unemployment rates were double those of whites throughout the postwar period.[17]

Fair Work Programs in Hiatus

The demise of fair work programs after World War II was not a foregone conclusion. Quite the contrary. But none of the proposals came to fruition, and the programs lay dormant until the 1960s.

The National Resources Planning Board and the New Economic Bill of Rights

A permanent job creation program similar to those of the New Deal was strongly advocated in the early 1940s by the National Resources Planning Board (NRPB), an executive-level agency established by President Roosevelt in 1933.[18] Roosevelt construed the NRPB's purview broadly to include both physical resources (for example, natural resources, buildings, dams) and human resources—that is, labor—as the agency published approximately 370 reports and helped plan and coordinate public works.[19]

By the late 1930s, the NRPB had come to serve as a central agency for people who believed that national planning was necessary to stave off long-term stagnation. They had ample cause for concern. While the massive government expenditures on World War II finally brought the nation out of the Great Depression, many worried that the end of the war would see a return to depression. Their fears were grounded in the severity and length of the Great Depression as well as in the post–World War I experience, as the very severe recession of 1920–1921 was attributed to that war's end.

The culmination of the NRPB's work came in reports planning for the postwar economy that were published in 1942 and 1943. Most important were *Security, Work, and Relief Policies*, written by the Committee on Long-Range Work and Relief Policies and strongly endorsed by the NRPB as a whole in a widely distributed four-page introduction, and the *Post-War Plan and Program* from the *National Resources Development Report for 1943*.[20] In these lengthy reports, the NRPB returned to the idea of Employment Assurance as proposed in the initial draft of the Social Security Act. Insisting that "our economy must provide work for all who are able and willing to work," the 1943 *Report* advocated a "New Bill of Rights" that would extend the political bill of rights in the U.S.

Constitution to enumerated rights for economic security.[21] It is instructive to recap their recommendations in order to have a complete story of work programs and to understand that the idea of the right to economic security has a history, and indeed was considered at the federal level, in this country.

Among the recommendations, the NRPB's New Bill of Rights included the following items:

> The right to work, usefully and creatively through the productive years;
>
> The right to adequate food, clothing, shelter, and medical care;
>
> The right to security, with freedom from fear of old age, want, dependency, sickness, unemployment, and accident.

It also included the right to fair play, education, and "rest, recreation, and adventure."[22]

In order to put these principles into practice, the NRPB recommended strengthening the social insurance and public assistance programs, in part by federalizing most programs, as well as establishing a permanent public employment program. It advocated improvements for the social insurance programs, not only by raising payments but also by expanding coverage through reducing the earnings requirements and including agricultural, domestic service, and other workers who were not covered. Unemployment compensation would be enhanced by replacing the federal-state system with an entirely federal apparatus and by financing payments primarily from general revenues instead of the regressive payroll tax. Public assistance would be extended through federal financial aid for general relief, strengthening the special public assistance programs (Aid to Dependent Children, Old Age Assistance, and Aid to the Blind) through strict federal controls, and providing aid in cash instead of in kind.[23] The NRPB also proposed establishing a national health care program and social insurance programs for industrial accidents and diseases, and committing funds for public housing, which would also provide jobs through the work program.

A job creation program integrated with social insurance and public assistance was considered critical to postwar economic and social policy. It would continue along the lines of the 1930s programs in order to provide work for the "employable" unemployed, mostly white men, and thereby "retrieve for society at large an otherwise wasted national resource—its labor power."[24] The 1942 *report* discussed the problems encountered by the "dual nature" of the WPA as both a relief program and a work program.[25] As a relief program it was mandated to provide as many jobs as possible with the allocated funds, while as a work program it was supposed to provide useful work in an efficient manner. These problems would be solved as they had been in the CWA. As explained in the 1943 *Report,* this would involve the "[f]ormal *acceptance by the Federal Government of responsibility* [emphasis in original] for insuring jobs at decent pay to all those able to work regardless of whether or not they can pass a means test," and would include a permanent "Work Administration" that would carry out "all kinds of *socially useful work* [emphasis in original] other than construction."[26] In other words, the work program would be divorced from relief; arts projects and production-for-use could be developed; the program would include both labor-intensive projects (as in the FERA, CWA, and WPA) and capital-intensive projects (similar to the PWA); and the program would be permanent as opposed to the temporary emergency work programs of the 1930s. These plans were never developed into legislative proposals, however. Not only that, but the NRPB itself was terminated in 1943 when Congress refused to allocate further funds.

Yet the idea of an economic bill of rights was not ignored. In fact, it was advocated by President Roosevelt in his 1944 state of the union address. Asserting that "true individual freedom cannot exist without economic security and independence," he included in his recommendations the "right to a useful and remunerative job," the "right to earn enough to provide adequate food and clothing, and recreation," and "the right to adequate protection from the economic fears of old age, sickness, accident and unemployment."[27] It remained only rhetoric, however.

The 1945 Full Employment Bill and the Employment Act of 1946

The commitment to national planning was incorporated into the Full Employment Bill of 1945. Declaring that "all Americans able to work and seeking work have the right to useful, remunerative, regular, and full-time employment," it would have committed the federal government to ensure full employment.[28] An annual National Production and Employment Budget would effectuate national planning, estimating the amount of both public and private expected investment and the level of spending needed for full employment. The federal government would fill this investment gap, if necessary with deficit spending.[29] Although the Full Employment Bill did not contain public employment programs, an opening existed through establishment of an agency similar to the NRPB.

But the results were minimal, as the Full Employment Bill of 1945 became the watered-down Employment Act of 1946. Instead of an unequivocal commitment to full employment, there was only tempered support for "maximum employment," which, in the context of the debates, was clearly understood as less than full employment.[30] In place of the National Production and Employment Budget and its planning mechanism there was only an advisory body, the Council of Economic Advisors, and an annual report to the President. And instead of the obligation that federal deficit spending would be used, if necessary, to increase demand and create jobs, there was only a declaration to create favorable economic conditions.[31] As Ohio Senator Robert Taft explained to fellow Republicans, "I do not think any Republican need fear voting for the bill because of any apprehension that there is a victory in the passage of the full employment bill, because there is no full employment bill anymore."[32]

Support for the intensive federal planning and investment included in the 1945 bill was undercut by economic and political events. First, the expected postwar recession did not materialize. Instead, the U.S. economy began almost three decades of substantial growth. Second, a strike wave in 1946 marshaled antilabor sentiment. In place of guaranteed employment, Congress in 1947 passed the Taft-Hartley Act, which restricted union activities.

Third, and most fundamentally, the evisceration of the Full Employment Bill was caused by antipathy toward national government planning.[33] Planning was portrayed as antithetical to American values of freedom and democracy and was eschewed in favor of the "free market." Likened to the state control that existed in communist and fascist societies, this view fed on and contributed to the growing anticommunism that flourished after the war. (This fear of planning and federal control also explains the death of the NRPB.) Furthermore, the growing numbers of conservatives elected to Congress in 1942 made it easier to defeat more progressive policies. Opposing all measures they saw as eroding local control and interfering with labor markets, the stronger conservative coalition effectively joined together agricultural and small business interests to keep the federal government out of the economy and maintain low wages.[34]

Instead of planning for a range of socially useful projects, the U.S. developed a form of military Keynesianism as billions of dollars were spent on the military. 'his had two main effects, shoring up the U.S. position as hegemonic country and increasing the demand for government goods and services. In contrast to the 1930s work programs, military Keynesianism was consonant with production-for-profit. While the FERA, CWA, and WPA developed production-for-use projects and construction projects that could have been contracted out to private-sector firms, the military projects did not decrease demand for any goods and services. Instead they were a bottomless pit—some general could always be counted on to assert that more was needed.

It is important to note that all of these debates about full employment implicitly dealt with white men. Although the need to create work for young people was asserted, there was no mention of the right of women or people of color to work. Low-wage labor was not discussed as a problem; the focus was only on the availability of decent work for all Americans. And there was no mention of the difficulty that women encountered trying to combine unpaid caretaking work in the home with wage labor. Yet this simply followed from the historical focus on white men in job creation work programs and shows again that unless race and gender are explicitly addressed white men become the primary concern.

Discussions of more broadly construed labor market policy continued throughout the 1940s and 1950s. Instrumental in this ongoing process was the National Manpower Council, a private organization that was funded by the Ford Foundation and had close ties to the Department of Labor.[35] Established during the Korean War in response to worries that the U.S. was not adequately prepared for the Cold War era, the Council's fears were confirmed when the USSR launched Sputnik in 1953. Reiterating the NRPB's focus on the unemployed as a wasted national resource, the Council was particularly concerned about structural unemployment among white men. This type of unemployment, which renders some skills obsolete because of changes in production processes or demand for products, led to an emphasis on training programs, primarily by private firms and unions, as well as issues such as labor mobility.

To its credit, the National Manpower Council went beyond the boundaries of its name and also examined labor problems encountered by women. Concern was generated by a recognition of the important role women had played during World War II and of the factors that might impede women's participation in the labor force in the event of another national emergency. In a volume entitled *Womanpower,* the Council noted the increasing numbers of women in the labor force, the continuing wage gap between women and men, and the societal disapproval of women with young children working outside the home unless economic necessity compelled them to do so. Eschewing government programs, the Council's recommendations for women included encouraging expanded educational and training opportunities, setting up government commissions to review policies, and urging employers and unions to hire, train, and promote people regardless of their gender.[36] Labor market problems faced by people of color received little attention, and no volumes were devoted to them.[37]

Following the dissolution of the NRPB there was little discussion of job creation programs. While the low unemployment during World War II undercut the perceived need for work programs similar to those of the 1930s, the sharp periodic recessions beginning in 1948 again sent unemployment to high levels. In spite of this, neither the National Manpower Council nor other organizations (such as the Upjohn Institute) established to study manpower policy gave much attention to public employment programs. Instead, they maintained a focus on training and other narrowly construed labor market interventions.

Restrictive Relief Policies

As discussions about fair work program policy became divorced from relief, all policies connected to it became increasingly restrictive. The new Aid to Dependent Children (ADC) program, established as part of the Social Security Act, became the main vehicle through which poor women could receive public assistance. During that program's early years, regulations were implemented to limit this aid to women who were considered deserving. "Suitable home" requirements, supplemented by "substitute father" or "man in the house" rules, defined many poor, primarily African-American, women as violating social norms and therefore being undeserving of relief. And "employable mother" rules allowed relief departments to deny aid when work was available; the rules thereby functioned as a type of informal work requirement.

The situation of poor people was indeed abysmal. The level of ADC payments remained exceedingly low, although it did increase 76 percent during this time period. From an average monthly payment of $333 (in 1994 dollars) per family in 1940 the amount rose to $390 by 1945, to $431 by 1950, and to $521 by 1960.[38] Three main factors contributed to this expansion: an increase in the average size of ADC families from 3.4 in 1940 to 3.8 in 1960 (reflecting the baby boom in the general population); a 1950 policy change that allowed the mother herself, in addition to her dependent children, to receive a grant; and a general rise in the level of other cash assistance payments (such as Old Age Assistance and Aid to the Blind).[39]

Furthermore, in spite of the restrictions, the numbers of people on ADC more than doubled during this time—from 349,000 families in 1940 to 644,000 in 1950 and to 787,000 by 1960.[40] Yet these numbers should have been even higher and, indeed, grew tremendously during the late 1960s and early 1970s. The growth of the rolls in the 1940s and 1950s was caused by several factors that expanded the pool of people eligible for ADC: general population growth; higher fertility rates, and the consequently larger size of families throughout the general population (also a reason for higher payments); increasing rates of divorce, separation, and desertion resulting in a higher percentage of families headed by women; the increase in the percentage of births outside marriage; and increased economic dislocation of African-Americans from the rural South.

Economic displacement, especially of African-Americans, by far the largest group of people of color in the U.S. during these decades, impacted the third and fourth factors listed above. Mechanization of southern agriculture exacerbated the migration of blacks to the cities, where racial discrimination meant that men had difficulty finding employment, and when they obtained jobs, they were usually paid low wages. As a result, a high percentage of black women were drawn into the labor force, often into very low wage jobs as domestic service workers.[41] This, in turn, contributed to marital disruption and the increase in births outside marriage, as men were often reluctant to form families when they felt they could not support them financially.[42]

The increases in the amount of payments and in the numbers of people on the rolls did little to alleviate poverty. Indeed, the insufficiency of all government assistance programs was reflected in the poverty rate, which stood at 22.4 percent in 1959, when nationwide poverty rates were finally measured.[43]

The Withdrawal of Federal Control over Relief Policy

In stark contrast to the massive federal government intervention in relief policy during the 1930s and early 1940s, the postwar years were marked by very little federal control, as the states were given a lot of latitude in developing relief policies. Under the watered-down prescriptions of the Social Security Act—that ADC and the other forms of public assistance would be provided "as far as practicable under the conditions in such State"—the rights of the poor, especially people of color, went largely unprotected.

Restrictive policies developed from efforts to limit ADC to women seen as "deserving" of public aid. This followed from ADC's origins in the Mothers' Aid programs earlier in the 1900s, which had also taken pains to differentiate between the "deserving" and the "undeserving" poor.[44] Women were considered "deserving" if they conformed to societal norms as elaborated through the family ethic. In addition, in order to qualify for aid they had to show that they were unable to obtain sufficient income from other sources. Thus, rules were developed to try to ensure both that ADC was given primarily to women who followed societal norms of the traditional family and that it would not become an alternative to low wage labor. Restrictive regulations were bolstered by cumbersome intake procedures and general harassment of ADC recipients.[45] The main targets of these exclusionary rules and punitive policies were African-American women, especially in the South. Low ADC payments, or none at all, left them little choice other than low-wage labor and/or marriage.

Several events contributed to the attack on relief. Mimi Abramovitz suggests that the punitive policies were in part a response to the gains made by women and people of color during World War II and to emerging movements for women's rights and African-American civil rights that took shape after the war.[46] Although no legislation was enacted, both an Equal Rights Amendment and an Equal Pay Bill were introduced in Congress. And even during this conservative era, the 1954 Supreme Court school-desegregation ruling of *Brown* vs. *Board of Education* was an important victory for African-Americans, although not until 1970 was it widely implemented in the South.

"Suitable Home" Rules

The primary mechanism used to enforce societal standards of the traditional family were "suitable home" requirements. Under these rules, developed by individual states shortly after the Social Security Act was passed in 1935 and expanded in the 1940s and 1950s, families considered "unsuitable" could be denied ADC. Codifying societal norms of the traditional nuclear family, suitability was determined almost exclusively by the marital status of the mother: homes were considered unsuitable when women had children outside marriage, and the children were termed illegitimate. The patriarchal nature of this concept is striking, as "illegitimate" children clearly have mothers; only the identity of the father is an issue. These requirements were not intended to help children, since they were rarely removed from supposedly unsuitable homes. In fact, the Bureau of Public Assistance (BPA), the federal agency that oversaw relief policy—to the limited extent that this was done during the post–World War II era—declared in 1945 that "suitable home" provisions were not aiding children and recommended their repeal.[47] Although fifteen states followed the BPA's advice, as the 1940s and 1950s progressed other states added "suitable home" requirements, and those in existence were enforced with increasing rigor.

Instead of trying to protect children, "suitable home" policies were primarily used to punish poor African-American women who bore children outside marriage. Concern about "illegitimacy" among blacks was heightened by the changing composition of the ADC rolls, as African-Americans came to make up a growing percentage of those on ADC throughout the 1940s and 1950s. Also increasing during this time was the percentage of families headed by women who had never been married. Simultaneously, the percentage of widows on ADC fell, as many of them became eligible for social security survivors' benefits in 1939.

Although statistics on the racial composition of the ADC rolls were gathered only sporadically in the 1940s and 1950s, they clearly show an increase in African-Americans, by far the largest group of people of color on relief. Between 1942 and 1948, a study conducted in sixteen states found that, on average, the numbers of blacks on ADC rose from 21 percent to 30 percent, a trend that continued through the 1950s in almost every state in the country.[48] For example, in Michigan, African-Americans made up 30 percent of the ADC rolls in 1948, 44 percent in 1953, and 55 percent in 1961. This trend was also apparent in the South. In Alabama, for example, blacks made up 37 percent of the rolls in 1948, their numbers growing to 55 percent in 1953 and to 62 percent by 1961.[49]

The rise in nonmarriage among women on the ADC roles, and the consequent increase in "illegitimate" children, was perceived as a serious problem by most whites. In fact, several reports were commissioned by state relief agencies, as well as the BPA, to study the growing trend of births outside marriage and its relationship to ADC.[50] The statistics were indeed arresting. While the percentage of births outside marriage increased in the general population during the 1940s and 1950s—from approximately four in each hundred live births to about five in each hundred live births—it skyrocketed in the ADC population. By 1958 approximately 20 percent of all ADC families were headed by unmarried mothers. Yet the children of never married mothers made up only 16 percent of all of the children on ADC, reflecting the fact that unmarried mothers on the rolls tended to have fewer children than those who were married.[51]

"Illegitimacy" on ADC was considered a problem because it was primarily black women who kept the children they gave birth to outside marriage; most white unwed mothers put their babies up for adoption. As stated in the BPA report, in 1958 while 70 percent of white children born to unmarried mothers were placed in adoptive homes, only 5 percent of African-American children in similar situations were put up for adoption.[52] Yet unwed motherhood was not seen as a problem until ADC made government funds available—only then did it become a taxpayer issue, open to moralizing and societal proscriptions. In fact, unmarried black women had been keeping their babies since slave times, and although they faced problems, the community accommodated both mother and child. In opposition to the mores of dominant white society, it was considered immoral for African-American women to give their babies up for adoption.[53] Not surprisingly, it was more difficult for unwed black mothers than for whites to get on the ADC rolls. This is

shown in the statistics: almost one-third of all children born to unmarried white women, but only one-sixth of the children born to black
unwed mothers, received ADC in 1958.[54]

Since federal funds could be withheld from states that excluded
children from ADC on the basis of their birth status alone, "suitable
home" requirements were enforced through regulations specifying factors other than "illegitimacy" that were seen as constituting unsuitabil-
ity.[55] The main types of regulation, other than gross neglect, which was
very rarely found, were "man-in-the-house" or "substitute father" rules.
Enacted by many states, these gave rise to what Winifred Bell, in her
classic study of ADC, mockingly called "the search for the elusive man
in the home."[56] "Substitute father" rules were founded on two interrelated assumptions: if a welfare recipient had a relationship, even a short-
term one, with a man, he was supposed to support the woman and her
children, thereby absolving the state of its responsibility to provide assistance, and he was (supposedly) living on the relief money. These ideas
persisted even though studies showed that fathers most often left the
home because they had no jobs and could not support their children.
Bell summarized these findings, explaining that "even the most vigorous
law enforcement does not create income."[57]

The Myth of "Chiselers" and Purges of the Relief Rolls

Punitive policies toward ADC recipients were carried out with the support of the general population. Just as the attacks on relief in the 1820s
and 1870s had been accompanied by a barrage of criticisms of relief and
its recipients, so too the assault of the 1940s and 1950s made use of time-
worn arguments and presaged the "war on the poor" in the 1980s and
1990s. Although the increase in the rolls was caused by a variety of
factors (most importantly, economic dislocation, changing marital patterns, and population growth), the attacks on relief focused on the rising
costs of the program and the moral character of the recipients. Implicit,
and sometimes explicit, in these attacks were race and the changing
racial composition of the rolls. Racism was used to substantiate further
the idea that the rolls were filled with "chiselers" who did not deserve to
receive public assistance, as numerous stories in the media painted pic-
tures of undeserving—read African-American and unmarried—ADC
recipients living off the public largesse.

Central to these attacks on ADC were the special investigating units
(SIUs) established by local relief departments to ferret out "welfare
cheats," and to their coverage in the media. Virginia Franks, assistant
supervisor of social service in St. Louis, Missouri, described the components of what she termed the new "detective method of investigation":

[I]nvestigations made without the knowledge and consent of the public assistance applicant, unauthorized interviews with employers, friends, acquaintances, and organizational heads of the family or individual in question; "surprise" home visits to applicants and recipients for the purpose of "catching" them in an "unstaged" situation; caseworkers representing themselves as something other than what they actually are as they make contacts with family, friends, and acquaintances.[58]

Not surprisingly, the unauthorized and deceitful aspects of these investigations bear a resemblance to the methods used during that era in the anticommunist witch hunts.

A critically important target of the special investigating units was the searches for "substitute fathers." Trying to find a man in the house was sometimes carried out through surprise midnight raids, in which welfare workers arrived at a client's home during the middle of the night—one knocking on the front door and the other going around to the back to catch anyone who might try to leave—and demanded to be let in. Even if a man was a boarder or in a casual relationship with an ADC recipient, he could be considered a substitute father. His presence was sometimes "proved" by the presence of a large shirt or a pair of shoes.[59]

The focus on "substitute fathers," generally portrayed as deadbeats and malingerers, went hand in hand with the concern about "illegitimacy" and the rising numbers of black ADC recipients who bore children out of wedlock. However, as has been true of the special investigating units in the 1980s and 1990s, these earlier searches were primarily intended to harass those already on the rolls and to dissuade others who might be eligible for ADC from applying. The results were hailed as a success as the rolls were reduced and tax dollars were saved. In 1957, for example, all relief agencies that had special investigating units, with the exception of the state of Maine, reported these benefits.[60]

Exposés of "substitute fathers" and discussions in the media about increased "illegitimacy" were critical in marshalling public opinion against relief recipients. In fact, this has always been easy to do, since the idea that relief recipients are taking advantage of people who are working for wages has a long history. Despite the reality that most relief recipients to this day go in and out of the labor force, often taking low-wage jobs, the widespread belief continues that they remain at home having more children in order to increase their grants.

Widespread media coverage was given to the periodic attempts to rid the ADC rolls of "chiselers" who supposedly did not deserve assistance. Purges of the rolls had two targets, reflecting the importance of maintaining both low-wage labor markets and the family ethic: recipients who were "able-bodied" and should work for wages; and recipients who were "morally unfit" and had homes that were not considered "suitable." Racism was central to most of these actions, as the perception that the ADC rolls were being inundated by African-American women who bore children out of wedlock and should work for wages instead of receiving relief increasingly gained credence in the public view.

Two of the best-known instances of purges of the ADC rolls occurred toward the end of this period—one in Louisiana and the other in Newburgh, New York. The Louisiana crisis, as it was sometimes called, took place from July through September 1960, when almost 30 percent of those on the ADC rolls were dropped. The basis of this action was the "suitable home" rule, as homes were considered unsuitable if the mother gave birth to an "illegitimate" child, became "illegitimately" pregnant after receiving an ADC, or was living in a stable relationship without the sanction of marriage. Not surprisingly, although 66 percent of the ADC caseload in Louisiana had been African-American, they represented 95 percent of those taken off the rolls. However, public sympathy was aroused, since no other aid was given to the thousands of children denied relief, and the federal government responded the following year with the Flemming ruling that assistance could not be denied if no other source of support was available.[61]

The other case that attracted a great deal of attention was in Newburgh, New York, in the spring of 1961. A widely publicized program was implemented to remove "chiselers" from the rolls by doing the following: paying recipients with vouchers instead of cash; denying aid to unwed mothers who had additional children out of wedlock; denying relief to able-bodied men who refused any job and assigning others to forty-hour-per-week work assignments; limiting aid to three months per year; restricting the amount of the grant to the take-home pay of a city employee with the same size family; and placing children in a foster home if their home was considered "unsuitable."[62]

Race and illegitimacy were central to discussions of the events in Newburgh. City Manager Joseph Mitchell, the primary force behind these actions, explained that welfare was attracting "the dregs of humanity into this city" in a "never ending pilgrimage from North Carolina."[63] Although the New York State Supreme Court prevented the program's implementation, widespread support for it was evidenced. As the *Saturday Evening Post* wrote about the Newburgh events, "Surely a community should have some defense against Bankruptcy by Bastardy."[64] The contribution of the Newburgh incident to antiwelfare ideology is instructive. Even though it was subsequently shown that the "facts" were false—the majority of recipients were white and only one man, who was disabled, was on the rolls—much of the damage had been done in terms of public perception of the supposed unworthiness of those on relief.

Work Requirements

The "suitable home" and "substitute father" rules excluded many poor, primarily African-American, women from the ADC rolls. Thus the rules functioned as a type of informal work requirement, since poor women were pushed into the labor market to support themselves and their children. Furthermore, without the cushion of relief, poor women were even more vulnerable to employers' demands that they work for low wages and under oppressive conditions, thereby helping keep costs of production low. These policies were supplemented by formal work requirements designed to prevent relief from serving as an alternative to wage labor. Most important were "employable mother" rules, which allowed relief departments to remove recipients from the ADC rolls when their labor was needed, usually on a seasonal basis for agricultural work.

Low Payments as Informal Work Requirements

Even though the level of ADC payments rose throughout the 1940s and 1950s, it remained low enough to make work usually more attractive than relief. This was especially true for blacks, who continued to receive lower payments than whites, if they could get on the rolls at all.[65] These racial differentials persisted into the mid-1960s. In hearings held in February 1967 by the Mississippi State Advisory Committee to the U.S. Commission on Civil Rights, it was pointed out that the average monthly relief payment received by an African-American family of four in Mississippi was thirty-six dollars, substantially below the maximum of fifty dollars paid to most whites.[66]

"Employable Mother" Rules

"Employable mother" rules were perhaps the most important means of ensuring adequate seasonal supplies of low-wage labor. Winifred Bell notes that "employable mother" policies to provide additional low-wage labor for agricultural employers were most often developed in areas where these jobs were filled by African-Americans.[67] In 1943 Louisiana became the first state to implement such a rule, decreeing that all ADC recipients could be refused aid if work was available in the cotton fields. This policy was applied not only to adult recipients of aid, but to their children as well. In one Louisiana parish, children as young as seven were required to work in the fields along with their mothers. Not surprisingly, "most if not all" of the families dropped from the rolls to work in the fields were black.[68]

In 1952 a detailed "policy package" was developed in Georgia. Along with a primary focus on "suitable home" provisions it had an "employable mother" policy: "Able-bodied mothers with no children under 12 months of age are expected to find employment if work is available, and so long as work is available in the area, their families are not eligible for ADC."[69] And the state of Arkansas adopted a "farm policy" that sent women and children into the fields when their labor was needed.[70]

Although most states did not have explicit "employable mother" rules, such rules were followed informally throughout much of the country, as aid was routinely denied when work was available. This was made clear in some of the hearings held in the mid-1960s by the U.S. Commission on Civil Rights, which looked into relief policies as well as other topics of concern to African-Americans. Showing that these policies were not confined to the southern states, participants in hearings held in Cairo, Illinois, described similar practices. A Reverend Cobb stated that the Cairo relief department regularly sent blacks, but not whites, to the fields, where they were paid only fifty cents an hour.[71] And Mr. L. V. Jones explained that he was on ADC in the winter but received a letter every May telling him that his grant would be cut since he could obtain full-time employment. He pointed out, however, that relief officials never checked to find out whether people actually obtained jobs, but simply assumed that this would happen.[72]

This simply shows that in order to maintain low agricultural wages the supply of people desperate for work needed to be greater than the number of jobs available. The fact that many people who were excluded from the rolls could not find jobs was known by others who did have jobs. Consequently, they felt lucky to have any income at all and were reluctant to risk their jobs in collective action to improve their wages and working conditions.

The importance of maintaining a large supply of people with no recourse other than low-wage jobs was made clear by policies that prevented the supplementation of wages with relief. This was a change from New Deal programs, which provided relief to augment low wages. Indeed, the state of Georgia not only prohibited the supplementation of wages but also forbade the augmentation of child support payments with relief.[73]

Trying to ensure that relief payments would remain lower than wages was also part of the ill-fated Newburgh proposals. Most pertinent was the policy that the level of relief should be set below the take-home pay of the lowest-paid city employee with the same size family. Although the intent of this policy was implicit in the way relief payments were determined throughout the country, in the Newburgh plan it was actually spelled out.[74]

Conclusion

In the conservative environment of the post–World War II era, the only type of government work programs that existed were punitive and mandatory. Proposals to establish a work program that would provide a job for everyone who wanted to work as part of an economic bill of rights were buried with the end of the WPA. And instead of the 1945 Full Employment Bill, which would have committed the federal government to maintain full employment, the Employment Act of 1946 merely affirmed that the federal government would use macroeconomic policies to try to create the *conditions* for maximum employment.

Work requirements connected to relief replaced the massive New Deal job creation programs. Welfare recipients were made available for work through "employable mother" policies when their labor was needed and by simply denying aid to African-American recipients at times of high seasonal demand for agricultural workers. Supplemented by "suitable home" and "substitute father" policies, poor, mostly black, women who bore children outside marriage were periodically removed from the relief rolls. Their only recourse was wage labor—at virtually any wage— or marriage. However, government work program policy was about to change, as the 1960s witnessed a flowering of fair work programs.

4

The 1960s: The Flowering of Government Work Programs

The 1960s brought a tremendous expansion in AFDC and an array of new government work programs. There was a sense during this time among policymakers that all that was needed was to come up with the right programs—that the U.S. possessed the will and the capacity to eliminate poverty and simply had to develop programs that would be effective. In contrast to the punitive policies of the postwar period, resumed during the 1980s and 1990s, the 1960s focused on "human reclamation."[1] As in the past, however, the fair work programs were based on the male pauper model: the belief that poverty could be ended by providing jobs that allowed a "breadwinner"—understood to be a man—to support his family. Again, women were marginalized.

The Economic Boom of the 1960s

The 1960s were a time of unprecedented economic prosperity. Following a series of recessions from the late 1940s through the early 1960s, the years 1961 through 1969 saw uninterrupted economic expansion. Based on a stable set of economic and political institutions and fueled by high government spending on the Vietnam War and social programs at home, production of goods and services grew 45 percent throughout the decade and unemployment fell, remaining below 4 percent of the labor force from 1966 through 1969.[2] The sustained low unemployment increased workers' ability to obtain higher wages and better working conditions, since they could not be replaced as easily, and average weekly earnings (adjusted for inflation) continued the rise that had begun after World War II, growing another 15 percent during the decade.[3]

As in the past, the prosperity of the 1960s was not equally shared by all groups in society. Women compared to men, and people of color compared to whites, consistently experienced lower average earnings and higher rates of unemployment. Earnings differentials between women and men worsened throughout the decade as the ratio between women's median income and men's median income for year-round, full-time workers) shrank from 61 percent in 1960 to 58 percent by 1969. When considering all female and male workers, the differential is nearly twice as great, reflecting women's greater likelihood of working part-time and/or part-year. Yet it improved slightly through the decade, from 30 percent to 33 percent, as women took advantage of the increased employment (both in hours per week and weeks per year) created by the economic expansion.[4] The ratio between black and white median family income improved more significantly, from 55 percent in 1960 to 61 percent by the end of the decade.[5]

Racial and gender inequality was also seen in comparative unemployment rates. During the recession of 1961, which preceded the expansion, while the unemployment rate for white men was 5.7 percent but 6.5 percent for white women, 12.8 percent for men of color (black and other racial minorities), and 11.9 percent for women of color. Furthermore, while unemployment rates for all groups fell as the economic expansion of the 1960s continued, the gaps between the groups widened. By 1969, after eight years of robust expansion reduced the unemployment rate for white men to 2.5 percent, the lowest rate since World War II, rates for the other groups were significantly higher: 4.2 percent for white women, 5.3 percent for men of color, and 7.8 percent for women of color.[6]

Women's responsibility for maintaining families continued its steady increase during the 1960s. Between 1960 and 1970 the percentage of families headed by women grew from 8.1 percent to 9.0 percent for white women, from 21.7 percent to 27.4 percent for African-American women, and from 11.9 percent to 13.4 percent for Hispanic women.[7] Among other results, this meant that in conjunction with their higher unemployment rates and lower earnings, greater numbers of women met the eligibility requirements for welfare.

Growing employment opportunities along with a heightened awareness among white middle-class women that they could combine work in the home with wage labor led to a continuing rise in the labor force participation rate for white women—from 36.5 percent in 1960 to 41.8

percent by 1969. The ongoing difficulties faced by African-American men in obtaining jobs and their lower wages compared to white men helped maintain higher labor force participation rates for black women (and other women of color). These rates increased slightly, from 48.2 percent in 1960 to 49.8 percent by 1969.[8]

The Burgeoning of Fair Work Programs

The 1960s witnessed a veritable explosion of fair work programs. In the context of the liberal domestic social policies of the Kennedy and Johnson administrations, these manpower programs were seen as an investment in human beings, reclaiming human resources that would otherwise be lost. By the mid-1960s, they had become an accepted, and many believed permanent, policy tool of the federal government.[9]

Fair work programs sprang from two different types of concerns and led to an emphasis on different program components and target populations. Worries about structural unemployment (caused by changing technology or decreased demand for products, which rendered some skills obsolete) among mostly white male heads-of-household led to an initial focus on skill development and training. Increased attention to poverty, especially among young African-American men who were in the forefront of the urban ghetto riots, led to a shift in priority to work experience and support services, as well as education, job market skills, and outreach. Although women were included, the term "manpower policy" was quite accurate, and the main focus of the programs remained on men.

The Area Redevelopment Act

The concept of training programs was kept alive throughout the post–World War II era by policy institutes. They were worried about the periodic recessions and accompanying increased cyclical unemployment, as well as the persistent high structural unemployment that remained even when the economy expanded. As in the past, white male heads-of-household were their primary focus.

By 1959 these concerns led the U.S. Senate to convene a Special Committee on Unemployment Problems. Apprehension was intensified by the sharp 1957–1958 recession, the most severe since the 1930s, as the overall unemployment rate rose to 7.6 percent and the rate for white men climbed to 6.1 percent.[10] The 1960–1961 recession was all that was needed to prod the government to take action. In hearings convened by the Special Committee, legislators and policy analysts worried about stagnationist tendencies in the U.S. economy as evidenced in the periodic recessions. While fiscal policy to stimulate the economy and create jobs was considered critically important, it was agreed that these macroeconomic policies did not adequately address the situation of people whose skills were no longer needed. While employers spoke of the lack of skilled workers, workers said they could not find jobs. The problem was seen as one of "square pegs and round holes," and the answer was thought to be retraining.[11]

Federal employment and training programs began on a small scale with the 1961 Area Redevelopment Act (ARA). This bill, which had been passed by Congress and vetoed twice by Eisenhower, provided monetary incentives for employers to locate in depressed rural areas. One of the incentives was federally subsidized training, which it was believed would provide a more suitable workforce.[12] At last, some recommendations of the National Resources Planning Board and manpower institutes interested in work and training programs had come to fruition.

The Manpower Development and Training Administration

The ARA was the first of the 1960s work programs, but it was the Manpower Development and Training Administration (MDTA), passed in 1962, that really got manpower policy off the ground. It provided two types of training: institutional training, also called classroom training (CT), and on-the-job training (OJT). CT was based on the same premise as vocational education, as new vocational skills were learned in a classroom setting. Operating out of skill centers, sometimes as part of the public schools, the MDTA provided participants with training allowances for up to one year. The average stipend was only $35 per week, however, even less than the minimum wage, and so low that as the economic expansion of the 1960s gained steam increasing numbers of white men left the program for higher-wage jobs.[13]

OJT involved training while people were working. Since they were paid a wage, additional government stipends were not necessary. Increasing in importance over the decade, OJT was promoted as a cost-effective way to provide up-to-date training, since employers already had the machinery and presumably kept up with technological developments. Employers received a subsidy, seen as part of the trainee's wage, as an incentive to hire OJT participants. It was argued that these subsidies were necessary to counteract the costs of red tape and to compensate employers for hiring "less desirable workers."[14]

Throughout the discussions of the MDTA, attention centered on men. They were seen as the target population—heads of families with at least three years of labor market experience, as well as heads of families with low incomes (less than twelve hundred dollars annually) living in rural areas.[15] It was understood that participants would predominantly be white, male, and married.

Soon after it began, the MDTA's focus shifted to young African-American men. While one factor was the increased employment opportunities for white men that accompanied the economic expansion, the other and more pressing reason was the eruption of riots in urban ghettos. The evolving change in emphasis was officially recognized in the 1966 MDTA amendments, as distinctions were made between training for each group. Thirty-five percent of the funds were to be spent on "job-oriented" skill training, primarily for the original target group; the remaining 65 percent of the funds would be used for "person-oriented" training that would be "directed to reclaiming the hard-core unemployed."[16]

The MDTA remained one of the largest work programs of the 1960s, with annual enrollment averaging 209,900 participants.[17] Yet the changing priorities were reflected in its relative size, and the by the end of the decade it was overshadowed by the youth programs, primarily the Neighborhood Youth Corps (NYC).

While most of the fair work programs of the 1960s focused on men, they were far more balanced in terms of race than their predecessors. This is not surprising, since they were intended primarily as antipoverty programs.

The program that showed the greatest gender and racial inequality was the MDTA. This was evident not only in the higher participation rates for whites and for men compared to other programs but also in the disparities between the CT and the OJT components. Through 1972, men made up 55 percent of those in the classroom training programs and 70 percent of OJT participants, and African-Americans made up 39 percent of the participants in CT and 28 percent of those in OJT.[18] This is an issue because participants benefited more from OJT than from CT; OJT enrollees were more likely than those in CT to obtain a job, and at a higher wage, when their time in the program ended.[19]

Gender and racial bias in the MDTA was also bolstered by the failure to challenge existing patterns of occupational segregation. Thus women were overrepresented (compared to their total enrollment in the MDTA) in training for clerical and other service work. African-American men were similarly overrepresented in training for service occupations, but underrepresented in training for professional, technical, and skilled work.[20] These lower-level service jobs have historically paid lower average wages than manufacturing. Although program administrators claimed that they were simply training people for the jobs they were most likely to obtain, their acceptance of occupational segregation helped replicate gender and racial inequalities in the program.

The Rise of Protest and the Debate Over the War on Poverty

The decade of the 1960s was marked by often tumultuous social protest. Erupting in the mid-1950s, the civil rights movement expanded in the early 1960s as a variety of tactics forced the federal government to protect the rights of African-Americans, especially in the clearly segregated South. Sit-ins at lunch counters, freedom rides in which blacks and whites traveled together on buses, protest marches, boycotts of white-owned businesses, freedom schools, and voter registration drives were the main tactics that eventually brought federal intervention, most importantly through the Civil Rights Act of 1964 and the Voting Rights Act of 1965.[21]

The civil rights movement was the most important impetus for the War on Poverty. By the early 1960s the movement was branching out from its initial campaigns as activists addressed economic issues. Organizing was both local, through rent strikes, boycotts, and demonstrations, and national, through the massive March on Washington for Jobs and Freedom in August 1963. In response, President Kennedy set up a task force to explore the economic and social concerns of African-Americans and begin to develop antipoverty policies. Federal officials were especially worried about the masses of blacks who left the rural South and migrated to cities in both the South and North as the mechanization of agriculture after World War II eliminated the demand for much of their labor.[22] In fact, the rise in juvenile delinquency caused by the breakdown of community ties and bleak employment prospects was addressed before the War on Poverty was even conceived, in the 1961 Juvenile Delinquency and Youth Offenders Control Act.

The War on Poverty was conceived in fertile ideological and economic ground. Indicative of this attitude, Michael Harrington's *The Other America,* which documented the widespread existence of poverty in the U.S., was widely read in the Kennedy White House. After Kennedy's assassination, President Johnson campaigned vigorously for the Economic Opportunity Act. Signing the bill in August 1964, he affirmed the commitment of a "great nation . . . to eradicate poverty among its people."[23]

The robust economy made it easier politically to implement social programs intended to alleviate poverty. It was perceived that as a nation the U.S. could afford antipoverty programs. And in the wake of the riots that began in August 1965 in the Watts section of Los Angeles, many believed that the nation could ill afford not to do something. As the cities burned, programs were developed and expanded.[24] Thus the tenor of the 1960s debates was the antithesis of the 1980s and 1990s, as administrators searched for policies they thought would improve people's lives and eliminate societal ills.[25]

The focus of the War on Poverty was a topic of debate during its early years. Some government officials argued that the programs should concentrate on job creation, with adults as the primary target population. They lost on both counts. Instead, the War on Poverty programs concentrated on services and on youths.

Most government administrators agreed that the "jobs problem" would be solved through a general fiscal policy of tax cuts and increases in government spending. This would expand the economy and create jobs, enough for everyone who was able to work.[26] Then, analogous to skills training through the MDTA, the "disadvantaged" would need "supplemental boosts"—via training and ancillary services—in order to compete effectively in the labor market. This focus on a "service strategy" was grounded in the belief that with the proper education and training the poor would be able to obtain decent jobs.[27]

Not everyone believed that the private sector would necessarily create enough jobs, and many voices were heard advocating job creation as a centerpiece of the War on Poverty. Willard Wirtz, secretary of labor in the Johnson administration, argued strenuously for public-sector job creation to alleviate the strains of a 35 percent subemployment rate in the inner cities.[28] The AFL-CIO emphasized job creation, stating that "half of American's poverty problem is directly related to the lack of enough jobs at decent pay."[29] Job creation would both alleviate poverty and increase the demand for labor, thereby helping maintain higher wages. Many Democratic senators supported job creation, seeing it as a key to making the training programs effective.[30] What good was training if people could not find jobs when they were done? Job creation was also part of the "Freedom Budget," which was developed in 1966 by the A. Philip Randolph Institute and signified the continuing focus of the civil rights movement on economic justice.[31]

There was substantial support for job creation from the general public. A Harris poll taken in the wake of the 1967 riots found that 66 percent of whites and a full 91 percent of African-Americans favored massive job creation as a preventative strategy.[32] This was echoed in the Report of the Kerner Commission, which investigated the riots and recommended the creation of one million jobs in the public sector.[33]

Large-scale public sector job creation did not come about until the 1970s, however. Three main factors figured in this postponement. First, the expanding economy led more and more government officials to believe that jobs really would be created by the private sector for all those able to work. Furthermore, they worried that labor markets would become too tight—that is, demand for certain types of labor would be greater than the supply—which would drive up wages and set off inflation. Second, the escalating Vietnam War was causing budgetary pressures, as many officials came to believe that the war took precedence over domestic spending. Finally, there was a knee-jerk reaction whenever job creation was mentioned. The dreaded specter of the WPA as a boondoggle was raised, and job creation programs were denounced as make-work and leading to dead-end jobs. Even those who supported job creation tried to differentiate their recommendations from the generally accepted assessments of the WPA. For example, the Kerner Commission Report stated, "Emphasis should be placed on employing trainees to improve rundown neighborhoods and to perform a variety of other socially useful public services which are not make-work.' "[34]

As the War on Poverty got under way, the focus on African-American men was further reinforced by Daniel P. Moynihan's widely publicized 1965 report published by the Department of Labor, *The Negro Family: The Case for National Action.*[35] Generally known as *The Moynihan Report,* it theorized that the "steady disintegration of the Negro family structure" was caused by discrimination and by the development of a matriarchy among black women. In other words, black women were too strong. According to Moynihan, this led to a "tangle of pathology" affecting youths, from alienation to dropping out of school to juvenile delinquency. His solution, embedded in the male pauper model, was to restore the position of black men as family "breadwinners," since this would promote family stability and better socialize young people.

The Economic Opportunity Act and the Variety of Fair Work Programs

The cornerstone of the War on Poverty was the 1964 Economic Opportunity Act, which set up the Office of Economic Opportunity (OEO) and provided the institutional basis for most of the antipoverty programs and policies.[36] Based on the earlier Mobilization for Youth (MFY), the programs were intended to bring the "economically disadvantaged" into the mainstream of U.S. society, and primarily targeted the urban poor, mainly African-Americans. While some of the programs included a focus on women, they were predominantly aimed at men.

The programs included a variety of components. Classroom training and on-the-job training were carried over from the MDTA. "Work experience" provided jobs in public sector and nonprofit agencies. Intended more as an income transfer program than as skill training, it came closest to what could be construed as job creation during this decade. Work experience was also provided in the private sector, with employers receiving a subsidy, theoretically for training, and participants being paid a wage. Educational components focused on remedial and basic education for adults. "Employment skills" training, also called prevocational training, primarily involved socialization regarding work habits and attitudes, as well as job search skills. Participants in these education and training components were usually paid a stipend. An array of support services was developed to enable people to make use of the programs. Most important were subsidies for work-related expenses, including child care and transportation, small subsidies (usually under one hundred dollars) for medical expenses necessary to obtain jobs (for example, eyeglasses or physical exams), and counseling. Job placement assistance helped people find jobs upon completion of education and training.

Community action agencies were the most innovative aspect of the OEO. By 1967 more than one thousand of these multiservice neighborhood centers had been set up. Mandated to operate with "maximum feasible participation" of the poor, the agencies developed policies, directed people to social services, provided paid employment for community workers, offered legal assistance on an individual and group basis, and organized community residents to demand services provided by other local government agencies. Men were usually the visible leaders, but most of the day-to-day organizing and provision of services was done by women.[37]

Participation in the community action agencies was often empowering. As one woman explained; "It's like the women are starting to feel good about themselves. . . . They have great potential. But they've always been in the house. . . . It amazed me that people had not even been out of the community because they're scared. And they grew up."[38]

The role of women in the community action agencies was facilitated through the New Careers program established in 1966. (In 1970 it was replaced by Public Service Careers.) New Careers was intended both to meet some of the increased demand for social services and to provide work experience for low-income adults. Designed to offer an "alternative career path" that did not require the extensive training mandated by traditional professional work, indigenous community residents served as a bridge between middle-class professionals in agencies and the low-income population. More importantly, as Nancy A. Naples explains, New Careers and the community action agencies offered the first state-sponsored support for the community work of low-income women. In a sense it was too successful, and bureaucratic regulations and increased emphasis on credentials soon circumscribed the program's effectiveness.[39]

Programs for Youths. Low-income youths of color (age sixteen through twenty or twenty-one) were the focus of two programs spawned by the Economic Opportunity Act, the Neighborhood Youth Corps (NYC), and the Job Corps. The NYC was the largest of all the War on Poverty programs, enrolling almost half a million young people in 1970 and continuing to expand until it served more than one million people each year.[40] The Job Corps is the only one of the War on Poverty work programs still in existence; it currently receives limited federal support through the Job Training Partnership Act (JTPA).

The NYC was one of the first programs set up under the Economic Opportunity Act. Designed to keep youths in school, help them return to school, or increase their employability if they dropped out, the NYC was intended to provide positive labor market experiences and thereby decrease teenage crime in the present and "welfare dependency" in the future. Offering work experience, remedial education, skills training, prevocational training, placement assistance, counseling, and support services, the NYC also functioned as an income transfer program for the poor. Three separate program components evolved. The program for youths who had dropped out of school focused on work experience and prevocational training in order to "establish work habits and attitudes that will stand them in good stead for their whole working lives."[41] The in-school program targeted potential dropouts who were still enrolled in school, offering part-time work experience and related services. By the late 1960s these components were overshadowed by the summer program, which provided work experience for youths who were still in school, as the NYC grew to dwarf not only the MDTA but all of the other antipoverty programs as well. Participation by gender was relatively balanced in the NYC: almost half the enrollees were women. Reflecting the concern about African-Americans, almost half of the participants were black.[42]

The Job Corps set up residential centers to provide education and training for youths who were considered more seriously disadvantaged and most likely to become juvenile delinquents. When it was first planned, the Job Corps was intended only for young men.[43] Although Congress broadened the program to include women, most of participants were black male youths from urban ghettos.[44] Compared to the NYC, the Job Corps remained small, serving an average of only forty-two thousand people a year through the early 1970s.[45]

Additional War on Poverty Programs. Additional programs were developed as part of the War on Poverty to reach different target populations. Two programs were established in 1964 to help African-Americans obtain jobs and training. The Opportunities Industrialization Centers (OIC) offered skill training and prevocational training to place urban blacks in entry-level jobs. Counseling and outreach were important in drawing people into the program, and more than two-thirds of the OIC's enrollees were women. Both the improving labor markets and the lack of stipends meant that people often left the program after a short time to accept jobs. The Apprenticeship Outreach Program (AOP), financed through the MDTA, helped young people of color qualify for apprenticeships, especially in the construction industry. Although the AOP did not offer training, it acted as a clearinghouse—recruiting, disseminating information, providing intensive tutoring to help prepare for entrance examinations, and serving as a labor exchange. It was understood that participants would be males.[46]

Operation Mainstream was all that was left of the calls for "massive funding of public employment" as part of the Economic Opportunity Act.[47] However, instead of a large job creation program, only a small amount (ten million dollars initially) was appropriated for a narrowly defined program. Providing community service work for chronically unemployed older adults in predominantly rural areas, it served primarily white men and remained small, enrolling fewer than one hundred thousand people through 1972.[48]

The Concentrated Employment Program (CEP), developed in 1967 under both the MDTA and the Economic Opportunity Act, epitomizes the 1960s search for policies to alleviate poverty. Designed to reach the "severely disadvantaged," the CEPs provided a multiple set of remedial manpower services, including counseling, employment skills training, job development, and outreach. Set up in areas of high unemployment and poverty, primarily inner cities, the CEPs often functioned as the manpower arm of the local community action agency. Almost half a million people, two-thirds of them African-American and two-fifths of them women, were served through 1972.[49]

By 1968, private-sector employers, spurred to action by the shortage of labor caused by the prolonged economic expansion, developed a job training program for the poor. Under the aegis of the National Alliance of Business (NAB) in conjunction with the federal government, Job Opportunities in the Business Sector (JOBS) was created to hire, train, and retain the "disadvantaged," almost two-thirds of whom were African-American and two-thirds male. As in the MDTA, employers received a subsidy for hiring JOBS participants.[50]

JOBS was generally seen as a failure. Although there was much enthusiasm for the program when labor markets were tight, this attitude changed with the advent of a recession in 1969. As unemployment increased, many of those hired through JOBS were among the first to be fired. JOBS was also criticized for providing little or no skill training, but wage subsidies to employers for hiring people in primarily unskilled jobs. Furthermore, only 5 percent of the funds allocated by Congress were spent in the first year, leading many government officials to believe that even with government subsidies the private sector could not create sufficient numbers of jobs. This became important in 1970, when a large-scale public employment program was finally enacted.[51]

Federal Work Programs for Welfare Recipients

The welfare system underwent some dramatic changes in the 1960s. An explosion in the AFDC program increased the numbers of people on the rolls as well as the average payments. Federal work programs for welfare recipients were also developed during the 1960s through the 1962 Community Work and Training (CWT) program, replaced in 1964 by the Work Experience and Training (WET) program, which in turn was supplanted in 1967 by the Work Incentive (WIN) Program. In contrast to the work programs since 1971, however, these were primarily voluntary and focused disproportionately on men. In addition, informal work requirements remained in effect, as African-Americans were still removed from the welfare rolls during planting and harvesting seasons.

Protest and the "Welfare Explosion"

The rise of protest was critical not only to the War on Poverty as a whole but also to the "welfare explosion." Realizing that the AFDC system was a large untapped source of funds for poor women and children, organizers through the Mobilization for Youth (MFY) informed potential recipients of their right to receive welfare. This idea was broadcast by Frances Fox Piven and Richard A. Cloward, authors of *Regulating the Poor,* whose involvement in MFY led them to draft "A Strategy to End Poverty" in late 1965. In it they argued that if all those entitled to AFDC received their full payments, the resulting fiscal and political crises would lead national officials to federalize the system and assure a minimum income.[52]

    The upshot of these efforts was the National Welfare Rights Organization (NWRO), chronicled in Guida West's comprehensive history of the movement as "the social protest of poor women."[53] Declaring that "welfare should be a right, not a privilege," tactics were adopted from the civil rights movement, as welfare recipients informed others of their right to receive welfare, staged sit-ins at welfare offices, deluged welfare departments with requests for funds, and, in general, empowered women to demand to be treated with dignity and respect. Johnnie Tillmon, one of the NWRO leaders, explained why she saw welfare as a women's issue:

> The truth is that A.F.D.C. is like a supersexist marriage. You trade in a man for *the* man. But you can't divorce him if he treats you bad. He can divorce you, of course, cut you off anytime he wants. But in that case, *he* keeps the kids, not you.

She went on to declare the importance of organizing:

> There's one good thing about welfare. It kills your illusions about yourself, and about where this society is really at. It's laid out for you straight. You have to learn to fight, to be aggressive, or you just don't make it. If you can survive on welfare, you can survive anything. It gives you a kind of freedom, a sense of your own power and togetherness with other women.[54]

As welfare applicants became more indignant and insistent, existing procedures were relaxed, and both the numbers of people on the AFDC rolls and the amount of the payments themselves substantially increased.[55]

The explosion in AFDC was significant. From 1960 through 1970 the rolls almost tripled—from 787,000 families initially to 2,208,000 at the end of the decade. (The rolls continued to increase, to 3,588,000 families, through the high point in 1977.) Average monthly payments per family (adjusted for inflation) increased 35 percent from 1960 through the maximum in 1968 (to $706 in 1994 dollars) and fell slightly thereafter. This was partially offset by a steady decline in the average size of welfare families—from the peak of 4.2 in 1965 to 2.9 in 1979. In fact, contrary to a widely held belief, the average size of AFDC families has remained 2.9 since 1979—one adult and slightly less than two children.[56]

The increases in numbers of recipients and payments were accompanied by other developments in welfare, all of which were part of the broadly construed antipoverty policies. The first of these came in 1961 with the expansion of the ADC program to Aid to Dependent Children-Unemployed Parent (ADC-UP). While the old regulations only allowed families with one parent present to qualify for ADC, ADC-UP gave states the option of including two-parent families as well. As a result, in some states poor families with unemployed fathers could now qualify for welfare.

The following year saw a further expansion in the welfare system through amendments to the Social Security Act, generally referred to as the Social Service Amendments. The program's broader scope was seen in its new name, as Aid to Dependent Children, or ADC, was changed to Aid to Families with Dependent Children, or AFDC. (ADC-UP then became AFDC-UP.) A major new program, Medicaid, was established in 1965, providing health care to AFDC recipients as well as others in poverty. (Medicare was set up at this time for the elderly.) And by the late 1960s, courts had declared illegal residency requirements, "suitable home" rules, and "employable mother" regulations, resulting in a further expansion of welfare eligibility.[57]

Work Programs for Welfare Recipients

By the early 1960s, concerns about growing "welfare dependency" engendered by the post–World War II increase in the rolls, especially the rising numbers of African-Americans, led to the development of federal workfare programs. These began in 1962 with the Community Work and Training Program (CWT) and its 1964 successor, the Work Experience and Training Program (WET). Although implemented on a small scale, they served as prototypes for the Work Incentive (WIN) Program in 1967. Using a combination of "carrots," or incentives, and "sticks," or sanctions, these programs aimed to move welfare recipients into wage labor or to have them "work off" their welfare payments.

The rhetoric surrounding the 1960s workfare programs was similar to although milder than that of the 1980s and 1990s. As President Kennedy explained when he signed the Social Service Amendments establishing the CWT, they were intended to help the system provide "rehabilitation instead of relief, and training for useful work instead of prolonged dependency."[58] As in the past, this view was grounded in the male pauper model, since it was believed that families would be strengthened if a parent, presumably the father, worked for wages. In fact, even though African-American women were still forced off the rolls and into the fields when their low-wage labor was needed, discussions continued throughout the 1960s about whether all mothers—read white mothers—with young children should formally be required, or even encouraged, to work outside the home.[59] Reflecting this ongoing debate, as well as the prevailing norms of fair work, all three "welfare-to-work" programs stressed incentives instead of sanctions.

The Community Work and Training program

The Community Work and Training (CWT) program was included in the 1962 Social Service Amendments along with two additional provisions designed to "rehabilitate" welfare recipients. First, while the MDTA provided training primarily for unemployed heads-of-household regardless of their income, the Social Service Amendments supplied federal funds (on a matching basis of three federal dollars for each state-provided dollar) to provide services and training for welfare recipients. The funds were available for current recipients as well as former and potential ones. As in the MDTA, the primary focus—in terms of both rhetoric and services—was on unemployed fathers. Second, the amendments included a limited "work incentive": some work-related expenses (WREs), including child care, could be reimbursed.

The main provision for "rehabilitation" offered through the social service amendments was the CWT program. State or local governments could choose to implement CWTs, in which AFDC recipients considered employable could be required to "work off" their welfare payments. Hours of work were usually determined by dividing the welfare payment by the prevailing wage for the same type of work. (Typically, this was the minimum wage.) Fifty percent of the administrative costs were paid by the federal government, with the exception of "demonstration" projects, which were fully financed by the federal government and were most extensive in depressed coal-mining areas of eastern Kentucky.

Just as unemployed fathers on AFDC were the primary target of services and training, they were also the main focus of the CWT's mandatory work provisions. In addition, AFDC mothers could choose to participate. Much of the rhetoric surrounding the CWT concerned the creation of work relief projects to train and "rehabilitate" AFDC recipients and thereby "enrich and expand" the old "work-for-relief" programs. Yet government officials also admitted that the CWT would help counter criticisms that people who should work for wages were receiving welfare, a concern that increased when two-parent families were allowed on the AFDC rolls.

In spite of the grand intentions, the CWT remained a very small program. It had been adopted in only ten states (excluding the demonstration projects in Kentucky) by the time it was replaced two years later. Furthermore, instead of providing training and "rehabilitation" for welfare recipients, most CWT projects did in fact resemble the old "work-for-relief" programs. Much of the training was in work habits, and approximately 90 percent of the funds were used for work payments.[60]

The Work Experience and Training program

In 1964, the CWT was replaced by the Work Experience and Training (WET) program, implemented as Title V of the Economic Opportunity Act. Broadening the demonstration project component of the CWT, the federal government provided 100 percent of the funds. As explained in the Act, the WET program was intended to "expand the opportunities for constructive work experience and other needed training."[61]

Politicians had divergent goals for the WET program. Conservatives saw it as a way to get "malingerers" off the rolls, since they would have to work for their payments. Liberals focused on "rehabilitation," viewing the training, support services, and orientation in work habits as a way to help the poor obtain jobs. Still others saw WET as an income support program, believing that it would provide federal funds primarily to two-parent families with unemployed fathers in states without AFDC-UP.[62]

One hundred percent federal financing led every state except Alabama (and some territories) to implement the WET program. In spite of this, WET did not go far in meeting its goals. Only 150,000 people participated in the program, and much of the training continued to be of dubious value, consisting primarily of informal vocational training for low-wage jobs. Instead, as with the CWT, most of the activities consisted of the old-style "work-for-relief."[63]

The WET program in Mississippi was described in February 1967 hearings convened by its State Advisory Committee to the U.S. Commission on Civil Rights. Participants told of relief agencies providing African-American recipients to private-sector employers who were instructed to "use them any way you can." Black women on the rolls were put to work in dishwashing, heavy cleaning, hauling sacks of building materials, and cutting grass. Although women in the programs were theoretically trained for employment, Richard A. Cloward and Frances Fox Piven, who described these hearings in *The Nation,* commented that the training "scarcely equipped them for decent jobs, and furthermore, such jobs were not available for many people in Mississippi."[64]

"Training" that supplied AFDC recipients as low-wage workers was not confined to the South. For example, a "domestic service training program" was set up in Gary, Indiana. This seemed rather odd to many people. As one participant explained, "It seems rather unnecessary for a Negro to go to school to get a certificate to clean up someone else's house."[65]

The gender and racial composition of the WET program reflected the continuing economic boom. As the steady decline in unemployment led to an increase in workers' bargaining power, allowing them to secure higher wages and better working conditions, more people had alternatives to welfare. This was especially true for white men, and their numbers in the program steadily fell. While slightly more than one-third of the participants were African-American, the proportion of male participants dropped from 61 percent of the enrollees in December 1965 to 48 percent one year later. Federal administrators viewed the increasingly female composition of the program with dismay and urged project directors to "hold the line" and maintain a minimum of 50 percent of the positions for men.[66]

The Work Incentive Program

In 1967, WET was replaced by the Work Incentive (WIN) program, implemented through another set of amendments to the Social Security Act. The CWT, WET, and WIN all tried to move AFDC recipients off the rolls and into wage labor through a combination of training, support services, and monetary incentives. However, there were some important differences between the CWT and WET, on one hand, and WIN on the other. First, while the CWT and WET were optional, and indeed reflected the general experimental nature of the proliferating work and training programs, all states were required to implement WIN. Second, while participants in the CWT and WET worked only in exchange for their welfare payments—not wages—WIN moved AFDC recipients into wage labor. Third, while the CWT and WET contained some reimbursements for work-related expenses, WIN included much more fully developed monetary incentives in terms of both work-related expenses and income.

The most critical incentive was the income disregard, also called the work incentive bonus. Before the inception of WIN, all earnings from employment were deducted from recipients' welfare payment, effectively taxing them 100 percent. This provided no inducement to work for wages, since people ended up with the same amount of money whether they received it entirely as AFDC or had their wages supplemented with a lower AFDC payment. Since it is economically rational to work for wages only if people earn more in wages—after deductions for child care, health care, and work-related expenses—than they receive in welfare, it made sense to develop a monetary incentive for wage labor.

The income disregard did just that. If an AFDC recipient obtained a job, the welfare department would not count—that is, would disregard—the first thirty dollars plus one-third of the remaining income in the computation of the welfare payment. Work-related expenses, most importantly child care, transportation, meals, and uniforms, were also reimbursed. This provided a monetary inducement to work for wages, since recipients now ended up with more money from welfare plus wage labor than they had previously.[67] In addition, WIN paid a stipend of up to thirty dollars per month for participating in training programs, and it offered employment placement and skills assessment.

Supplementing these enhanced incentives for training and wage labor, WIN mandated the referral of AFDC recipients considered employable, primarily fathers in two-parent families. Debates about encouraging or requiring mothers to work outside the home apparently were not settled when the WIN program was passed, and the criteria for referral left room for a good deal of variation.[68] In addition to exempting recipients who were under age sixteen, attending school, ill or incapacitated, or needed in the home due to the illness or incapacity of another household member, state welfare agencies were allowed to adopt additional criteria.[69]

Discussions of WIN at the time it was passed focused on the age-old claim that "welfare dependence" should be replaced by wage labor, as this would be better for people's morale and would allow them to "earn their keep." Yet there were four underlying factors that led to its development in 1967. First, in the context of the proliferating manpower programs, WIN continued along the lines of the CWT and the WET to channel work and training more effectively toward AFDC recipients, especially adult men. Initially, sanctions were not often used; WIN's voluntary components were primary. Second, WIN was a reaction to the explosion of the AFDC rolls, both to the growing cost and to the changing composition of the AFDC population, particularly the increasing numbers of African-American women.[70] Third, although debates continued about whether mothers of young children should work outside the home, as increasing numbers of white, middle-class married women entered the labor force in the 1960s, work outside the home became more widely accepted, especially for mothers of school-age children.[71]

The final reason concerned the supply of low-wage labor. Since courts struck down "employable mother" and similar policies that had enabled welfare departments to remove people from the rolls when their labor was needed, other mechanisms were developed to try to ensure a sufficient number of people available to work in low-wage jobs. This became even more critical as the economic boom of the 1960s continued and unemployment fell, decreasing the supply of low-wage (and other) labor, which increased workers' job security and allowed them to obtain higher wages and better working conditions. Thus, by expanding the supply of low-wage workers the WIN program could both meet employers' immediate needs for workers and help dampen workers' bargaining power.

Results of WIN

The first phase of WIN, sometimes known as WIN I, lasted through 1971. While WIN I focused on incentives and only required the referral of eligible AFDC recipients, as we will see in the next chapter, WIN II mandated registration instead of referral and generally tightened the program.

WIN I was only slightly larger than the CWT and WET had been, enrolling 81,000 people in 1969, 93,000 in 1970, 112,000 in 1971, and 121,000 in 1972. As in the earlier programs, men in two-parent families were overrepresented in relation to their numbers on the rolls, making up 37 percent of all WIN participants. Racial composition was more balanced, as approximately one-fifth of the enrollees were Hispanic and two-fifths were African-American.[72]

WIN was the target of a great deal of criticism during its early years. Conservatives complained that too few people participated and that WIN did little to reduce the dreaded "welfare dependency"; liberals worried that not enough was done to pull people out of poverty. Both points were valid. Although referral to the program was mandatory for those considered employable, many exemptions were granted. Although 1.6 million cases were reviewed for referral to WIN during the program's first twenty months, only 10 percent were found to be suitable.[73] And even people who were referred to the program but did not participate faced little in the way of sanctions. Piven and Cloward explain that local officials in urban areas were reluctant to enforce the mandatory provisions for fear of sparking riots.[74] Instead, the expanding AFDC rolls and rising payments successfully siphoned off some protest, as the government was shown to be responsive to people's needs.

Liberals' complaints were also well founded, as WIN did little to "rehabilitate" welfare recipients. Again the situation was worse for women. Department of Labor studies of people who completed WIN training programs found average postprogram wages of $1.98 to $2.12 per hour for women and $2.43 to $2.76 for men.[75] Since women realized a greater percentage increase between their preprogram and postprogram wage rates compared to men, most of those conducting the studies claimed that WIN was a greater success for women than for men. However, these wages were barely enough to pull a family of four (the average family size in the 1960s) out of poverty even if someone worked full-time and year-round.[76] And since most AFDC recipients, especially women, could only find part-time and/or part-year work, they usually remained in poverty, and, often, still on welfare.

Conservatives' complaints that WIN did little to reduce welfare dependency were borne out by low placement rates for those enrolled in the program. Studies showed that only 24 percent of the men and 18 percent of the women who participated in WIN training had a job upon completion of the program.[77] The low numbers of people in the program, low placement rates, and low earnings meant that WIN did virtually nothing to halt the unprecedented growth of the AFDC rolls. Thus, it became an easy target for reform in the early 1970s.

Informal Work Requirements

Informal work requirements, which had been commonly used since the beginning of poor relief in colonial America, continued into the 1960s. In hearings held in 1966 in Cairo, Illinois, by the U.S. Commission on Civil Rights, African-Americans described how they were removed from the welfare rolls and told to get a job in the fields. One person told of his experiences:

> I is on farm labor during the summer, and during the winter I am on ADC, and in May every year, May, I get a letter that my grant will be cut off because, due to full-time employment. I mean they never comes out to check to see if my employment have started, they just send the letter saying your grant will be cut off. They don't know when my employment even starts, which everyone knows this year the month of May it rained practically all the month, but still I got the same letter, the same type of letter saying that I would be cut off due to full-time employment. I think they should see if my work really have started before they cut me off, but they don't do it. I mean they cut me off each year completely.[78]

Such obvious forced-work methods were ended when "employable mother" rules were declared illegal.

Conclusion

The 1960s were a time of expansion of the welfare state and experimentation with social programs. The explosion in the welfare rolls and increase in welfare payments provided more adequate support for millions of people, mostly poor women and their children. Fair work programs flourished in the fertile soil of protest and liberal domestic policies, as government administrators tried to develop a variety of programs to meet the needs of the poor.

As in the past, the fair work programs focused on men, initially white male heads-of-household, and, as the War on Poverty got underway in the mid-1960s, young African-American men. While women were not as marginalized as they had been in past fair work programs, men remained the primary focus. Yet some of the War on Poverty programs, especially New Careers, demonstrate the possibilities of programs in meeting women's needs. And the community action agencies illustrate the potential outreach and mobilization that can draw people into programs and empower those working in the agencies, as well as people in the community. Reviving similar programs could help provide a needed antidote to the individualism and outright greed of the 1980s and 1990s.

5

The 1970s: The Revival of Job Creation Programs

The 1970s saw the further evolution of government work programs. Workfare was beefed up through the Work Incentive (WIN) program and Community Work Experience Programs (CWEPs). And as the developing economic crisis brought recession and increased unemployment, job creation was revived after an almost thirty-year hiatus, first in the Public Employment Program (PEP) from 1971 to 1973 and then under the Public Service Employment (PSE) program of the Comprehensive Employment and Training Act (CETA) from 1973 through 1981. Not surprisingly, while workfare was lauded by the business sector, PEP, and especially PSE, came under almost continual attack. These criticisms became a mantra—repeated over and over as the generally accepted assessment of the programs. Yet PEP and PSE were even more seriously constrained than their 1930s predecessors. The earlier programs provided work in construction, the arts, and production of consumer goods, but PEP and PSE, as their names imply, could only provide service work. However, services are even more susceptible than goods production to charges of inefficiency and makework. The ongoing criticisms were reflected, in part, in the programs' size. Whereas the 1930s programs provided work for 1.4 to 4.4 million people each month, the maximum in the 1970s programs was only 742,000—even though the labor force had doubled since the 1930s and government at all levels had grown substantially.

Also consistent with the earlier programs, PEP and CETA continued to focus on white men—even though the 1960s term "manpower" was replaced in the early 1970s by the gender-neutral "employment and training." By the late 1970s, however, some innovative although short-lived training programs were developed for women—for "displaced homemakers," teenage mothers, and training in "nontraditional occupations" (NTOs)—illustrating the possibilities of education and training programs in meeting women's needs.

Women and Economic Hard Times

The economic prosperity that characterized the post–World War II era came to an end by 1973, as underlying structural problems led to economic hard times.[1] The recession, which began in November of that year and lasted through March 1975, was the most severe since the Great Depression of the 1930s, causing a 4.3 percent decline in the production of goods and services and an increase in unemployment to 9.1 percent of the labor force.[2] Workers were put on the defensive as high unemployment weakened their bargaining power, reversing the steady rise in wages that began after World War II and leading to a 7.5 percent decline in average weekly earnings (adjusted for inflation) from 1973 through the end of the decade (and another 11 percent in the 1980s).[3]

The economic crisis was manifested in higher rates of both unemployment and inflation. This heretofore unseen situation led economists to coin a new term, "stagflation," to describe the simultaneous *stag*nation and in*flation*.[4] Although government officials and the business community were very concerned, especially about inflation, the federal government's primary response was one of muddling through with traditional fiscal and monetary policy tools.[5] Although the problems are much clearer in hindsight, their institutional causes were neither understood nor addressed. President Nixon, for the brief time he was in office after the crisis began, was so caught up in the Watergate scandal that he had relatively little attention for other matters. And neither President Ford nor President Carter had the political consensus or the analysis to implement policies that could begin to address the underlying problems. In fact, not until 1981, when Ronald Reagan became President, were some of the underlying issues dealt with—in the interests of capitalists.

Local governments faced an additional problem. While rising unemployment led to lower tax revenues, legislative initiatives throughout the country brought limitations in property taxes. These "taxpayer's revolts," from Proposition 13 in California to Proposition 2 1/2 in Massachusetts, reduced local tax revenues and wreaked havoc with government services through the 1990s.

The decline in workers' earnings had two main effects on women's economic status. First, in order to maintain family income, even more women entered the labor force. Consequently, in the 1970s the labor force participation rate for white women increased 19 percent—from 42.6 percent to 50.5 percent—and the rate for women of color rose 7 percent—from 49.5 percent to 53.1 percent.[6] Second, women's median earnings fell, along with those of men, and the ratio between the earnings of women and men who worked year-round and full-time remained between 57 and 59 percent throughout the decade.[7] As had been true historically, unemployment rates remained higher for women than for men, and for people of color compared to whites, throughout the 1970s. In 1979, while the unemployment rate stood at 4.5 percent for white men, it was 5.9 percent for white women, 11.4 percent for black men, and 13.3 percent for African-American women.[8]

This bleak situation for women was somewhat alleviated by social welfare policies implemented during the 1960s. The expansion of AFDC was especially important, as poverty rates fell to their lowest levels ever in the U.S. The low of 11.1 percent was reached in 1973, the year in which the economy hit its peak, and rates between 11.1 percent and 12.6 percent marked the entire decade.[9] Furthermore, African-American women made significant progress, reflected in the ratio between black women's median income and white women's median income, which narrowed from 82 percent in 1970 to 91 percent by 1980. This advance was largely due to federal affirmative action policies and was seen in the growing numbers of black women obtaining government jobs. The income gap between African-American men and white men also narrowed, though far less substantially than for women, increasing slightly from 68 percent in 1970 to 72 percent by 1979.[10]

Women's responsibilities for families continued to increase, reflecting the steady rise of female-headed families. Between 1970 and 1980, the proportion of households headed by women rose from 9.0 percent to 10.6 percent for whites, from 13.4 percent to 15.9 percent for Hispanics, and from 27.4 percent to 37.2 percent for African-Americans.[11]

Workfare Programs

Government work programs for welfare recipients shifted from their 1960s focus on voluntary components to emphasize mandatory policies. The backlash to the continuing growth of the AFDC rolls and concern about "welfare dependency," the increasing participation of white middle-class women in the labor force, the end of informal methods of removing people from the rolls when their labor was needed, and employers' continuing need for large supplies of low-wage labor combined to strengthen the belief that welfare recipients should work outside the home. Just as the antipoverty programs of the 1960s were instigated by the civil rights movement and developed in the more open atmosphere of the Kennedy and Johnson administrations, the 1970s constriction was part of the law-and-order ideology and emphasis on self-reliance that undergirded the repressive policies advanced by the Nixon administration. The changes in government work programs were part of the general tightening of social welfare programs that began shortly after Nixon became president in 1969. Stressing an ideology of self-help, his administration immediately began to restrict the programs developed as part of the War on Poverty. The community action agencies were quickly brought under federal control, and the Office of Economic Opportunity was decimated, as its funding was cut and most of its programs were moved to other departments.[12] Following the defeat of Nixon's welfare reform proposal, the Family Assistance Plan (FAP), the Work Incentive (WIN) program was tightened and some experimental work programs were developed, most importantly the Supported Work Demonstration (SWD) project and the notorious Community Work Experience Program (CWEP), better known as workfare.

Expansion and Restriction in AFDC

The early 1970s saw a continuation of the "welfare explosion," as the AFDC rolls increased dramatically, from 2,208,000 families in 1970 to 2,762,000 in 1971 and 3,049,000 in 1972. They rose more slowly through 1977, as higher unemployment forced more people to turn to welfare, to a maximum of 3,588,000 families. Thereafter, reflecting the overall restrictiveness in federal government policies beginning in 1978, the rolls declined slightly, to 3,509,000 families in 1979.[13]

Average (inflation-adjusted) payments per family continued the decline that began in 1966, falling another 23 percent during the decade. This was partially offset by the ongoing decrease in the average number of people in AFDC families, which fell from 3.8 members in 1970 to 2.9 to 1979—one adult and slightly less than two children—where it remained through the early 1990s. Thus, average monthly payments per recipient (adjusted for inflation) increased 8 percent from 1971 through 1977, falling back to the original level by 1979.[14]

The Family Assistance Plan

The Family Assistance Plan (FAP) was introduced into Congress soon after Nixon took office.[15] It had two main components. The first involved establishing a minimum income paid by the federal government, initially set at sixteen hundred dollars per year for a family of four (five hundred for each adult and three hundred for each child). This amount could be supplemented by individual states at their discretion and would be available to all of the "working poor," both those with children and single adults (who were not eligible for AFDC).

The second basis of FAP was its work provisions. The Nixon administration and advisors, notably Daniel P. Moynihan, were particularly worried about what they saw as the disintegration of society. At a meeting on the welfare crisis, Moynihan reiterated the concerns expressed in his 1965 *Report on the Negro Family* and exhorted the government to take action:

> Among a large and growing lower class, self-reliance, self-discipline, and industry are waning; a radical disproportion is arising between reality and expectations concerning job, living standard, and so on; unemployment is high but a lively demand for unskilled labor remains unmet; illegitimacy is increasing; families are more and more matrifocal and atomized; crime and disorder are sharply on the rise.[16]

Their solution again drew on the male pauper model, assuming that work would increase family stability, cure social pathologies, and reduce "welfare dependency."

The FAP aimed to intensify both incentives and sanctions to compel AFDC recipients to work. Incentives would be bolstered by raising the income disregard to the first fifty dollars per month (up from thirty dollars) plus one-half of the remaining earned income (up from one-third), as well as disregarding work-related expenses in the computation of AFDC payments. Thus, the new income disregard, or work incentive bonus, would be fifty dollars and one-half instead of thirty dollars and one-third.

The incentives were augmented by work requirements. Welfare recipients would be required to register with the state employment service for work, as well as for training and support services. Exceptions would be made for mothers who had children under age six, were needed in the home to take care of a sick or disabled family member, or whose husbands were registered or working full-time, as well as for adults who were sick or disabled or already working full-time.[17] Jobs could pay less than the minimum wage. And people who failed to comply—not registering, not accepting a "suitable" job offer, or not participating in training programs—would be sanctioned by having their portion of the AFDC payment cut, although the family would continue to receive the remainder of the payment.

The FAP engendered considerable debate, primarily over the federal minimum income. While it was supported by liberals in Congress, as well as by mayors and governors who wanted some fiscal relief from the federal government to help pay for the ever-increasing costs of AFDC, progressives criticized the minimum as too low and conservatives lambasted it as too high. Indeed, the $1,600 figure was less than half of the poverty-level income $3,743 for a family of four when FAP was introduced in 1969 and $4,275 in 1972 when it was finally defeated.[18] In fact, the National Welfare Rights Organization (NWRO) began a campaign to "ZAP FAP" and proposed an alternative federally guaranteed "adequate income plan" of $5,500 for a family of four, raised to $6,500 in its 1971 proposal.[19] From the other direction, Southern conservatives complained bitterly that the guaranteed income was too high and would unduly disrupt labor markets.[20]

Work requirements were less contentious than the federal minimum income. In fact, there was a general consensus that welfare recipients should work, and wanted to work, although welfare rights advocates insisted that compulsion was not necessary. As the NWRO explained, "No forced work requirement is necessary. Recipients will work if given a good opportunity."[21] Others responded by implicitly redefining work in the home. Mrs. Bessie Moore, of the Milwaukee County Welfare Rights Organization, explained how this could easily be accomplished: "If the government was smart, it would start calling AFDC 'Day and Night Care,' create a new agency, pay us a decent wage for the service work we are now doing, and say that the welfare crisis has been solved because welfare mothers have been put to work."[22]

Charles and Dona Hamilton attribute the FAP's defeat to the NWRO and claim its opposition was misguided, since the FAP would have federalized AFDC payments and provided a foot in the door to higher payments.[23] However, it is easier to make these criticisms with the knowledge of hindsight; in the context of the gains made in social welfare policy from the mid-1960s on and the empowerment of welfare recipients, opposition to a low minimum payment and advocacy of an adequate amount seemed to make sense at the time.

The Talmadge Amendments and WIN II

Although the FAP was defeated, its forced work provisions were incorporated into amendments in the AFDC program. Generally known as the Talmadge amendments, after Senator Talmadge of Georgia who pushed them as an alternative to FAP, they were signed into law in December 1971 and became effective the following July.

The Talmadge amendments inaugurated the second phase of the WIN program, sometimes known as WIN II. They strengthened the WIN "stick," requiring registration for all those suggested under the FAP. Thus they settled the debates about whether mothers should be required to work, as women were considered employable if their youngest child was age six or over—that is, in school.[24] In addition, people who were not required to register could choose to participate. Also, as proposed in the FAP, non-compliance with WIN could be sanctioned with the loss of the offending recipient's portion of the welfare payment.

Beginning a trend that continued into the 1980s and 1990s, WIN II stressed immediate job placement and deemphasized training. Thus, although the allowance was increased for vocational training in a classroom setting, it remained low—$1.50 per day and another $2 for work-related expenses. And the time in training was limited to one year for any single participant, and to an average of six months or less for all participants.[25] There was a further focus on on-the-job training (OJT) and public service employment for welfare recipients. This followed from studies showing that OJT had higher placement rates at higher wages than CT and therefore would allow more people to leave the welfare rolls. In a similar line of reasoning, government officials believed that since PSE was a form of "work experience" it would also move more people off the rolls than CT did.

In spite of the stricter requirements, WIN failed to deliver on its promise of ending "welfare dependency." Studies showed placement rates for WIN participants ranging between 20 and 25 percent, but most people who obtained jobs through WIN were paid such low wages that they continued to receive AFDC as well. Furthermore, there were no studies of the many people who found jobs without participating in WIN. In an extensive review of WIN surveys in the late 1970s, Jesse E. Gordon concluded that the program was not cost-effective, since more was spent to operate it than was saved in reduced welfare payments. Echoing the earlier statement by the NWRO, Gordon noted that WIN participants were already motivated to work and needed jobs.[26] This sentiment was reiterated in the summary of another review of WIN research conducted by the Department of Labor: "In general, welfare recipients and other low-income persons (along with most Americans) have a strong work ethic, want to work, and when feasible, do work."[27]

Gender and racial bias continued from WIN I into WIN II. Men in two-parent families remained the focus of the program, representing from 25 to 30 percent of the enrollees, although WIN's racial composition was relatively balanced, reflecting the make-up of the AFDC rolls.[28] Furthermore, women and people of color were less likely to participate in OJT, leading to better outcomes for white men.[29] Job placement rates and wage rates were consistently higher for men compared to women and for whites compared to African-Americans (and to hispanics when separate data were gathered).[30] Yet all rates remained low. In 1976, for example, fewer than 9 percent of all participants in

WIN training programs found jobs.[31] And wage rates remained too low to bring most people out of poverty. Average hourly wage rates in 1978 for WIN participants entering jobs were $4.01 for men compared to $2.97 for women and $3.43 for whites, compared to $3.08 for blacks.[32]

Thus WIN was still seen as a failure. Even though enrollment increased from its early years, with 14 to 16 percent of all adults on the AFDC rolls involved in the program, conservatives complained that participation rates were too low. Liberals also criticized the program, charging that its mandatory components penalized people unfairly and the paucity of education and training did virtually nothing to reduce poverty. The general consensus that WIN was not working left it open to punitive reforms in the 1980s.

The Supported Work Demonstration project

Although the profusion of innovative programs that characterized antipoverty policy in the 1960s was not entirely absent in the 1970s, the programs scope was narrowed. Given the attention to "welfare dependency," AFDC recipients were a primary focus of experimental programs. An important target group was women who had received AFDC for many years and had little job experience, education, or training. Concerns that they faced severe barriers to finding and maintaining employment led to the development of the Supported Work Demonstration (SWD) project. It was based on time-limited (twelve to eighteen months) employment in a supportive and closely supervised work situation in order to help participants acquire skills, habits, and credentials that would enable them to find and keep jobs. Evaluation of the SWD was considered important and led to the establishment of the Manpower Demonstration Research Corporation (MDRC), a nonprofit organization that became very influential in welfare reform during the 1980s.[33]

Four groups of people were selected for the SWD project—long-term welfare recipients, unemployed ex-offenders, former addicts, and young school dropouts. The studies found that AFDC recipients benefited far more than the others (compared to control groups). Although most jobs obtained by participants were low-wage, their employment rates, hours of work, and earnings were significantly higher than those in a control group, results that were sustained for several years. Even the bottom line was positive, as the benefits outweighed the costs of the program.[34] This project showed, not surprisingly, that provision of additional resources to long-term welfare recipients helps them find and retain employment. Confirming earlier statements by NWRO members, researchers, and Department of Labor officials, it offers an alternative to punitive, mandatory policies.

The Community Work Experience Program

Yet it was the punitive work programs that prevailed. In fact, the most influential experimental program in the 1970s was not the SWD, but the Community Work Experience Program (CWEP). Hearkening back to the workhouse, CWEP was a fundamentally punitive program based on sanctions. Ignoring the value of caretaking work in the home, welfare recipients were forced to labor outside the home in order to "work off" their welfare payments. Hours of work were usually determined by subtracting any earned income from the AFDC (or food stamp) payment and dividing the remainder by the federal minimum wage. The basic problem was, and remains, that in CWEP people receive only welfare payments—no wages—for their work. Sanctions have always been critical: noncompliance could result in control of the recipients' payment reverting to a third party, or in suspension or termination of the offender's portion of the payment.

CWEPs began on a small scale in 1972. Developed as demonstration projects in states as diverse as Massachusetts, California, and Utah, they served as precursors to the "workfare explosion" of the 1980s. California's CWEP, in existence from 1972 to 1974 under the guidance of then-governor Ronald Reagan, was the best-known of these early programs. Welfare recipients considered employable—that is, fathers in two-parent families and mothers with children over age six—were required to work up to eighty hours per month in community service jobs in public-sector or nonprofit agencies.[35] Training was diminished in order to allow the maximum number of people to rotate through the work slots, and participants received only their welfare payments in exchange for this work.

The basic goal of California CWEP, as described in the grant application approved by the Department of Health, Education, and Welfare, was "to have AFDC recipients reach self-sufficiency . . . by securing regular employment." This would be manifested in four main ways. First, there would be a reduction in the current AFDC caseload as people moved into jobs. Second, revealing the underlying punitive nature of the program, there would be a decrease in "the rate of new applications by encouraging potential applicants who are employable or have an employable family member to seek out other means of support." In other words, potential recipients would become aware of CWEP and would not bother to apply. Third, the savings, in terms of both the average level of payments and numbers of people on the rolls, would exceed the costs of operating the program. And, fourth, CWEP would be "administratively feasible and practical."[36]

The California CWEP failed miserably on all four goals. For starters,

participation was very low. In 1974, the year of maximum implementation, only 2.6 percent of the recipients available for CWEP were placed in
work assignments. This was only 0.2 percent of the total AFDC caseload
in CWEP counties.[37] Although researchers cautioned that the low level of
participation meant that the findings might not be warranted, they stated
quite clearly that "the statistical indicators . . . do not show that CWEP
achieved any of its impact objectives."[38] Comparing CWEP counties to
control counties, in which CWEP was not implemented, they found "no
significant difference" in either the number of cases discontinued as a
result of employment or in the level of average welfare payments. And in
a reversal of expected results, the numbers of people applying for AFDC
showed a "significantly greater increase" in CWEP counties compared to
those without CWEP! Thus researchers concluded that CWEP "did not
prove to be administratively feasible and practical."[39]

There was considerable resistance to CWEP. Opposition was voiced
by some program administrators, staff implementing the program, and
welfare rights advocates. In fact, in Contra Costa, a populous county in
the San Francisco Bay area, community groups protested so effectively
that it was difficult to find CWEP placements in public agencies.[40] Furthermore, there was a general consensus among social service department personnel who supported CWEP that it should only be continued
on a voluntary basis.[41]

In the late 1970s, the Department of Labor reviewed research on
CWEPs and other "welfare-to-work" programs. Not surprisingly, it was
found that the greatest improvement occurred when people received
training and other services instead of direct placement in work situations. Summarizing the findings on CWEPs, the Department of Labor
concluded that the programs were "costly, inefficient, and resented by
work supervisors as well as participants."[42] This negative evaluation was
ignored, however, and CWEP was extended. The Food Stamp Act of
1977 mandated the development of workfare demonstration projects, in
which food stamp recipients in some areas would be required to perform
public service work in exchange for their food stamps. In other words,
payment would be given in food stamp coupons—not even through a
welfare check.[43]

The Program for Better Jobs and Income

Requiring welfare recipients to work was the centerpiece of the Carter
Administration's 1977 welfare reform proposal, the Program for Better
Jobs and Income (PBJI). A comprehensive plan that sparked a great
deal of debate, just as the Family Assistance Program (FAP) had done a

few years earlier, it also included a national minimum standard along with work requirements.[44]

The essence of the PBJI was the differentiation between those expected to work (ETW) and those not expected to work (NETW). People in the NETW category remained the same as they did under the WIN program—aged, blind, and disabled adults, and single mothers with children under age seven. They would be able to receive the upper-tier minimum income, $4,200 for a family of four. Although this was relatively closer to the poverty line ($6,191 for a family of four in 1977) than the FAP had been, it included the cashed-out value of food stamps and so would still leave people deeply in poverty. All other adults would be in the ETW category, eligible for only the lower tier minimum set at $2,300 per year for a family of four. Under this proposal, mothers with children between the ages of seven and thirteen would be required to work part-time, presumably while their children were in school. Incentives to work for wages would be bolstered by increasing the income disregard, as well as the Earned Income Tax Credit (EITC). The "stick" was a mandatory annual job search, during which time the recipient's AFDC payments would be reduced. Since it was understood that not everyone would be able to find jobs, the PBJI included a significant increase in "work experience" positions, accomplished through an expansion of PSE.

Alternatives to parts of the PBJI were advocated by legislators, policy analysts, and groups interested in welfare reform. The more conservative proposals recommended reducing the minimum income, leaving as much discretion as possible to individual states, and strengthening the work requirements. In addition, work positions would be expanded through WIN instead of PSE, reflecting the workfare character of WIN in contrast to the fair work nature of PSE. The more progressive proposals supported the federally guaranteed minimum income and often suggested higher amounts, stressed work incentives instead of requirements, and advocated that work program participants should receive "equal pay for equal work" compared to other public-sector workers.[45] However, the PBJI met the same fate as the FAP and was also defeated.

Fair Work Under CETA

Fair work programs were a critically important and generally accepted component of the government policy mix in the 1970s. The most significant development was the revival of large-scale job creation programs. After remaining dormant since the WPA ended in 1943, job creation was resumed through the 1971 Public Employment Program (PEP), replaced in 1973 by the Public Service Employment (PSE) program that was part of the Comprehensive Employment and Training Act (CETA).

People were put to work in a variety of socially useful jobs—for example, setting up screening programs in hospitals, providing additional personnel for law enforcement agencies, developing community programs in arts and recreation, helping staff battered women's shelters and child-care centers, and weatherizing low-income homes. All of the work was in services, in contrast to the 1930s programs, which developed work in construction and production-for-use as well as services. PEP and PSE often had a profound impact on participants' lives. Sue Hamlin described the importance of her CETA job as a teacher's assistant in the Shawnee County Youth Center in Topeka, Kansas, in 1976 and 1977: "It got me into a field that I have a lot of skills in. I don't know what I would have done without CETA."[46] CETA projects in many community-based organizations also provided the potential for progressive activities. For example, the National Congress of Neighborhood Women, a multiracial community organization in Brooklyn, New York, used CETA funds for its own staff as well as to support women activists throughout New York City in projects such as Healthright and Women Make Movies.[47]

The job creation programs were intended to meet multiple goals, most fundamentally the "double benefit" of providing both jobs and social services.[48] Further, in terms of jobs, they had two primary economic and social motivations: to serve the "disadvantaged," furnishing work experience as part of a transition to unsubsidized employment for those who faced labor market barriers, and to function as a countercyclical employment program during recessions for people who could more easily obtain jobs when they were available. By the mid-1970s, PSE was also seen as a substitute income-maintenance program that would put people to work instead of simply providing cash payments, an alternative to AFDC for the poor and to unemployment insurance (UI) for the recently unemployed. As was true of the 1930s programs, the jobs were meant to be temporary and transitional to private sector employment.

Also following the earlier programs, PEP and PSE existed in a similarly contentious atmosphere and were subjected to a familiar litany of criticisms—that wage rates were too high, that the programs were inefficient and unnecessary make-work and were riddled with fraud and abuse. Unlike the 1930s programs, however, PEP and PSE were plagued by charges that federal CETA funds were substituted for state and local tax revenues and that CETA workers displaced regular government employees. These were serious issues that, if valid, would affect the expansionary impact of the programs—replacing regular employees with CETA workers did not create additional jobs. It was a particularly important issue for public-sector unions, wary of CETA being used to replace union members with PSE workers. Although a careful study later in the 1970s found substitution rates of 11 to 18 percent, estimates as high as 90 percent were repeated in Congress and the media and helped fuel increasing constraints on the program.

Although issues related to the logic of production-for-profit were less contentious than they had been in the 1930s, since production-for-use was omitted entirely, alleged interference with labor markets provided an ongoing source of tension. Trying to avoid these contradictions, meet the sometimes disparate program goals, and address conflicting demands—of workers, especially in public-sector employee unions, who wanted job protections; of local program administrators who wanted flexibility; and of the business community, which pressed for restrictions—regulations were frequently changed.[49] As a result, the policies were often internally contradictory, especially those concerning the determination of wage rates and allowable projects; this in turn helped fuel the criticisms.

Racial and gender discrimination were apparent in the job creation as well as the training programs, in both numbers of participants and in payments. All programs exhibited gender and racial income gaps, as men compared to women and whites compared to people of color were trained for higher-wage jobs and/or placed in higher-paying positions in PEP and PSE. Continuing from their performance in the 1960s, the programs were more biased in terms of gender than race, as proponents reiterated the importance of providing jobs and training for men.[50] The training programs continued to target both white men and men of color. And the job creation programs initially focused on white men, but became more balanced with respect to both gender and race as the decade progressed. This was accomplished, in part, through more stringent criteria regarding eligibility, payments, and project type and duration, as PSE increasingly focused on the "disadvantaged," often women and people of color.

The Changing Fortunes of the Programs

The sharp recession that began in December 1969 and ended the long expansion of the 1960s finally brought the return of clearly defined job creation programs. As unemployment climbed, causing tax revenues to fall and consequent cuts in public services, several arguments emerged in favor of public-sector job creation. The failure of the Job Opportunities in the Business Sector (JOBS) program in the late 1960s—only one-third of the projected number of jobs were created, and numerous placements used government subsidies to hire unskilled workers who would have been hired anyway—convinced many government officials that job creation could not be left solely to the private sector. Increasing numbers of congressional representatives supported job creation, coming to view it as the key to making training programs work. Mayors, especially of large cities, saw job creation as a way to relieve some of the strains of declining public services and increasing unemployment and underemployment. And organized labor, especially the AFL-CIO, continued to press for job creation to increase the demand for labor and thereby help shore up wages.[51]

In response to these pressures and arguments, an Emergency Employment Act authorizing a public service employment program was passed by Congress in mid-1970. President Nixon vetoed the bill. Conjuring up negative images of the 1930s work programs, he criticized public service employment as "dead-end jobs in the public sector" and went on to declare, "WPA-type jobs are not the answer for the men and women who have them, for the government which is less efficient as a result or for the taxpayers who must foot the bill. Such a program represents a reversion to the remedies that were tried 35 years ago. Surely it is an inappropriate, an ineffective response to problems of the 1970s."[52]

Unemployment remained high, however, and Congress passed another Emergency Employment Act in April 1971. With an election coming the following year, Nixon signed it.[53] Thus, the Public Employment Program (PEP) was created. A clearly temporary program, it provided work for an average of 224,300 participants during each of its three years.[54]

In December 1973, the proliferating employment and training programs were combined to form the Comprehensive Employment and Training Act (CETA), the largest and most innovative fair work program since the 1930s. CETA was truly comprehensive, amalgamating work and training programs formerly carried out under the Manpower Development Training Administration (MDTA), the Economic Opportunity Act, and PEP. Title I authorized comprehensive manpower programs along the lines of the MDTA. This included educational programs, most importantly high school equivalency degrees (GEDs), English as a Second Language (ESL), and adult education, as well as vocational training programs in the classroom and on the job. Title II continued the PEP, renamed Public Service Employment (PSE). Title III implemented federal programs for specific groups, primarily Native American Indians and migrant and seasonal farm workers, and authorized research, evaluation, and experimental and demonstration projects. Title IV continued the Job Corps, and Title V established a National Manpower Commission.[55] The federal government developed regulations and appropriated funds, and the program was carried out on the local level through prime sponsors.

PSE through Title II was initially conceived as a small program creating only 50,000 jobs. It was intended to provide work for people who were structurally unemployed in "areas of substantial unemployment" (ASUs), localities where the unemployment rate was above 6.5 percent for three consecutive months. Yet no sooner was CETA enacted than the recession that began in November 1973 increased unemployment to its highest levels since the Great Depression. In December 1974 Congress added Title VI, a countercyclical employment program intended to replace some of the jobs lost through the recession. As PSE grew to almost 369,000 participants by 1976, regulations were added to limit the duration of most Title VI projects and to target more clearly the long-term, low-income unemployed as well as welfare recipients.

Presidents Nixon and Ford were ideologically constrained in their responses to the unfolding economic crisis, but Jimmy Carter, who became President in 1977, was freer to pursue more expansionary policies. Shortly after taking office, he proposed a two-year, $31.2 billion economic stimulus package, $20.1 billion of which was passed by Congress.[56] Much of this money went to CETA. Some of the funds were used to develop new programs. The Youth Employment and Demonstration Projects Act (YEDPA) funded experimental programs for youth employment and training and grew steadily to serve almost 500,000 young people in 1980.[57] The Skills Training Improvement Program (STIP) and Help through Industry Retraining and Employment (HIRE) provided training in the private sector And PSE underwent a dramatic increase, more than doubling size and reaching its maximum of 742,000 participants by March 1978.[58]

Time-worn criticisms of job creation programs intensified, exacerbated by the growing economy and consequently reduced unemployment. Thus, while PSE participants were 4.5 percent of the unemployed in March 1977, they were 12.0 percent of the unemployed in March 1978 and 12.6 percent by the following June.[59] Although this was still very low—especially in comparison to the CWA, which provided work for one-third of the unemployed at its maximum—it was greeted with alarm by a business community worried that a reduction in unemployment would further fuel the fires of inflation. Thus, just as quickly as PSE had been expanded, it was cut.[60] The 1978 CETA reauthorization restricted PSE, reducing wages, placing limits on the amount of time people could remain in the program, and mandating performance standards (PSs). It also more clearly differentiated between Title II, now renamed Title IID, which became a permanent program combining public employment and training for the structurally unemployed, and the more troublesome Title VI, which continued as a countercyclical program intended to be increased during recessions and reduced during economic expansions. Title VI was slashed from a total of 1,017,000 participants throughout the entire year of 1978 to 791,000 in 1979 and 410,000 in 1980.[61] Finally, the Private Sector Initiative Program (PSIP) was implemented as Title VII, more clearly institutionalizing the role of the private sector in CETA.

The restrictions on CETA were carried out in the context of Congress' developing conservative policy bent. They were mirrored in other government policies—including the beginnings of reductions in AFDC payments and numbers on the rolls, tax cuts for corporations, antilabor policies, the military buildup, and industrial deregulation—all of which were intensified in the 1980s. PSE continued to decline until it was ended by President Reagan shortly after he took office. In contrast, the PSIP grew, serving as a prototype for the Job Training Partnership Act (JTPA), which replaced CETA entirely in 1982.

Eligibility and Targeting

The main determinants for participation in PEP and PSE were the length of time a person was unemployed, the level of family income, and status with respect to AFDC or unemployment insurance (UI). These eligibility criteria became increasingly restrictive throughout the 1970s as the programs focused more clearly on the "disadvantaged." In addition to the generally defined long-term, low-income unemployed, guidelines were adopted throughout the decade to target specific priority groups, most importantly veterans.

Eligibility criteria in the PEP were quite loose. One result was that gender discrimination was very clear: 72 percent of the enrollees were men, and only 28 percent were women. Racial bias was less pronounced: 60 percent were white, while 24 percent were African-American and 13 percent were Hispanic.[62]

When PSE began in 1974 it continued these loose rules, basing participation only on the length of time a person was unemployed. Set at thirty days when the program started, it was shortened the following year to fifteen days in areas with unemployment rates of 7 percent or more. However, in 1976 the criteria were tightened, as five main concerns led to targeting the long-term, low-income unemployed.

First was the belief that the available resources should be used primarily for those who were most in need. Since participants in the PEP and early PSE programs had been disproportionately white, male, not economically disadvantaged, and had at least a high school education, stricter eligibility criteria were thought to be necessary.[63]

Second, many legislators considered it important to shift the costs of transfer payments, specifically AFDC and UI, to programs that would place people in jobs leading to unsubsidized employment. In regard to AFDC recipients this sentiment was intensified by increased worries that the "undeserving poor" were becoming increasingly "welfare dependent," a view that also led to tightening WIN in 1971 and to the proposed but defeated Family Assistance Plan and Program for Better Jobs and Income. UI recipients presented a different concern, related to the costs of the program and to the generally accepted view that these former jobholders were "deserving poor." In the wake of the severe 1973–1975 recession, Congress had extended UI benefits so that in some areas, depending on the state unemployment rate, they could be collected for sixty-five weeks (five quarters). In spite of the extension, however, lingering high levels of unemployment led to estimates that more than two million people would exhaust UI in 1976. Thus, expanding PSE and targeting it to UI recipients and exhaustees was seen as an alternative to yet another UI extension.[64]

Third, as explained in a report by the Congressional Budget Office (CBO), a focus on the long-term, low-income unemployed would reduce substitution of CETA workers for normal government operations, since they would be "less likely to have the skill characteristics of those who would normally be hired."[65] Fourth was the "percolator effect" of "bubble-up" policies: targeting the disadvantaged would get money into the pockets of people who would quickly spend it, increasing the demand for goods and services and thereby stimulating the economy. Fifth, targeting the disadvantaged would keep the program from further reducing the supply of skilled workers and helping boost their wages. Many politicians, along with those in the business community, believed that higher wages were an important factor contributing to inflation, widely seen as the most critical economic problem throughout the 1970s.[66]

Thus, additional criteria were adopted for the new Title VI projects.[67] First, the length of unemployment was increased considerably, to fifteen weeks. Second, localities were mandated to have an "equitable allocation of jobs" among four groups: people who had received UI for fifteen weeks; those not eligible for UI; people who exhausted their UI payments; and AFDC recipients. Third, income level became an additional criterion, as people were considered low-income if their family earned less than 70 percent of the Bureau of Labor Statistics (BLS) "lower living standard."[68]

Even though these criteria were adopted, verification procedures were often loose—in contrast to the scrutiny given AFDC recipients. This slackness increased during the rapid PSE buildup in 1977–1978, as an estimated 12 percent or more of the participants were not eligible, fueling widely publicized accounts of fraud and abuse.[69] However, most of those who were ineligible failed to meet the unemployment criteria.[70] In other words, they had not been unemployed long enough. Yet they needed, and wanted, to work.

In addition to the overall focus on the long-term, low-income unemployed, other groups were also targeted for PSE. The 1976 act mandated that veterans make up 35 percent of the new hires. This was expanded in the 1978 reauthorization, which included a long list of priority groups: displaced homemakers (DH), single parents, the disabled, youths, older workers, offenders, and those with limited English or limited education. In addition, women—presumably all women—made up their own category![71]

As a result of these new criteria the percentage of women and African-Americans in PSE increased. Participation rates for women rose from 34 percent in 1974 to 47 percent in 1980 and 1981, and rates for blacks increased from 23 percent in 1974 to 33 percent by 1980.[72] Although the numbers of women in general increased, this success was not shared by all of the targeted categories of women. Most importantly, the mandate to include welfare recipients in proportion to their numbers in the local eligible population was never met. Although at the March 1978 peak 48 percent of all those eligible for PSE received AFDC, they filled only 11 percent of the positions. Finding a general bias against women, and more specifically against welfare recipients, researchers reported that project sponsors were reluctant to place women in jobs traditionally filled by men and furthermore felt that AFDC recipients lacked the skills needed to do the work.[73]

Wage Rate Policies

Like the eligibility criteria, PSE wage rate policies also became increasingly restrictive throughout the 1970s. Reflecting the logic of labor markets, the changes were fueled by continual charges from the business community that PSE wages were too high, attracting people away from private-sector employment and undermining PSE's mandate to provide temporary and transitional jobs. Two groups pressed for higher payments, however. Public-sector unions argued for higher wages to prevent replacing union members with lower-cost CETA workers, and local program administrators advocated higher payments so they could develop a greater variety of projects and have a greater choice of applicants. Wanting as much flexibility as possible in setting up projects and filling the positions with people who could do the job well, they felt that lower PSE wages led some of the most capable people out of the program.[74]

Throughout the duration of the programs, PEP and PSE were mandated to pay "prevailing wages" for similar work in the same agency.

Additional criteria were also adopted. Through 1978 CETA funds could be used to pay a maximum wage of $10,000 per year. In order to give sufficient flexibility to agencies in high-wage areas, they were allowed to supplement this $10,000 by as much as they chose from their own funds. However, total supplementation and total payments were constrained by a mandate to keep the national average CETA wage below $7,800. This proved effective, and in 1977 the median PSE wage, including supplementation, was $7,700, which was 78 percent of the median national wage for all wage and salary workers.[75]

Wage rates were further restricted in the 1978 CETA reauthorization. Although the $10,000 ceiling was retained (and could be increased to $12,000 in high-wage areas), supplementation was now limited to 10 percent of the maximum wage in each area (and to 20 percent in high-wage areas), and the average nationwide payment was reduced to $7,200 (to be increased each year according to the rate of inflation).[76] Intended to make PSE less attractive compared to private-sector employment, these changes would help focus on the long-term, low-income unemployed, who were assumed to have fewer labor market options, and would also inhibit the substitution of CETA workers for normal government employees.

The wage constraints were augmented by time constraints. Reviving a WPA policy developed as part of the 1939 restrictions, individuals could remain on PSE for a maximum of eighteen months. Officials explained that this would help maintain the transitional nature of the program.[77]

Lower wages and tenure limits succeeded in making private sector jobs relatively more attractive than PSE, but they also created serious problems. First, PSE became a less rational economic option for AFDC and UI recipients, since they already had a source of income. Yet these were some of the people that Congress most wanted to reach. Furthermore, the wage limitations reduced flexibility, restricting the types of projects that could be developed by agencies in high-wage areas. Since they were still required to pay "prevailing wages" for the same work, projects involving high-wage jobs were no longer feasible.[78] However, public employee unions claimed that the "prevailing wage" provision was sometimes circumvented, as agencies classified CETA workers in categories that allowed payment of lower wages.[79]

Although a great deal of attention was devoted to constraining PSE wages, little was done to narrow the PSE wage differential between women and men. Indeed, program administrators generally claimed that women did well on PSE since the ratio of women's earnings compared to men's earnings on PSE was significantly higher than it was for the general labor force. In 1977, for example, in the projects targeting the long-term, low-income unemployed, women's payments averaged 91 percent of men's payments. However, average payments were higher for men than for women in every occupational group, from professionals to laborers, illustrating the institutional basis of gender discrimination in wages.[80]

Projects in Public-Sector and Nonprofit Agencies

A critical difference between the 1930s and the 1970s work programs concerned the nature of the projects. Although their predecessors in the 1930s developed a range of projects in construction and in production of goods and services, PEP and PSE were restricted to service work in public-sector and nonprofit agencies. Furthermore, there was a significant difference in allowable service work between the two eras. While maintenance and repair of public buildings, equipment, streets, and sidewalks were prohibited in response to charges of make-work when the CWA ended in 1934, these tasks provided an important source of work for unskilled men in the PEP and PSE. And, of course, both construction of new roads and public facilities and production of consumer goods, which provided much of the work in the 1930s, were prohibited in the 1970s.

In spite of the restriction on services, a wide variety of socially useful work was accomplished in the PEP and PSE. Public works projects included maintenance and repair of buildings, equipment, streets, sidewalks, and sewers; cleaning streets and alleys; collecting garbage; flood and erosion control; and conservation, including weatherization and repair of low-income homes. Parks and recreation projects included the development and maintenance of facilities, as well as operating recreational programs. Educational services, too, involved maintenance of school buildings and grounds, as well as instruction-related projects for teacher's assistants. New programs and services, such as low-cost meals on wheels delivered to the elderly in their homes, and community arts programs, were set up, and surveys of community needs for social services were conducted. Additional workers were provided to expand services in existing agencies, including day care centers, shelters for battered women and their children, legal aid, hospitals (for example, setting up hypertension screening programs and treatment programs for alcoholics), and law enforcement agencies.[81] In fact, many institutions developed during the 1970s, such as food cooperatives and women's health clinics, ran on shoestring budgets and depended on CETA workers to remain in operation.

Throughout the decade, PSE projects were subjected to changing restrictions. The greatest concern was preventing the substitution of

CETA projects for normal government operations and displacing normal government workers with CETA workers. This clearly makes sense in terms of the goal of creating new jobs. If work programs are substituted for work that would normally be done, new jobs are not created but merely funded from federal instead of state and local sources. Furthermore, this can jeopardize existing jobs and currently employed workers. Public-sector unions were particularly attentive to this issue, worried that CETA workers were being used to weaken unions by replacing union members. Their concerns were expressed by an official of the American Federation of State, County, and Municipal Employees (AFSCME) in congressional hearings: "We do not want a Federal policy which, while bringing some people off the unemployment rolls, at the same time forces public employees onto the unemployment rolls. This sort of job recycling would be cruel and counterproductive."[82]

AFSCME urged its members to be alert to "budget games" of unnecessary layoffs and subsequent hiring of new CETA workers in similar positions.[83] (Some laid-off workers could be rehired with CETA funds.) In cities such as New York and Philadelphia, where public-employee unions were sufficiently strong, CETA workers could be required to join the union.[84] By 1976, some AFSCME officials questioned the practice of separately identifying CETA workers, claiming that this fostered a dual personnel system that was not under the union's purview. The officials suggested that reducing or eliminating the distinction between CETA workers and regular workers would be preferable.[85]

Some substitution and displacement did occur. Allegations that it was rampant led to congressional action, as the 1976 legislation tightened the criteria for new Title VI projects. Three requirements were adopted. First, the new projects were limited to twelve months' duration, although they could be renewed, or "recycled," for another twelve months. (This time limit was also intended to facilitate reductions in PSE when the economy revived.) Second, emphasis was placed on "new or separately identifiable tasks" instead of extensions of existing activities. Third, a "substantial portion" of the funding was to be used by nonprofit organizations instead of government agencies, since this would avoid normal government operations.[86]

The mandated PSE buildup quickly led local program administrators and agency officials, who developed the jobs, to plead for a more relaxed definition of projects in order to give them greater flexibility. Thus, by May 1977, when the PSE expansion began, projects had been redefined as tasks that would be completed within a year; have a public service objective; result in a specific product or accomplishment; and would not otherwise be done.[87] Although these looser criteria made it easier to expand PSE, they also made some projects more marginal, and consequently more vulnerable to make-work criticisms. The 1978 CETA reauthorization tried to reduce this marginality, lengthening the time limit on projects from twelve to eighteen months and allowing an eighteen-month extension). In spite of the changes in project requirements, charges of fiscal substitution and job displacement continued.

CETA Training Programs

Training programs that were set up during the 1960s under the MDTA and the War on Poverty were continued and expanded as part of CETA.[88] Providing classroom training and on-the-job training, they were often bolstered by additional activities, including outreach, pre-employment services, counseling, peer support groups, life skills workshops, job search assistance, and supportive services, most importantly payments for child care and other work-related expenses (WRES). These activities were especially significant for women who had been marginal to the labor market.

Training programs were an important focus of the 1978 CETA reauthorization. Under pressure from women's groups, notably Wider Opportunities for Women (WOW), some innovative programs were developed. Most significant were programs for teenage mothers, displaced homemakers, and women in so-called nontraditional occupations (NTOs). (These occupations are seen as nontraditional only because women have historically been underrepresented in them, but are more accurately labeled "male-dominated occupations," or MDOs, reflecting the greater percentage of men and consequently higher average wages.)

The Displaced Homemaker (DH) program is particularly noteworthy. It was designed for women who followed the family ethic and performed unpaid caretaking work in the home but were widowed, separated, or divorced. Possessing few marketable skills and too young to receive social security dependent benefits, they were labeled the "new poor." A typical story was told by a woman in the Baltimore DH program: "After nearly forty-two years of happily married life, I was widowed in 1975. I had only worked outside my home for six years during my life. . . . For the first time in many years, I had to live on next to no income. I applied for widow's pension, but I was not yet eligible."[89]

The fruits of a movement formed in the mid-1970s to advocate for government programs and services for these "women who, like refugees, were forcibly exiled from their homes and into the labor market," the DH program provided the entire range of training and support activities.[90] Chani Beeman, who found herself deserted with an infant and a four-year-old, described the impact of CETA's DH program on her life:

"Before CETA I didn't see myself as capable of learning or succeeding. I had been beaten down by the marriage and desertion . . . the DH program gave me confidence that I could take care of myself and my kids."[91]

Women made gains in CETA training programs, especially after the 1978 reauthorization. However, as in the job creation programs, they fared worse than men. This was most apparent in the bottom line—on average, women continued to earn less than men when they left the program. Chani Beeman notes that while her participation in the DH program was critically important in getting her back on her feet, she never used her training as a stenographer since "the pay was too low to support my family."[92]

The programs were touted as a success for women, however. Women who went through CETA training earned more than women who did not participate, in contrast to men, who showed negligible income gains.[93] Yet as pointed out by Sharon L. Harlan, Lynn C. Burbridge, and by Linda J. Waite and Sue E. Berryman, these increases need to be placed in perspective.[94] Women showed a greater percentage income gain compared to men in part because their preprogram wages were so much lower—the female/male earnings ratio of 57 to 59 percent in the overall economy meant that the same absolute increase translated into a larger percentage gain for women than for men. Furthermore, the focus on comparing pre- and postprogram wages ignores job placement rates, which were consistently higher for men than for women.

Three factors were important in maintaining gender discrimination in CETA training programs. First, as had been the case in the Manpower Development and Training Administration (MDTA), women were placed in classroom training (CT) programs more readily than in on-the-job training (OJT), even though OJT participants had higher placement rates and higher average earnings than those in CT (see chapter 4 of this book). Second, although a variety of activities were theoretically available, they were not always adequately developed. Especially important was the insufficiency of support services for women, particularly child care. This was the case even though after 1978 between 30 and 40 percent of the total funds for training were spent on child care and other support services.[95] It still was not enough.

Third, prior to the 1978 CETA reauthorization, institutional factors that historically limited women's employment opportunities were generally ignored. Stereotypical views of the types of work considered appropriate or inappropriate for women were accepted; women were largely excluded from higher-paid, male-dominated fields and channeled instead into lower-wage "women's work," primarily in services.[96] In fact, while some of the increase in women's earnings was attributable to a change in occupations—from very low paid service work to slightly higher wage clerical work—the jobs were still "women's service work" and still underpaid.[97]

The focus on implementing training programs to meet women's needs as part of the 1978 reauthorization was a welcome change and showed that with resources and some commitment more helpful programs can easily be developed. However, these gains were soon swept away as the Reagan administration allowed CETA to expire in 1982.

The Private Sector Initiative Program

The 1978 CETA reauthorization also developed a new training program, the Private Sector Initiative Program (PSIP). A response to charges of inefficiency, fraud, and abuse, the PSIP was based on the belief that the private sector is inherently more efficient than the public sector.[98]

The centerpiece of the PSIP was Private Industry Councils (PICs), groups of local employers and government and community officials who advised local program administrators on training and placement programs. The PSIP was hailed as a success by business groups, who claimed that the greater involvement by the business community led to higher placement rates in unsubsidized jobs than had been achieved in other CETA programs. However, this success was partially due to "creaming"—compared to the other CETA components, PSIP served a slightly higher percentage of whites and males, who did not face gender and racial discrimination, while people who were more disadvantaged were often screened out.[99] Most important to the perception of PSIP as a success was the simple fact of private sector involvement, and the belief that the private sector is more efficient, and therefore better, than the government. Thus, although the PSIP received only 5 percent of CETA funds in 1980 and 12 percent in 1981, it served as a model for the 1982 JTPA, the only component of CETA continued, albeit in an altered form, in the 1980s.[100]

The Humphrey-Hawkins Full Employment and Balanced Growth Act

PSE's declining fortunes were reflected in the evisceration of the Humphrey-Hawkins Full Employment and Balanced Growth Act. Just as the heart was removed from the 1945 Full Employment Bill in its metamorphosis into the bland Employment Act of 1946, so the original Equal Opportunity and Full Employment Act introduced by Representative Augustus Hawkins (D-Calif.) in 1974—and again in 1975, this time combined with the Balanced Growth and Economic Planning bill sponsored by Senator Hubert H. Humphrey (D-Minn.)—was finally passed in 1978 as the watered-down Humphrey-Hawkins Full Employment and Balanced Growth Act.[101]

Harkening back to the 1945 Full Employment Bill, the original bill proposed to "establish and guarantee the rights of all adult Americans able and willing to work to equal opportunities for useful paid employment at fair rates of compensation."[102] Seeming to draw on the 1942 and 1943 reports of the National Resources Planning Board, it mandated systematic federal planning of production and investment in order to fulfill "human and national needs" in a variety of areas: conservation; housing; antipollution and recycling activities; health care; education; day care; infrastructure construction (for example, railroads, subways, and other mass transportation); and "development of artistic, esthetic, cultural, and recreational activities." Drawing on the 1960s ideology behind the War on Poverty, it further called for "the virtual liquidation of poverty, substandard wages, and substandard conditions of employment in the United States within a decade."[103]

The centerpiece of the original bill, as well as the 1975 and 1976 versions, was a countercyclical public service employment program. The government would serve as the employer of last resort for people unable to find jobs through the labor market, establishing a program that would go into effect when the unemployment rate fell below 3 percent of the labor force. Wages would be set at "fair rates of compensation": the highest of prevailing local wage rates, the minimum wage, or wages specified in existing collective bargaining agreements. And attention was given to combating discrimination based on race, gender, age, and physical and mental capacity.

Reminiscent of the original 1945 Full Employment Bill, the President would submit an annual "Full Employment and National Purposes Budget, which would "set forth national goals related to full employment and other national purposes, and the major policies and programs to achieve these goals."[104] The Employment Service would be transformed into a Full Employment Service, and a Job Guarantee Office would be established in each state. An enforcement provision was also included; people who felt they had not been adequately served by the Job Guarantee Office could sue the government in federal court.

From the outset care was taken to assure the importance of efforts to control inflation. Furthermore, the bills criticized anti–inflationary measures then in use as ineffective and argued that full employment would increase productivity and relieve bottlenecks and shortages, thereby reducing "cost-push" inflation.[105] Additional benefits of full employment were enumerated in the bills. Economic impacts included increased aggregate demand, which would counteract recessions, rescuing labor power that would otherwise be lost and reducing the cost of transfer payment programs. Social benefits focused on increasing people's self-esteem and avoiding the distress that accompanies unemployment, as well as mitigating societal unrest. Indeed, the not-too-distant urban ghetto riots served as vivid reminders of the social costs of unemployment and poverty.[106]

But the opponents won the day. Senator Jake Garn (R-Utah) argued that the Humphrey-Hawkins Bill was "interference in the private sector without parallel, a bigger dose of socialism all at one time, than we have ever seen." Asserting that "the major problems in the economy are Government caused," he advocated keeping the politicians out of the private sector.[107] Senator John Tower (R-Texas) warned that the bill would lead to an "economic police state," and the Chamber of Commerce denounced it as a "government power grab" and an "engine of inflation."[108]

The Humphrey-Hawkins Full Employment and Balanced Growth Act was finally passed in 1978 as an amendment to the Employment Act of 1946. "Balanced growth" meant that real full employment was sacrificed. In fact, similar to the 1946 act, this one only established "as a national goal the fulfillment of the right to full *opportunities* for useful paid employment at fair rates of compensation of all individuals able, willing, and seeking to work [emphasis added]."[109] Yet even this declaration was toothless, as the law contained no mechanisms for achieving full employment. Instead, it would simply "require the President to initiate, as the President deems appropriate, with recommendations to the Congress where necessary, supplementary programs and policies to the extent that the President finds such action necessary to help achieve these goals."[110] Full employment was further watered down by adding other policy goals—most importantly, a decrease in the rate of inflation, as well as a balanced federal budget, and minimizing federal expenditures as a percentage of GNP. Public employment job creation was restricted. Greatest emphasis was placed on job creation in the private sector, and a means test was added as an eligibility requirement, as the right to a job was transformed into a privilege.[111]

Once again a commitment to full employment was gutted, and even this minimal measure was not enforced. As tight monetary policy cooled off the economy in the early 1980s, President Reagan simply ignored the Humphrey-Hawkins Act, focusing on reducing inflation, in part by allowing unemployment to rise to 10.7 percent of the labor force.[112] The Humphrey-Hawkins Act was all but forgotten.

Public Employment Programs in the 1970s: Success or Failure?

The PEP and PSE were hounded by some of the same criticisms that plagued their 1930s counterparts. As in the earlier era, charges that they were too expensive, that fraud and abuse were rampant and payments too high, and that the projects themselves were inefficient and unnecessary make-work led to changes in policies and constrained the programs. Also problematic were complaints that federal CETA funds were substituted for local tax revenues as CETA workers allegedly displaced regular government employees. The overall constraints were most clearly seen in the program's size. Although the labor force had doubled and government at all levels had grown substantially in the intervening years, at its maximum PSE provided work for 742,000 people, less than 12 percent of the jobless—compared to the CWA high point of 4.4 million jobs for more than one-third of the unemployed.

Again, as was true of the 1930s programs, these accusations warrant a closer look. Criticisms of expense are regularly lodged at government programs. Similar criticisims, however, have not impeded high military expenditures or bailing out large corporations or savings and loan institutions and banks.

Charges of fraud and abuse were given credence by their repetition in the media. In fact, media accounts often focused on blatant abuses— political patronage, as politicians' relatives were sometimes placed on the rolls, and "mismanagement" or embezzlement of CETA funds, often by small agencies that were supposed to provide training.[113] Although this type of obvious fraud was not common, it served to obscure the program's accomplishments and to sidetrack debate of critical issues.

Most allegations of fraud and abuse had to do with the presence of "ineligibles" on the PSE rolls, a situation that was exacerbated during the rapid buildup. The reasons for ineligibility are telling. In some cases people's income was not low enough, and in others people had apparently been preselected for the position before the job was officially created. However, the main reason was that they had not been unemployed long enough. In other words, participants were still low-income and still unemployed, but they did not meet the increasingly strict criteria targeting long-term, low-income individuals. Although this is clearly far different from kickbacks or outright embezzlement, descriptions of such situations were often couched in similar terms.

Repeating problems faced by the New Deal work programs, the gist of the remaining criticisms had to do with whether the jobs created were "real work" or "make-work." Indeed, the 1975 *Manpower Report of the President* explained that "the WPA was criticized for sponsoring "leaf-raking" make-work—a criticism that has endured to haunt present debates over public employment programs."[114] (In fact, this characterization was wrong, as the New Deal programs were prohibited from providing leaf-raking or any other maintenance work after April 1934.)

Debates about real work versus make-work reflected a tension that intensified throughout the decade. On one hand, there were pressures to focus more clearly on the "disadvantaged," who were needier than those more able to find jobs on their own and who could be paid less than skilled workers. This reduced interference with labor markets by lessening the risk of creating PSE jobs that were more attractive than private-sector jobs and prevented the program from contributing to a shortage of skilled workers and thereby fueling inflation. However, the increasingly restrictive criteria regarding eligibility, payments, and project design and duration meant that more of the jobs were marginal and easily construed as make-work. In contrast to those arguing for more restrictions were local agency administrators, who wanted more flexibility—in order to develop socially useful projects and hire the most qualified workers. The increased restrictions clearly complicated their efforts.

Thus, criticisms that wages were too high, which reflected capitalists' worries that PSE would present a more attractive alternative than private-sector employment, were countered by people in other positions who argued for increased wages. Agency administrators who hired CETA workers wanted to be able to offer higher wages in order to attract the most qualified workers, especially for skilled positions. Members of public-sector unions wanted CETA workers to be paid union wages so they would not be used to replace union workers. And, obviously, those on the program wanted to receive higher wages. Yet the constraining arguments prevailed, and changes in the 1978 reauthorization were primarily designed to appease private-sector employers.

These tensions were also seen in charges of inefficiency. In fact, these stemmed from the ideology that government provision of services is not efficient simply because it is not based on profits. Acceptance of this view led to the development of the PSIP in 1978 and to the increasing privatization of public-sector services throughout the following decade, as services from operating prisons to collecting garbage were contracted out to private-sector firms.

Criticisms of make-work were virtually assured by a Catch-22 situation that existed in the 1930s and applied to the 1970s job creation programs as well. In order to prevent substitution of funds and displacement of workers, the programs were not supposed to be used for normal government operations. However, requiring that the work would not ordinarily be provided makes it extremely susceptible to make-work charges.

Yet this points out a fundamental problem: it is difficult to determine what work is extraneous to "normal" government operations. Is work considered substitution if it would be provided by the government if the funds were available? In the context of the fiscal crises that hit cities beginning in the mid-1970s, is work considered substitution if it *had* been provided but could no longer be funded due to declining revenues? And, in a broader context, what services *should* government provide? Are community arts and recreation projects extraneous simply because they improve the quality of life but are not "necessary," as garbage collection is?

The strident charges of fiscal substitution and job displacement led to studies designed to gauge the extent of the alleged abuses. Researchers arrived at estimates ranging from 20 percent to 90 percent of the jobs created, depending on the assumptions used.[115] Most of these studies were macrolevel analyses that calculated substitution and displacement based on the estimated impact of PSE funding on total state and local government spending.[116] However, this methodology overestimated the extent of displacement: it ignored jobs subcontracted to nonprofit agencies, failed to account for other causes of slowed growth of tax revenues (most importantly, tax limitation initiatives), and glossed over microlevel aspects of the actual jobs.

These concerns were addressed in a careful study of PSE from 1977 through 1980 carried out through the Brookings Institution and Princeton University. Instead of macroestimates, they conducted field studies in cities and counties throughout the U.S. to ascertain whether actual PSE positions constituted job creation or job displacement.[117] The first survey, conducted in July 1977, found that 82 percent of PSE positions were job creation and 18 percent were job displacement. By the last survey, in December 1980, when slowed economic growth and tax limitation led to lower tax revenues and to fiscal crises in some large cities, 89 percent of PSE positions were classified as job creation, as many cities and towns used PSE to provide services that otherwise would have been cut.[118]

Even though the employment and training programs underwent significant modifications in the 1970s, sometimes in response to these criticisms, they were carried out in the context of job creation as a permanent feature of national employment and training policy. In fact, by 1978, more than 5 percent of all state and local government workers were funded through PSE.[119] Policy analysts and program administrators taking part in these discussions throughout the decade could probably not have imagined the changes that were about to begin in 1981, as fair work programs were narrowed in scope and reduced in size while workfare programs proliferated.

6

The 1980s: Workfare for the "Truly Needy" and Prosperity for the "Truly Greedy"

The 1980s witnessed another era of conservative social and economic policies. Fair work programs were almost nonexistent; President Reagan axed the Public Service Employment (PSE) program soon after he took office in 1981 and allowed authorization for the entire CETA program to expire the following year. The collectivity and compassion of the 1960s and 1970s was gone, limited though it had been, replaced by ideologies grounded in individualism, self-help, and outright greed. Taxes were cut for the rich while working people experienced a decline in their standard of living as the purchasing power of wages continued to fall and the social welfare safety net was slashed. Drawing on sexist and racist stereotypes of welfare recipients, "poverty-by-choice" theorists decried the "welfare dependency" purportedly created by the past two decades of social welfare policies and provided the social rationale for punitive welfare reform, as the Reagan administration cut welfare payments (adjusted for inflation), tightened eligibility requirements, and supported an array of workfare programs.

Right-Wing Policies as a Solution to Economic Hard Times

Reagan took office as President in 1981 with a mandate to solve the economic problems. He began with the "Reagan recession" in 1981–1982, the most severe since the 1930s, as production of goods and services fell 3.4 percent and peak unemployment reached a depression-level

126

10.7 percent of the labor force. As always, measured unemployment was higher for African-Americans—18.9 percent in 1982 and 19.5 percent the following year—compared to 8.6 percent for whites in 1982 and 8.4 percent in 1983.[1] High unemployment made it more difficult for workers to demand increased wages and better working conditions—they could easily be replaced if they complained. In order to cut wages further and thereby expand profits, labor discipline was addressed through additional policies: a rabid anti-union stance, industrial deregulation, and the gutting of social programs.[2] As a result, wages continued the slide that began in 1972, falling another 11 percent in the 1980s.[3]

Profits, as well as income for the rich in general, received a further boost from supply-side tax cuts. Promising that cutting taxes for the rich would give them an incentive to increase savings, which would be used by corporations to expand investment and thereby create jobs—the wealth would "trickle down" to the rest of the population—the top income tax rates were cut in half, capital gains taxes were slashed, and corporate profit taxes were lowered. However, the rich simply became richer. While the income of the poorest fifth of the population fell 5.2 percent (adjusted for inflation) between 1980 and 1990, the income of the richest fifth increased 32.5 percent. The numbers are even more astounding at the very top. The richest 5 percent of the population saw its income increase by 50.6 percent, and the richest 1 percent experienced an 87.1 percent increase in income.[4]

An important component of the Reagan administration strategy to decrease wages involved cutting social programs, since they provide a cushion in times of unemployment. If people have something to fall back on, they will be less desperate to find a job and will be able to hold out longer for employment that pays higher wages and provides better working conditions. The expansion of social welfare programs in the 1960s and 1970s did, in fact, provide a more adequate cushion, and so, from the capitalist perspective, it needed to be eroded.

Arguments that high social welfare expenditures during the previous decade were an important cause of the burgeoning federal budget deficit provided justification for slashing the social "safety net."[5] A range of programs were cut: AFDC, food stamps, Medicaid, housing assistance, energy assistance, child nutrition programs, WIC (Women, Infants, and Children program, which provides food supplements to pregnant and nursing women and to young children), disability compensation, Supplemental Security Income (SSI), family planning, and legal aid.[6] The transparency of this argument became apparent as the gutting of social welfare programs was accompanied by the largest peacetime increase in military expenditures; inflation-adjusted funding for the military grew 50 percent from 1980 through 1987.[7]

"Poverty by Choice," AFDC, and Women's Economic Status

Economic arguments for cutting the theoretical safety net were accompanied by social rationales for punitive welfare reform. Time-worn arguments were trotted out as welfare itself was blamed for the increase in the AFDC rolls. Right-wing "poverty by choice" theorists claimed that generous welfare payments in the 1960s and 1970s led millions of women to choose welfare rather than working for wages or remaining in a marriage relationship. Instead of acknowledging the structural causes of poverty, "welfare dependency" was seen as a behavior or a condition that had been heightened by misguided government policies.[8]

An influential proponent of this thesis in the early 1980s was George Gilder, whose *Wealth and Poverty* was purportedly one of President Reagan's favorite books. Integrating "poverty by choice" with "culture of poverty" theories, Gilder described what he saw as the problem:

> [W]elfare, by far the largest economic influence in the ghetto, exerts a constant, seductive, erosive pressure on the marriages and work habits of the poor, and over the years, in poor communities, it fosters a durable "welfare culture." Necessity is the mother of invention and upward mobility; welfare continuously mutes and misrepresents the necessities of life that prompted previous generations of poor people to escape poverty through the invariable routes of work, family, and faith.[9]

In terms of costs and benefits, Gilder wrote, "Our welfare system creates moral hazards because the benefits have risen to a level higher than the ostensible returns of an unbroken home and a normal job."[10]

Gilder worried about the resulting "increasing reluctance of the poor to perform low-wage labor," which had been a step out of poverty for previous generations.[11] He deplored "the increase in the independence of black women, secured by both welfare and jobs," which led to more female-headed families, black male poverty, and children raised without fathers.[12]

While Gilder decried the alleged effects of AFDC, Charles Murray used regression analysis to purportedly prove that the increased spending on social welfare programs through the War on Poverty only heightened the extent of poverty. In *Losing Ground: American Social Policy, 1950–1980*, he claimed to document that higher AFDC payments led to "labor supply disincentives," as women chose poverty levels of welfare over wage labor or marriage.[13]

The scourge of "welfare dependency" needed to be replaced with the "independence" that comes from wage labor, something that could be accomplished by making welfare less attractive—cutting payments (or ending welfare entirely), tightening eligibility requirements, and forcing welfare recipients to work outside the home. Alternatively, welfare recipients could get married, since dependence on a man in a traditional nuclear family was considered desirable by "poverty by choice" proponents.

Conservatives' fears were fueled, in part, by the continuing rise in female-headed families, whose numbers had almost doubled since the 1960s. By 1989, 13.3 percent of all white families, 44.6 percent of all black families, and 22.8 percent of all Hispanic families were headed by women.[14] The main concern, again, was African-American women. Although studies showed that the most important factor in the rise of black female-headed families was high unemployment among black men, the blame remained focused on welfare.[15] AFDC did, however, affect living arrangements, as greater numbers of single women lived on their own, a situation addressed in the early 1990s through programs denying welfare to teenage parents who did not live with their own parent(s). (See chapter 7 of this book for a discussion of these programs.)

AFDC was immediately targeted by the Reagan administration through the 1981 Omnibus Budget Reconciliation Act (OBRA), which tightened eligibility requirements, cut payments, and encouraged individual states to develop WIN Demonstration programs.[16] Average monthly AFDC payments per family (adjusted for inflation) continued the slide that had begun in 1977, falling another 8 percent from 1980 to 1982, recovering only 1 percent of this loss by 1988, and decreasing another 5 percent between 1988 and 1990. Perhaps even more shocking, the number of families receiving AFDC fell from 3,835,000 in 1981 to 3,542,000 the following year even though the nation was in the midst of the severe Reagan recession.[17]

The results of this "war on the poor," in conjunction with the severe recession, quickly became clear.[18] Reflecting the movement of AFDC payments, the overall poverty rate increased 31 percent between 1979 and 1983, rising from 11.7 percent to 15.3, recovering to only 12.8 percent by 1989, and then again beginning to rise, reaching 13.5 percent in 1990.[19] The disastrous effects on women and their children were clearly seen. Mirroring the other trends, the poverty rate for children under age eighteen in families headed by women rose from an already high 48.6 percent in 1979 to 55.5 percent in 1983, declining only slightly to 50 percent by 1989 and rising again to 52.1 percent by 1990.[20] The numbers are even more startling for families headed by women of color. By 1990, the poverty rates for children under age six in female-headed families were 50 percent for whites, 69 percent for blacks, and 72 percent for Hispanics.[21]

In spite of these increases in poverty rates, the public was told that women were doing better economically because the ratio of women's median earnings divided by men's median earnings for year-round, full-time workers increased from 60 percent in the late 1970s to 70 percent by 1990.[22] However, this gave little cause for cheer, since it was not due to a marked improvement in women's economic status but instead to a severe decline for men. The deindustrialization of the early 1980s saw the eradication of more than a million jobs in basic industries such as steel and autos. These relatively high-wage union jobs, which had been held mostly by men, were never replaced, and men's wages fell commensurately.[23] Yet the 70 percent wage ratio tells only part of the story. If all workers are taken into account, instead of only those who worked full-time and year-round, the wage ratio rose to only 50 percent (from 40 percent), reflecting the fact that women are more likely than men to work part-time and/or part-year.[24]

Racial inequities continued as well. Yet while comparative wages between black men and white men remained fairly stable through the 1980s, at approximately 70 percent for males working year-round, full-time and 60 percent for all men, the gaps between black women and white women widened. The affirmative action policies of the 1970s did indeed have an effect, as the wage ratio between black and white women—both for those working year-round, full-time and for all workers—increased from 88 percent in 1971 to 93 percent by 1980. However, as right-wing economic policies led to gutting affirmative action mechanisms, this progress was reversed, and black women's income fell relative to that of white women. While the earnings ratio between black and white women working year-round and full-time widened slightly, to 89 percent by 1990, the ratio between all black and white women increased to 81 percent, reflecting black women's greater difficulties in securing year-round and/or full-time employment.[25]

These trends were also seen in labor force participation rates, which continued to increase for women and remain fairly stable for men. Between 1980 and 1989, the labor force participation rate for white women rose from 51.2 percent to 57.2 percent; it rose from 53.1 percent to 58.7 percent for black women. During these same years, the rate for white men fell slightly, from 78.2 percent to 77.1 percent, while the rate for African-American men reversed its downward slide and increased slightly, from 70.3 percent to 71.0 percent.[26]

The "Workfare Explosion"

Welfare policy in the 1980s was marked by the resurgence of workfare, as "poverty by choice" theories held sway and increasing numbers of welfare recipients were forced to work outside their homes. Most programs were accompanied by flowery rhetoric about providing education and training, as well as child care and other support services, to enhance women's skills and end "welfare dependency." The supposed benefits of California's Greater Avenues for Independence (GAIN) program were explained in a booklet for participants:

> The purpose of the GAIN program is to teach, train, counsel and help you find a job. When you become self-supporting, you and your children will enjoy a higher income and a better way of life. . . . GAIN is with you every step of the way, providing you with such important supportive services as child care, transportation and work- or training-related expenses. GAIN helps you get the skills that are needed in today's work force. You could become a technician, salesperson, assembler or any one of hundreds of other professionals. . . . Everyone wins. You gain a job and a future. Private industry and business gain a skilled work force.[27]

The benefits were primarily realized by businesses, however. The helpful components were routinely underfunded, and instead of providing training for high-wage jobs the programs helped push poor women into the ever-expanding low-wage service sector.

The 1981 Omnibus Budget Reconciliation Act Mandate and WIN Demonstration Programs

Mandatory government work programs and other punitive welfare policies were ushered in with great fanfare in 1981 through the Omnibus Budget Reconciliation Act (OBRA).

Eligibility for AFDC was restricted by tightening some of the requirements. The value of a family's assets was limited to one thousand dollars in property and fifteen hundred dollars in the value of an automobile; the amounts remained unchanged throughout the 1980s.[28] While the "sticks" requiring work outside the home were strengthened, the "carrots" were gutted, as severe limitations were placed on the WIN income disregard or work incentive bonus. The thirty-dollar/one-third income disregard was ended after the first four months of employment; it was based on gross instead of net income; unlimited deductions for work-related expenses were replaced with a flat monthly amount of $75 (prorated for part-time workers); and child-care subsidies were limited to $160 per month per child (as well as attendant care expenses for incapacitated adults).[29]

In light of the widespread acceptance of "poverty by choice" theories and pronouncements about the importance of work, these cuts in the

income disregard were clearly counterproductive, as it became more difficult to combine wage-labor and welfare. Immediately, 442,000 "working
poor" who were supplementing their low-wage jobs with welfare were
thrown off AFDC, resulting in the otherwise surprising decrease in the
rolls in the midst of the severe recession of 1981–1982. The loss of supplemental welfare payments, and, even more importantly, of Medicaid,
eventually led many of them back on welfare.[30]

"Poverty by choice" theories were most evident in WIN demonstration programs. As discussed in chapter 5, the WIN program, which had
been roundly criticized since its inception, was an easy target for reform. Compromising between conservatives who believed that welfare
recipients should "work off" their grants in forced work programs and
liberals who thought that education and training should be provided to
upgrade people's skills, the budget act encouraged individual states to
develop their own programs as alternatives to WIN. The result was a
proliferation of programs with enticing acronyms—GAIN (Greater Avenues for Independence) in California, JEDI (Jobs for Employable Dependent Individuals) in Maryland, MOST (Michigan Opportunities for
Skills and Training) in Michigan, and ET (Employment and Training)
Choices in Massachusetts, to name a few. Promising to end "welfare
dependency" by making people "independent" through wage labor,
WIN demonstration programs included some or all of the following:
education and training components, support services such as child care
and transportation allowances, job search, and, often, Community
Work Experience Programs (CWEPs), commonly known as workfare.
Most programs required AFDC recipients considered employable, generally those with children age three or over, to register. Even in ET
Choices, widely touted as a voluntary program, welfare recipients were
vulnerable and often subjected to subtle pressures to participate.[31] People failing to comply could be sanctioned, as their welfare grants could
be cut, given to a third party who would then pay the bills, or suspended
entirely.

Education, Training, Job Search, and Support Services. The education
components in some of the programs looked quite impressive. They
included General high school Equivalency Degree (GED), English as
a second language (ESL), remedial adult education, postsecondary
education, and vocational training, both in a classroom setting (CT)
and on the job (OJT). OJT was usually set up through Work Supplementation Programs (WSPs), in which a participant's wage was subsidized by the welfare department. This practice was sometimes called
"grant diversion," stressing the fact that part of a worker's welfare
check was "diverted" to the employer. When this type of training

included support by counselors or peers it was sometimes called "supported work."

Job search was carried out by individuals or in groups commonly known as "job clubs." Activities included help with résumé writing, practice in interviewing skills, access to the state computer job bank, and/or simply phoning employers who advertised job vacancies. Support services included subsidies for a portion of work-related expenses, primarily child care and sometimes transportation, lunch, and uniforms, as well as vocational and other types of counseling.

Many problems were apparent with these program components. One of the most important was that the beneficial activities—education and training, as well as support services, notably child care—were never adequately funded. Even though education and training are needed to increase employability and help women obtain jobs paying sufficiently high wages to keep them off welfare, a 1987 General Accounting Office study of sixty-one WIN demonstration programs in thirty-eight states found that only 10.4 percent of the participants received any education or training.[32] Only 2.3 percent of the total participants were involved in remedial or basic adult education, in spite of the high numbers of people known to need these programs. In California, for example, approximately 60 percent of those who attended GAIN registration sessions were found to require basic adult education.[33]

The 10.4 percent figure also included women in postsecondary educational programs, who could receive support services and sometimes tuition, and represented 1.6 percent of WIN demonstration participants. It included SIPs (Self-Initiated Programs), women who went to college after they registered for a WIN demonstration program, as well as women who were enrolled in college and then pulled into WIN demonstration programs. Even though studies show the importance of a college degree, especially a four-year degree, in ending "welfare dependency," obstacles were routinely placed in the paths of women trying to obtain degrees.[34] The amount of time they could remain in college was limited, usually to two years, and participants were often channeled into two-year vocational programs that would leave them in poverty. Regulations about allowable income and expenses sometimes led to reductions in payments, especially food stamps. And, reflecting the view that welfare recipients could not be trusted, many programs required participants to have their professors sign time cards confirming that they had attended classes.[35]

The problems created by the GAIN program in California led many AFDC recipients attending college to try to obtain deferrals to avoid participating in GAIN. Lori Richard's story is typical. She went on AFDC in April 1987 and enrolled in college the following year. In early 1989 she received a notice to report to the GAIN office, where she was told that she could only remain in college for another two years. According to Lori, "I wanted to be able to get ahead, to make a life for myself and my child. This meant finishing school, not being pushed into a low-wage job that would keep me in poverty. They didn't see that if I finished school I would get a better job and pay more taxes."[36]

Training was also limited. It was provided to only 2.3 percent of WIN demonstration participants nationwide, and the length of training was shorter than it had been in CETA.[37] Instead of developing their own training programs, most states utilized other resources, primarily through the Job Training Partnership Act (JTPA). However, assessment criteria mitigated against serving AFDC recipients who needed a lot of support services and were often difficult to place in jobs. Some states, such as Massachusetts, made use of Supported Work Programs, a form of on-the-job training, with the idea that participants would be hired as regular employees once their welfare subsidies expired. Employers were under no such obligation, however. An ET Choices participant described this imbalance: "Supported Work takes women on welfare and serves them on a silver platter to the private sector."[38]

Insufficient child care presented further complications. Although many programs formally required participation of mothers whose youngest child was over age two, this was often prevented by the lack of child care. In fact, a meager 6.4 percent, or approximately $22.30 per participant, of the median program's total budget was spent on child care.[39] Even in states that had a greater commitment to subsidizing child care, the amounts given were far too low to adequately cover expenses. In Massachusetts, which spent 32 percent of its budget on child care, more than any other WIN demonstration program, each participant received an average of only slightly over four hundred dollars for her entire time in the program.[40] In the mid-1980s this amount could perhaps pay for one month of full-time child care in the Boston area. In some programs, such as California and Massachusetts, subsidies for child care were also supposed to be provided for a three-month transitional period after participants left AFDC for employment. Although a good deal of attention was given to this provision, the amount was still too low, and after the transitional period expired people were again solely dependent on their own resources.

The other important support service was the provision of funds for transportation, primarily reimbursement for mileage or bus tokens. Yet these amounts were also very low, with the median program spending $24.41 per participant, or 7 percent of its budget, on transportation funds.[41]

The program component used most often was job search. It was both the least expensive way of getting people off the rolls—costing the median program only $183 per participant—but also showed quick results.[42] However, most people who participated only in job search ended up with low-wage jobs that left them in poverty, and often still on welfare.

Community Work Experience Programs (CWEPs). Many of the WIN demonstration programs included a Community Work Experience Program (CWEP), in which welfare recipients were forced to work in jobs designated by the welfare department in public or nonprofit agencies in exchange for their welfare checks. The number of hours of work was usually determined by dividing the welfare grant by the minimum wage. In addition to being a component of WIN demonstration programs, CWEPs were also sometimes set up as programs in their own right, both for AFDC recipients and for people on general assistance and food stamps. Clearly punitive, mandatory work programs, CWEPs force people to work for welfare payments, not for wages. A job—almost any job—can look better in comparison.

CWEPs were the favored program of the Reagan administration. In fact, the administration's initial 1981 welfare reform proposal involved eliminating WIN and requiring all states to replace it with a CWEP.[43] In the compromise, the income disregard was severely restricted and states were given the option of setting up a variety of work programs, including a CWEP.

Reasons given for implementing CWEPs drew on both the economic and social rationales used in the 1980s attack on welfare. Some CWEP supporters cited the importance of "providing services of value to local communities in return for their expenditures on welfare." Others stated that CWEPs would improve participant's employability, both directly through acquiring new job skills and indirectly by "instilling a sense of responsibility, or the work ethic.' "[44] As explained by Mickey Kaus, another widely read "poverty by choice" proponent, work would enable people to "hold their heads up" and to obtain references from supervisors.[45] The importance of forcing the poor into wage labor was explained in the GAO study of WIN demonstration programs in words reminiscent of earlier attacks on relief: it would work by "deterring employable people from going on or staying on welfare." This, in turn, would have the beneficial result of "increasing public support for welfare by giving citizens cause to believe that all who can work are doing so."[46] In another often-cited study of WIN demonstration programs, the Manpower Demonstration Research Corporation (MDRC) explained that welfare should no longer be seen as an entitlement and that CWEPs could "change the terms of welfare, from a system of benefits conditional only on the recipient's level of income and wealth to one that also required the recipient's commitment to try to become self-supporting."[47]

What's Wrong with CWEP? CWEPs are, quite simply, the most punitive form of government work program. There are five major problems with them.

First, and most fundamentally, they ignore the value of women's work in the home raising children, requiring poor women to work outside the home in order to "work off" their welfare payments. It is instructive that the media applaud professional women who leave their careers to take care of their children, but that poor women are not given this choice.

Second, while the idea became widely accepted in the 1980s that welfare recipients had an "obligation" to work outside the home and could be sanctioned if they failed to comply, no corresponding punishment was meted out to welfare departments if eligibility workers made errors and mistakenly cut off a family's grant.[48] Compounding this imbalance, by the end of the decade welfare recipients faced charges of fraud for these mistakes.

Third, contrary to the claims of supporters that training would be provided, this was not borne out. In fact, the MDRC found that CWEPs provided little skill development "because most of the participants had the required general working skills at the time they began the assignment." Furthermore, the MDRC found that although participants generally felt they were making a positive contribution, they believed that the "employer got the better end of the bargain" and that they "would have preferred a real job."[49]

A fourth set of problems stems from the fact that CWEPs do not provide a "real" job. Participants have virtually no rights as workers. It is instructive that whereas workers in the 1930s programs and in CETA sometimes felt secure enough to stage strikes, this has not been the case for people on CWEPs. The threat of having their welfare payments cut or canceled has apparently, and not surprisingly, made them unwilling to take collective action. In addition, people on CWEPs, as with CETA workers, were sometimes used to undermine the position of public-sector workers and of public-sector unions. According to a spokesperson from the American Federation of State, Country, and Municipal Employees (AFSCME), this leads to "the creation of a subclass of low-paid employees, erosion of well-paid jobs, and a diminution in the quality of public services."[50]

There was evidence that regular employees were indeed replaced by welfare recipients. AFSCME cited a sizable decrease in the number of workers in some low-skilled job categories in New York City when a CWEP program was implemented.[51] And Shirley Ware, secretary/ treasurer of Service Employees International Union (SEIU) Local 250 in Oakland, California, stated that when GAIN began, many janitorial and clerical positions were staffed with people on workfare, and numerous positions as groundskeepers were eliminated and filled instead with "gardeners" on workfare.[52]

As was true of CETA PSE in the late 1970s, some CWEP positions were developed in programs that otherwise might well have been eliminated. For example, CWEP participants prepared food at a Head Start center in Beaufort County, South Carolina, were given work in meals on wheels and other low-income services in Salisbury, Maryland, and worked in schools, hospitals, parks, and welfare centers(!) in New York City.[53] In fact, MDRC studies found that some of these jobs had been paid positions under CETA.[54]

The final general problem with CWEP in the 1980s, as had been true in the 1970s, was that it was not cost effective. Although some supporters claimed that workfare both saved money for taxpayers and increased the income of participants, these conclusions were questioned.[55] There were several problems. Although welfare expenditures often were immediately reduced as a result of workfare programs, since recipients left the rolls for wage labor, most studies failed to follow participants for more than a few months to see whether they kept their jobs or returned to the rolls. Indeed, income gains for individual recipients evaporated after taking into account additional expenses for child care, transportation, and taxes, as well as the loss of Medicaid, leading many people back on AFDC. This was the case in the widely touted San Diego program. Men, especially, were found to be "net losers in the short run," experiencing losses from participation in the program.[56]

The San Diego CWEP warrants closer examination. One of the earliest WIN demonstration programs, it was pronounced a success in terms of costs, and indeed it provided an important basis for arguments that mandatory work programs should be made permanent. A closer look at the results does not support this conclusion, however. In addition to income losses for men, the program did little to reduce welfare rolls. Although 61 percent of those in the work program obtained a job, 55 percent of the people in the control group (on welfare but not in the CWEP program) also found work. In other words, it could only be claimed that 6 percent of those on welfare who might not otherwise have done so found jobs.[57] Furthermore, the programs proved very costly to administer, as they required a great deal of supervision.[58]

In spite of these problems, CWEP was widely hailed as a success. It seemed that evidence was far less important than the perception that welfare recipients were finally being forced to "be responsible" and work. And, indeed, many recipients did leave the welfare rolls, even if they later returned. This process, known as "churning," was actually cited as a benefit in an Illinois proposal for a Chicago CWEP, as administrators explained that it "would yield welfare savings because the program would both improve employment and 'increase eligibility-related case actions'—that is, speed up departures from the rolls, at least temporarily, because of sanctioning."[59]

Sanctions. The final component of most of the WIN demonstration programs, and one that did result in some of the "successes," was sanctions, since failure to participate could lead to the reduction or suspension of welfare payments. If the noncooperative recipient were from a two-parent family, the entire grant was cut. If the person was a single parent, only the amount of the payment designated for the parent was cut. The first offense for a single-parent family often resulted in turning the remaining payment over to another party (usually a relative, neighbor, or friend) who would pay the family's bills.[60] Further offenses led to suspending the remaining portion of the grant for three months, and then for six months. For two-parent families, the entire grant was suspended for three months for the first offense and six months for the second.[61] Although some states rarely used sanctions during the first few years of the programs, they became more frequent by the late 1980s. This was due, in part, to the states' worsening budget crises and to further efforts to reduce social welfare spending.[62] It also reflected the logical result of intensified antiwelfare ideology.

Results. It is clear that the 1980s programs did virtually nothing to help women. Supporters' claims that both taxpayers and welfare recipients benefited from the programs evaporate under closer scrutiny. Yet all studies of the WIN demonstration programs agree on one point: AFDC recipients most in need of education, training, and support services were those who had been on the rolls for many years, that is, people considered "highly welfare dependent." However, the funds necessary to implement programs of the magnitude needed by this population were not appropriated. In fact, if people in this category had been served in the early programs, claims of program effectiveness could probably not have been made at all.

Pronouncements that the work programs would lead to "independence" based on wage labor also proved false. The GAO study found that approximately half of all program participants ended up with entry-level, low-wage, often part-time jobs that left them with income so far below the poverty line that they remained on welfare.[63] In fact, these low-wage jobs have even less security than AFDC. In spite of all the cuts that were made in AFDC in the 1980s, it was still more predictable than jobs at the bottom of the economic ladder, in which hours can be cut or the job itself ended, often with little notice. In reality, workfare programs simply force people to exchange dependence on welfare for dependence on insecure, low-wage jobs.

Furthermore, the economic irrationality described earlier for CWEP participants extended to all WIN demonstration programs. This was borne out in a study by Christopher Jencks and Katherine Edlin, who found that a mother with two children working in a job that paid five dollars an hour lost almost four dollars a day compared to what she would receive on welfare after taking into account the loss of government benefits (most importantly, health care through Medicaid), as well as payment of taxes and work-related expenses (such as child care and transportation).[64] In spite of this irrationality, the increasingly punitive nature of welfare in the 1980s provided a strong incentive for people to stay off the rolls. According to the GAO study, "Despite the difficulties for low-income workers, there is evidence that AFDC recipients tend to choose work over welfare even when they suffer financially as a result. . . . But, despite the desire of AFDC recipients to work, personal crises with health care, child care, or transportation may precipitate their return to the welfare rolls."[65]

The Family Support Act of 1988: Institutionalizing the Experimental Work Programs of the 1980s

Extensive support for mandatory work programs led to their institutionalization as a permanent part of the AFDC program in the 1988 Family Support Act.[66] Originally titled the Family Security Act to reflect its initial rhetorical focus on security through obtaining a job, it was renamed the Family Support Act during committee deliberations. The support portion dealt with finding errant fathers, commonly berated as "deadbeat dads," and requiring them to pay child support.

Although the Family Support Act took its name from the efforts to force fathers to pay child support, its centerpiece was the work program, called Job Opportunities and Basic Skills (JOBS). Hailed as a "consensus" between conservatives and liberals, it combined conservatives' insistence on mandatory work with liberals' calls for education and training. However, as Nancy A. Naples explains, "The so-called 'new consensus' merely reflects the ideological success of the patriarchal position on social welfare."[67] Any notion that welfare was a right, as claimed by welfare rights organizations, was gone. Instead, there was a social contract—the government would provide welfare and the recipient would work, for wages if possible, and if not, then in a CWEP.

Yet this was a contract with no balance. The government could easily punish welfare recipients who did not fulfill their part of the bargain, but recipients had little recourse when the government made mistakes. Indeed, at the congressional hearings, some policy analysts reminded legislators of the government's side of the contract. Mary Jo Bane, former executive deputy commissioner of the New York State Department of Social Services and a professor at the John F. Kennedy School of Government, Harvard University, argued that welfare reform should involve "a genuinely mutual effort among all of us—government, business, and private citizens—that recognizes our mutual obligations." She went on to explain, "No significant progress can be made in reducing poverty and reforming welfare without increases in employment, improvements in the wages and benefits associated with entry-level work, better training and job readiness among the poor, and efforts to reduce discrimination in wages and employment."[68]

Instead of making any mention of the systemic causes of poverty, however, responsibility was laid squarely on individuals. Drawing on "poverty by choice" and "culture of poverty" theories, it was assumed that welfare recipients needed to learn the importance of work. As explained by the conservative Working Seminar on Family and American Welfare Policy, "No able adult should be allowed voluntarily to take from the common good, without also contributing to it." Only by meeting their "obligations" to society—through work—would the poor improve their "self-esteem" and reduce "behavioral dependency."[69] Senator Daniel Patrick Moynihan, a sponsor of the legislation, stated that since it was "now the normal experience of mothers to work, at least part time," AFDC recipients should also have to work outside the home.[70] This would also increase the supply of entry-level low-wage labor, an interest expressed by the Chamber of Commerce.[71]

Not allowing evidence of the failings of WIN demonstration programs to get in the way, work requirements were central to JOBS. In deference to liberals, JOBS continued the rhetoric of WIN demonstration programs, mandating that AFDC families would "obtain education, training, and employment necessary to help avoid long-term welfare dependency." Individual states could choose among an impressive array of educational activities: "high school or equivalent education (combined with training as needed); basic and remedial education to achieve a basic literacy level, and education for individuals with limited English proficiency; and job skills training; job readiness activities; and job development and placement."[72] In addition, each program was required to include two of the following components: group and individual job search; on-the-job training; work supplementation; and community work experience programs. We will see in the following chapter how the empty promises of WIN demonstration programs were carried over into JOBS, as beneficial components were underfunded and mandatory work requirements were supported by other punitive policies.

Probably the only bright spot in this decade of cuts in social welfare and resumption of punitive welfare policies was welfare rights organizing. Although small in scope, especially in comparison to similar activities in the 1960s, groups throughout the country—Welfare Warriors in Milwaukee, the Coalition for Basic Human Needs in Massachusetts, and the Women's Economic Agenda Project in California—organized against welfare cuts and other punitive policies. An umbrella organization, the National Welfare Rights Union, was established in 1987 to "rededicate ourselves to the pursuit of social justice for all members of our society, particularly those who have been excluded from the benefits of this nation."[73]

The Job Training Partnership Act: The Remaining Fair Work Program

Little was left of fair work programs in the 1980s. Public service employment programs disappeared completely, and the only reminder of the extensive 1970s employment and training programs was the Job Training Partnership Act (JTPA). Far more restricted in both scope and expenditures than its predecessor, the JTPA was enacted in 1982 when authorizing legislation for CETA expired, and began operation the fall of 1983. Modeled on CETA's Private Sector Initiative Program (PSIP), which was established in 1978 in response to ongoing criticisms of PSE, it allowed private-sector employers to develop training programs that met their needs. In harmony with the Reagan administration's economic philosophy, the bottom line was of paramount importance, and the JTPA's much heralded "success" in terms of low training costs and high job placement rates was attributed to selection of the most job-ready.

The constriction in fair work policy was reflected in the opening paragraphs of the JTPA legislation. The Act authorizing CETA declared it would "provide job training and employment opportunities for economically disadvantaged, unemployed, and underemployed persons, and . . . assure that training and other services lead to maximum employment opportunities," but JTPA's mandate was only "to prepare youth and unskilled adults for entry into the labor force" and to serve "those economically disadvantaged individuals facing serious barriers to employment."[74] In contrast to the strong federal leadership in fair work policy during the 1960s and 1970s, the federal government relinquished much of its control, as well as oversight, of education and training policy, and local communities developed training programs with little monitoring by either the state or federal government. The withdrawal of federal control was accompanied by a severe cut in federal funds. Throughout the 1980s, the JTPA received only one-third to one-half as much as had been allocated to CETA in the early 1980s, when it was much reduced from its 1978 maximum; only $3.7 billion or less was appropriated each year from 1982 through 1987.[75] Consequently, the main JTPA program provided training for three-quarter of a million people each year, only 4 percent of the nineteen million people who were eligible.[76]

Private Industry Councils (PICs) were the centerpiece of both the CETA PSIP and the JTPA. These were local groups composed of employers and other community representatives. CETA's prime sponsors became service delivery areas (SDAs) under the JTPA, each one governed by a PIC. Although the PICs had only an advisory capacity under CETA, they became policy-making councils in the JTPA. A majority of the members of each PIC, as well as the chairperson, had to come from the private sector, and it was the PICs, in conjunction with local elected officials, that determined which programs to fund.

The JTPA contained several titles, most of them carried over from CETA. The main one was Title II, which authorized programs for the "economically disadvantaged." Title IIA, which consumed approximately half of the funds allocated to the entire JTPA, established a year-round training program for disadvantaged adults and youths. Title IIB authorized a summer program for youths, Title III contained employment and training for "dislocated workers," the euphemistic term for people who lost their jobs due to plant shutdowns, and Title IV included federally administered programs for Native Americans, migrant and seasonal farmworkers, and veterans, as well as the Job Corps.[77]

The JTPA continued CETA's practice of targeting specific groups of people. There were two primary targets in the Title II programs. First, 40 percent of the funds were supposed to be spent on youth age sixteen to twenty-one. The second critical target group was AFDC recipients, who were to be "served on an equitable basis" in proportion to their numbers in the local population.[78] Indeed, JTPA training became an integral component of the efforts to "reduce welfare dependency" and was used by many WIN demonstration programs.[79] More generally, for most participants family income had to be below either the poverty line or 70 percent of the "lower living standard income level," although SDAs could request waivers of the income criterion for up to 10 percent of the participants who did not meet the income test but faced serious barriers to employment. The list was similar to CETA's 1978 reauthorization and included but was not limited to "those who have limited English-language proficiency, or are displaced homemakers, school dropouts, teenage parents, handicapped, older workers, veterans, offenders, alcoholics, addicts, or homeless."[80] Unlike the 1978 CETA list, however, "women" as a group were missing.

Education and training programs developed in the 1960s and 1970s were constrained in the JTPA, with the main emphasis placed on moving people into jobs quickly and at the lowest possible cost. Length of classroom training (CT) in basic education and specific job skills averaged a little over four months, one month less than in CETA. In spite of the need, far fewer people received remedial education—only 7 percent of JTPA participants in 1985 compared to 14 percent of CETA participants three years earlier. Furthermore, CT enrollees received a stipend in the 1960s and 1970s programs, but in the JTPA they rarely received anything.[81] On-the-job training (OJT) in private-sector firms was also continued. Participants were paid a wage, half of which was reimbursed by the government; this subsidy was widely seen as a windfall to businesses, since OJT continued to serve the most qualified, who might well have obtained a job without the program. In fact, the Houston PIC advertised that its OJT program was designed "for businesses that want to reduce labor costs and increase profits."[82] Work experience was primarily used for youths in entry-level positions in public and nonprofit agencies. Finally, there was job search assistance, sometimes called pre-employment training, or PREP. This could involve a range of activities, including values and skills assessment, life planning, time management, assertiveness training, academic brush-up, counseling, as well as job search techniques and support groups. Yet this, too, was limited compared to CETA, averaging two weeks or less.[83] The emphasis on the bottom line was also reflected in the changed program mix; there was a relative increase in job search and on-the-job training, while classroom training and work experience were reduced.[84]

Performance Standards

Measuring the success of the JTPA was considered very important. Indeed, the JTPA legislation declared, "The Congress recognizes that job training is an investment in human capital and not an expense. In order to determine whether that investment has been productive . . . the basic return on the investment is to be measured by the increased employment and earnings of participants and the reductions in welfare dependency."[85]

This led to a strong reliance on performance standards. Although performance standards had been brought into CETA as part of the 1978 CETA reauthorization, they were neither required nor even fully implemented. This changed under the JTPA; ongoing funding, as well as additional incentive payments for exceeding the standards and reductions in funds for failing to meet them, were contingent upon achievements as evaluated through the performance standards. There were three criteria for adults, three for youths, and one criterion specifically for AFDC recipients. They were, respectively, the percentage of adult participants who obtained a job at the end of the program, also called the "entered employment rate," or "placement rate"; the cost per adult participant who became employed; the average wage for adults who obtained jobs; the percentage of youth participants who obtained a job at the end of the program; the average wage of youths who obtained jobs; the "positive termination rate" for youths, that is, the percentage who continued in further education or training, entered the armed forces, or achieved specific "competencies" (educational, job-seeking, or occupational skills) designated by the PIC; and the percentage of welfare recipients in the program who obtained a job.[86]

The early JTPA performance standards were derived by taking 1982 CETA results as a baseline and adjusting them upward by approximately 10 percent. Reflecting the logic of capitalist production-for-profit, this was justified by a presumed "productivity improvement factor" caused by reliance on the private sector, which was assumed to be more efficient, and therefore yield better results, than the government.[87] Thus the initial performance standards for adults were set at the following levels: entered employment rate, 55 percent; entered employment rate for welfare recipients, 39 percent; cost per placement, $5,704; and hourly wage, $4.91. The monetary incentives worked, and, on average, SDAs exceeded most performance standards. In 1984, the entered employment rate was 67 percent for all adults and 57 percent for welfare recipients, and the cost per placement was $3,395. Only the actual hourly wage was lower, $4.85 per hour. The following year saw further "improvement": an entered employment rate of 69 percent for all adults, and the same 57 percent for AFDC recipients, an even lower cost per placement of $2,941, and an hourly wage of $4.91. By 1987 the entered employment rates had been increased to 62 percent for all adults and 51 percent for welfare recipients, while the cost per placement had been lowered to $4,374. The hourly wage remained the same.[88]

While the federal government gave a great deal of flexibility to SDAs in choosing training programs and services, there were strict limits on how funds could be spent. Reflecting the success of arguments by the Reagan administration that cash allowances and support services became a "disguised welfare program" under CETA, little money could be used for these purposes.[89] Federal legislation decreed that at least 70 percent of the funds had to be used for training and that a maximum of 15 percent could be used for administration, leaving only the remaining 15 percent available for support services and stipends.[90]

Women in the JTPA

The JTPA was hailed as a success—a cost-effective use of federal training funds. Indeed, it proved effective for business. As explained in a report by Wider Opportunities for Women, compared to CETA, the JTPA "simply switched beneficiaries from the economically disadvantaged to the private sector."[91] This view was echoed by a businessman involved in the program, who explained, "Our job is to make this JTPA System serve employers quickly and at the lowest possible cost."[92]

Yet the success was not shared by workers. Women, in particular, were ill served, especially in comparison to their treatment in CETA after the 1978 reauthorization. The JTPA's fundamental weakness was the centrality of performance standards, which led to reliance on brief low-cost training programs, as well as a general tendency to select the most job-ready who needed the least training and fewest services and could be most easily placed. As explained by Sar Levitan and Frank Gallo in their helpful study, "Poorly drafted performance standards may produce the appearance of program success without the substance and also cause unintended and deleterious side-effects."[93] This was clearly the case in the JTPA. Indeed, the performance standards ignored "impact evaluations," which measure the net effect of training programs and show that people who need the most costly education, training, and services, such as long-term welfare recipients, evidence the greatest net gain in earnings.[94] These problems specific to the JTPA were exacerbated by the overall right-wing attack on labor, especially the effort to maintain a low minimum wage, and the focus on "reverse discrimination," as employment barriers faced by women and people of color were ignored while "unfair treatment" of white men became a paramount concern.

We have already noted the shift from CETA to the JTPA in terms of program mix and length of training. OJT and job search assistance increased at the expense of CT and work experience, and the average length of all programs was shortened. Yet studies show that the initial earnings gains of job search assistance dissipate within a few years, or even months.[95] Furthermore, more intensive, longer-term training and education also have longer lasting effects. Emphasis on low cost per placement, however, led SDAs to opt for shorter programs with immediate results. A woman who completed JTPA training described the views of many participants:

> I know that some of the women feel they're allowed only so many
> classes and then they're pushed out into the marketplace as quickly as
> possible without thinking ahead to how well prepared they actually are.
> In other words you can get a job at minimum wage, but if staying an-
> other quarter or even a whole year would prepare you for a much better
> job, then it would seem to me to be worthwhile to do that.[96]

The focus on low cost per placement in conjunction with a high placement rate also encouraged creaming. Instead of adhering to the legislative mandate to serve the "economically disadvantaged" who had "serious barriers to employment," applicants more likely to be chosen for the program were those who were most likely to obtain jobs and needed few or no services. As a PIC member explained, "Let's be honest. To meet the performance standards, we have to cream the population."[97]

Creaming had the greatest impact on women, since they often needed child care. Not only would program funds have to be spent on child care, as well as other services, while women were in the program, but continued child-care responsibilities with no additional money for child care after their training ended made it more difficult for women to secure jobs. This was particularly problematic for teenage mothers, who needed assistance with childcare, and often transportation and counseling, and were less likely to find jobs, since they had little or no work history.[98]

This also created problems for AFDC recipients, especially those who had been on the rolls for many years and typically required many of services and were harder to place. In fact, although it is these "long-term, highly welfare dependent" women who are the targets of the most vitriolic right-wing diatribes, the resources necessary to move them into employment have not been forthcoming. Even though approximately one-fifth of JTPA enrollees were on AFDC, creaming was also evident among this population, who tended to be better educated and had a longer work history than the average AFDC recipient.[99]

Providing money for support services in the JTPA for welfare recipients and other women was constrained by the expenditure cap; only 15 percent of each SDA's funds were allowed to be used in this manner. This was a sharp contrast to CETA, in which 30 to 40 percent of the funds were used for support services, especially child care and transportation.[100] The cap proved unnecessary, however, as the focus on minimizing the cost per placement mitigated against spending even this small amount; every dollar that went into services was seen as a dollar less for direct training. Furthermore, some PIC members worried that providing support services only "promoted dependency."[101] Thus, in 1984 and 1985 an average of only 8 percent of the PICs budgets was spent on services.[102] This was indeed minimal. A 1985 GAO survey found that only one-sixth of all JTPA enrollees received any support services through the program, and the average amount was a mere $161 for each participant.[103] The paucity of support services directly provided by the JTPA was supposed to be offset by the use of support services provided by other programs, most importantly welfare agencies paying for child care and transportation for AFDC recipients.[104] This, too, was insufficient, however, and only one-fourth of AFDC recipients referred to the JTPA through WIN received support services from the WIN program.[105]

The emphasis on cost minimization also worked against women in another way. The 1978 CETA reauthorization focus on training for women in "nontraditional" occupations was not continued in the JTPA. In fact, in a nationwide survey of Women's Centers involvement with the JTPA, researchers concluded that "[NTO training] for women has to be near the top of the list of factors to be avoided since employer resistance to NTO women can make them hard to place."[106] Furthermore, the training itself is relatively costly and lengthy.[107]

Not only were women's needs for services and training for high-wage jobs slighted in the JTPA, but a gender imbalance that marked the MDTA and CETA was carried into the program; the percentage of women in CT was always greater than in OJT. A study of the JTPA's early years found that while women were 65 percent of CT enrollees, they were only 39 percent of OJT participants.[108] Yet, as had been true in the earlier programs, OJT was preferable because it led to a greater chance of obtaining a job than CT. Furthermore, it was the most common method of providing training for higher-skilled, higher-wage industrial jobs, whereas CT most often trained people for lower-wage service-sector jobs. Rather than challenging these inequities, the JTPA went along with them. A GAO report found that women were most often trained for clerical and sales jobs, whereas men received training in a variety of occupations, from custodial maintenance to truck driver to skilled trades such as construction, machine tools, and welding.[109]

Another gender disparity continued from the 1960s and 1970s programs was a female/male wage gap in the JTPA. Although men fared better than women, results for them also left much to be desired. Between April and June 1987, for example, the average employment wage for those who left the program was $4.51 an hour for women and $4.94 an hour for men.[110] Neither was sufficient to provide income (for someone working full-time, year-round) above the poverty line that year for a family of four. This made it even more difficult for AFDC recipients to remain off the rolls. In fact, intake workers sometimes recognized that the wages were too low and discouraged welfare mothers from enrolling in the program. As a local JTPA director clearly explained, "[W]e know that if we place her at $6.00 an hour and she has two kids, she's not going to make ends meet. In order for the placement to work, the person needs to come out ahead. And eventually she'll see that she's better off on AFDC than she would be in a job."[111]

Compounding the problem of low wages, many people who finished the program did not have any job. For example, from April 1987 to June of that year, 45 percent of the women and 39 percent of the men left the program without obtaining a job. And even those who left with jobs often did not keep them very long. A study by the Milwaukee PIC found that among participants who secured jobs upon leaving the JTPA, only 51 percent had those same jobs three months later.[112]

Problems faced by women and men in the JTPA were further complicated by a lack of data, especially detailed socioeconomic data on program participants.[113] More generally, this attitude led the federal government to cease publication of the information-filled *Employment and Training Reports of the President,* originally the *Manpower Reports of the President,* which had been published annually from the beginning of the MDTA through the end of CETA in 1982; these had provided a wealth of information about all of the government work and training programs. Although *Employment and Training Reports of the Secretary of Labor* were published by the mid-1980s, these were mere shadows of the earlier reports in both size and scope, and often did not appear until several years after the period studied.

Some changes were made in the JTPA in 1988. Recognizing that the performance standards adopted when the JTPA began did little or nothing to encourage placement of participants in stable jobs, four new standards were adopted. The data were gathered thirteen weeks after participants left the JTPA, and the standards and their target values were: adult follow-up employment rate, 60 percent; welfare follow-up employment rate, 50 percent; weeks worked during follow-up period, eight; and weekly earnings of all employed at followup, $177.[114] Expectations were indeed low, anticipating that enrollees would work less than two-thirds of the thirteen weeks and would earn only the minimum wage of $4.25 per hour, as well as some people losing their jobs entirely. It is clear that meeting these targets would do little to alleviate poverty.

Conclusion

The 1980s were a time of cuts in welfare and other social programs as right-wing social and economic rationales provided justifications for undoing many of the gains made in the 1960s and 1970s. Workfare became the norm, supplemented by tighter eligibility requirements for welfare and cuts in inflation-adjusted payments. The only remaining fair work program, the JTPA, was extremely constricted compared to the extensive and innovative programs of the previous two decades. The policies of the 1980s proved to be a precursor to the even more draconian measures of the early 1990s, as life on welfare became increasingly precarious.

7

The 1990s: The War on Welfare

The 1990s witnessed an intensification of policies begun in the 1980s. Ignoring structural causes of poverty, a "culture of poverty" analysis diagnosed "welfare dependency" as a disease that could be cured by absorbing basic American values of "work, self-reliance, and family."[1] Most distressing to conservative pundits was the increase in "illegitimacy" among whites as well as people of color, seen as the "royal road to poverty and all its attendant pathologies."[2] Liberals were not exempt from moralistic criticisms of welfare recipients, often espousing these views to prove that they, too, were "realistic."

Heightening the paternalism of the U.S. welfare system, the 1990s were characterized by four types of policies intended to instill "proper" values and teach "responsible" behaviors: cuts in payments; prosecutions for "welfare fraud"; an array of programs to modify behaviors; and continued emphasis on mandatory workfare. "Welfare fraud" prosecutions would cure dishonesty; programs from "learnfare" to "family caps" would lead recipients to "act more responsibly"; and payment cuts and forced work would teach the value of work. The most severe work incentive was terminating payments entirely, an idea captured by President Clinton in his promise to "end welfare as we know it" by stopping payments after two years on the rolls.

The Democrats also proposed some education and training, childcare subsidies, and workfare-type jobs to help AFDC recipients survive on wage labor. However, the November 1994 election sweep by Newt Gingrich and other reactionary politicians brought the Contract with America and the Personal Responsibility Act (PRA), which included proposals to substantially reduce or eliminate entirely most of the helpful components of AFDC along with other social welfare programs. The incentive was avoiding starvation—by wage labor or marriage.

There was also some discussion about community work programs—including a revived WPA. Yet these were not fair work. Instead of the voluntary participation, market-based payments, and innovative projects that characterize fair work programs, these were mandatory programs for welfare recipients and others considered undeserving.

Continuing Stagnation and the Legacy of Right-Wing Social and Economic Policies

The anemic recovery from the severe recession of 1981–1982 began to fizzle by 1990, and the economy slid into another downturn.[3] Yet even though the economy grew in 1992, 1993, and 1994, the underlying problems contributing to economic stagnation remained unsolved, and workers continued to suffer. Both the unemployment rate and the average length of unemployment remained high, and earnings resumed their downward course.

Unemployment continued to climb through 1992. In that year the rates were 6.0 percent for white females, 6.9 percent for white males, 13.0 percent for black females, and 15.2 percent for black males.[4] Yet the measured rates sorely underestimated the true extent of unemployment; increasing numbers of people became "underemployed," taking jobs below their skill level or part-time jobs when they preferred to work full time, and others became "discouraged workers," dropping out of the labor force altogether. Not only did unemployment rates increase after the recession technically ended, a common occurrence, but the duration of unemployment continued to rise as well. The average number of weeks a person was out of work in 1989 was 11.9; it steadily increased to 17.9 by 1992 and 18.1 in 1993.[5] Longer periods of time without jobs further increase workers' vulnerability and help keep wages down and the pace of work more intense.

The reduction in wages was reflected in several statistics. Average weekly earnings continued their downward course that had begun in 1973, falling another 2 percent from 1990 to 1993, to $254.87 (in 1992 dollars). This was a 19 percent drop from the high point in the early 1970s. And although additional family members in the labor force had been able to compensate for declining wages enough to maintain total family income during the 1970s and the mid- to late 1980s, this measure also fell in the early 1990s, decreasing 5 percent from 1989 through 1992, to $36,812, and taking almost $2,000 in purchasing power away from the average family. Since the ratio between black and white median income stood at 54 percent in 1992, the $2,000 decline had a greater impact on blacks. While median family income for whites fell 4.4 percent, to $38,909, it decreased 8.0 percent for African-Americans, to $21,161.[6] As a result, poverty rates also increased. By 1993 the poverty rate for the entire population stood at 15.1 percent, 29 percent higher than its level in 1979 before the advent of right-wing economic policies.[7]

Many economists were perplexed by the tenacity of high unemployment. A February 1993 cover story in *Business Week,* "Jobs, Jobs, Jobs," noted that the economy was experiencing a "recovery without a heart," since jobs were not being created in proportion to their usual increase.[8] The years of corporate streamlining and downsizing had an effect, as the bottom line was improved through layoffs of blue-collar and white-collar workers alike. Jobs were gone; three-fourths of those laid off during the recession did not get their jobs back.[9] The "virtual corporation," still only a trendy concept, was seen by many as the epitome of corporate flexibility, with a core of owners and managers, but with workers who were only contingent—part-time or temporary.[10] Indeed, the somewhat anomalous situation often occurred in which companies, in order to avoid paying benefits, required some employees to work many hours of overtime, while others were given only part-time work. And increasing numbers of employers used temporary workers.[11]

Not everyone suffered. The richer people were, the more their incomes increased through the 1980s and 1990s.[12] Income disparities were also reflected in the growing gap between the salaries of corporate chief executive officers (CEOs) and wage and salary workers. The average annual pay for a CEO was 42 times that of the average factory worker in 1980, but 149 times as high in 1993, as the average annual pay for a CEO stood at $3,841,273.[13] Not everyone was sanguine about this gap. Even *Business Week* warned that it was "a time bomb ticking."[14]

The widening gap between the rich and everyone else is generally recognized; what is less well known is that right-wing economics also failed to fulfill its promise—that is, restore savings and investment.[15] The main problem was that right-wing economics was so successful in keeping a lid on wages that people had less money to spend on goods and services. However, capitalists will only produce goods and services if they think they can be sold. Thus, with demand depressed, instead of investing in new plant and equipment and thereby creating jobs, capitalists bought luxury goods, speculated in the stock market and other financial assets, and bought other companies. (The relatively high interest rates also made speculation increasingly lucrative compared to investment in capital goods.) Furthermore, in the wake of mergers, new owners usually streamlined companies, causing even more people to lose their jobs.

State Budget Deficits

The recession and generally stagnant economy led to budget deficits in states throughout the country. Although increased unemployment during recessions results in both a decline in tax revenues and an increased demand for services, primarily unemployment compensation and a variety of social welfare programs, two factors exacerbated the normally occurring recession-induced deficits. First, tax cuts for the rich and for corporations since 1981 led to serious shortfalls of tax revenues on all government levels. In several states, notably Massachusetts and California, property tax limitation initiatives enacted in the late 1970s worsened the shortfalls. Second, on the expenditure side of the equation, the 1980s cuts in federal revenue sharing increased the responsibility of individual states to pay for services from their own funding sources instead of using federal funds. The need for social services would have been difficult to meet even if the economy were expanding, and the 1990–1991 recession placed an additional burden on the states as revenues declined further while the demand for services increased.

Women in the Economy

As in the past, women continued to shoulder the primary responsibility for taking care of children. Yet the effects of right-wing economic and social policies made this an increasingly difficult task.

Income differentials between women and men continued to narrow in the early 1990s; for those working year-round and full-time the ratio increased slightly from 69 percent in 1989 to 71 percent by 1992. For all workers (including those working part-time and/or part-year) the ratio changed more substantially, from 48 percent in 1989 to 52 percent three years later.[16] The smaller female/male income differentials reflected two main trends: more men than women were affected by plant closings and corporate downsizing; and some women did quite well, as the gap between low-income and higher-income women widened.

On average, however, women were not better off financially. The decline in everyone's wages meant that women's inflation-adjusted income fell along with men's, though much less precipitously. While women's real earnings declined 1 percent from 1989 to 1992, men's earnings fell 8 percent.[17] This was nothing to celebrate.

Racial inequities in earnings remained fairly stable during the early 1990s. The ratio of black/white earnings for women remained between 89 and 90 percent for year-round, full-time workers. It ranged between 80 and 82 percent for all workers, reflecting the greater difficulties experienced by people of color in securing employment that was full-time and/or year-round as opposed to part-time and/or part-year. And reflecting white males higher income compared to all other groups, the black/white earnings ratio for men varied between 70 and 73 percent for year-round, full-time workers and between 59 and 61 percent for all workers.[18] Yet most measures of earnings (adjusted for inflation) declined—people had less purchasing power, on average, in 1992 than they did in 1989.[19]

Labor force participation rates reflected the disillusion with the stagnant economy. The rates for men continued the decline that began after World War II, falling from 77.1 percent in 1989 to 76.1 percent by 1993 for whites, and a much more significant decrease for blacks, from 71.0 percent to a low of 68.6 percent. The rates for black women fluctuated during these years, varying between 57.0 percent and 58.7 percent. The only group that showed a consistent increase, though much slower than the preceding decades, was white women, whose labor force participation rate rose slightly, from 57.2 percent in 1989 to 58.0 percent by 1993.[20]

This overall decline in income was reflected in poverty rates, which increased among all sectors of the population. While the overall poverty rate rose from 12.8 percent in 1989 to 14.5 percent by 1993, the rates for female-headed families were much higher. Poverty rates for families headed by white women increased from 25.4 percent in 1989 to 28.4 percent in 1991 and decreased slightly, to 28.1 percent, the following year. Rates for families headed by African-American women were almost twice as high, rising from a two-decade low of 46.5 percent in 1989 to 51.2 percent in 1991 and falling to 49.8 percent in 1992.[21] Regardless of these fluctuations, the fact that approximately half of all families headed by black women are in poverty, and in a seriously underestimated measure of poverty, should be seen as a national calamity.[22]

Instead of recognizing that women's increasing impoverishment was exacerbated by economic stagnation and right-wing policies that eviscerated social welfare programs, women were blamed for their situation. Indeed, while the poverty rates remained fairly stable for black women since the early 1970s and increased slightly for white women during these decades, the percentage of families headed by women continued its steady rise, to 13 percent of all white families and 46 percent of all black families. The absolute number of female-headed families in poverty grew precipitously. In 1971, 1.2 million families headed by white women were considered poor; this number increased to 2.2 million families by 1992. And 0.9 million families headed by black women were poor in 1971; this figure doubled to 1.8 million families in 1992.[23]

The increase in the numbers of poor, female-headed families resulted from three main trends: the deterioration of worker's earnings; the steadily growing numbers of all families headed by women; and a "baby boomlet." These last two tendencies merit further commment, as they are present not only across all socioeconomic categories but also in countries other than the United States.[24] In fact, in what is sometimes termed the "independence effect," growing numbers of middle-class women are choosing to live without male partners and often choosing to bear children outside marriage relationships.[25] Reactions to Vice-President Dan Quayle's 1992 diatribe against television character Murphy Brown for having a child out of wedlock showed the limits of criticizing middle-class women for these life choices. Yet poor women remain acceptable targets.

AFDC: Increases in the Rolls and New Punitive Policies

Welfare policy continued along its path of the 1980s, becoming even harsher in the early 1990s. Existing welfare policies were blamed for encouraging the "underclass" to make choices that maintained a "culture of poverty." Conservatives were particularly concerned about the increase in "illegitimacy" among the poor. Recalling a similar focus in the 1950s, as well as the 1965 *Moynihan Report* on the "breakdown" of the African-American family, they voiced concern about out-of-wedlock births. One of the most notorious was Charles Murray. In a widely cited *Wall Street Journal* article published in November 1993, he noted that the black "illegitimacy rate" was now 68 percent, but he worried much more about the white rate of 22 percent. As he explained, "Illegitimacy is the single most important social problem of our time—more important than crime, drugs, poverty, illiteracy, welfare, or homelessness because it drives everything else." Welfare was seen as a misguided government program that perversely encouraged out-of-wedlock births. His solution was to end AFDC entirely, leading poor women to put their children up for adoption or place them in orphanages, which the government should fund "lavishly."[26] As explained by Charles Krauthammer, a Washington columnist who staunchly supported Murray's proposal, "the only realistic way to attack this cycle of illegitimacy and its associated pathologies is by cutting off the oxygen that sustains the system: Stop the welfare checks."[27]

The mean-spirited and punitive attitude underlying Murray's proposals was reflected in different types of policies. As the 1990–1991 recession caused states to became increasingly strapped for cash, the reaction against welfare that had been tapped throughout the 1980s was further energized. Using sanctions, along with a few incentives, to prod welfare recipients to learn "responsible behaviors," states throughout the country made outright cuts in payments, prosecuted recipients for "welfare fraud," set up an array of behavioral programs, and extended workfare.

These policies were further extended in the wake of the November 1994 elections and the ascendence of Newt Gingrich as Speaker of the House of Representatives. Although at this juncture in early 1995 the results are not precisely known, the contours of the proposals are clear. The Personal Responsibility Act, now being debated in Congress, tries to sweep away the remaining vestiges of the War on Poverty programs, ending their entitlement status, drastically reducing expenditures, imposing stringent restrictions, and allowing states to implement behavioral modification and other measuress with little oversight from the federal government.

The cuts in AFDC payments were supposed to function as a work incentive. They were particularly troublesome. While the decreases during the 1980s had been made by simply not raising payments and allowing the increase in inflation to reduce purchasing power, some of the cuts in the early 1990s were made in the actual money amount of the payments. California led the way; by the early 1990s it had more than twice as many AFDC recipients as any other state, and 17 percent of the national total.[28] AFDC payments were cut outright by 4.4 percent in 1991, another 5.8 percent in 1992, and an additional 2.7 percent in 1993, so that the grant for a family of three fell from $694 per month in 1990 to $663 per month in September 1991, $624 per month in November 1992, and $607 in September 1993.[29] Maryland, Tennessee, Vermont, and Washington, D.C., also made actual cuts in payments. In Wayne County, Michigan, the average AFDC payment was slashed 13 percent—from $525 to $459 per month—between January 1991 and January 1992.[30] Some states simply continued their low payments. In January 1994, the maximum monthly payments for a family of three were $184 in Texas, $164 in Alabama, and a mere $120 in Mississippi.[31]

Most states continued the strategy of the 1980s, failing to increase AFDC payments to keep pace with inflation. Yet the outright cuts were so severe that the actual median payment fell from $389 per month in 1990 to $377 per month in 1993.[32] When adjusted for inflation, this was a 13 percent fall in purchasing power in only three years.[33] The increase in food stamps did not come close to compensating for these reductions.

In fact, prices continued to rise, particularly for housing. In California, the fair market rent for a two-bedroom apartment increased from $715 in 1989 to $864 by 1993.[34] Even the fair market rent for an efficiency unit (that is, a studio apartment) was $570 in September 1993, only $37 less than the total welfare payment for a family of three and $80 more than the $490 per month AFDC payment for a family of two.[35] Housing was similarly expensive in other parts of the country, especially in metropolitan areas. For example, the monthly fair market rent for a two-bedroom apartment in 1993 was $854 in Washington, D.C., $809 in Boston, $692 in Chicago, $681 in New York City, and $630 in Seattle, amounts that were well above median AFDC payments in each area.[36]

It should be noted that even though the cuts in California were particularly severe, they were only a fraction of the amount requested by Governor Pete Wilson. Trying to hone his image as a presidential contender, he argued that reductions in AFDC payments were necessary in order to both increase work incentives and reduce the California budget deficit; he repeatedly proposed an immediate 10 percent cut in payments followed by another 15 percent cut six months later for families with able-bodied adults. If this had been enacted as part of the 1994–1995 budget, the AFDC payment for a family of three would immediately have fallen to $546 per month and to an outrageously low $464 six months later.[37]

Wilson's cuts were eventually halted, at least as of early March 1995. In response to a lawsuit filed by welfare rights advocates claiming that in an earlier Department of Health and Human Services waiver allowing a grant cut the Bush administration had acted "arbitrarily and capriciously," a California superior court judge enjoined the 2.3 percent reduction scheduled to take effect on September 1, 1994. Wilson appealed to Department Secretary Donna Shalala, imploring her to approve the cuts. As he put it, "Your administration has a choice—to encourage states in their bold and innovative reforms, or to further tighten the screws that trap millions in a lifetime of welfare dependency."[38] Wilson may well get his way. If the Personal Responnsibility Act passes it is likely that waivers from the Department of Health and Human Services will no longer be required, and the cuts supported by Wilson, along with a range of other state initiatives, will simply be implemented.

Cash assistance programs other than AFDC were also targeted by many states throughout the country. In 1991, Michigan did away entirely with its general assistance program, ended special needs payments for pregnant women, and reduced SSI state supplements to the elderly poor. Particularly deep cuts were also made by Ohio, Massachusetts, Illinois, Maryland, Maine, and the District of Columbia. It is of little surprise that most of the states involved had suffered from deindustrialization, and the resulting loss of jobs since the mid-1970s and were severely buffeted by the recession of the early 1990s. In addition, continuing a trend begun earlier in the 1980s, payments for Medicaid were further restricted, leading more and more physicians to refuse to treat

Medicaid patients at all since their reimbursements were so low. Other health and nutrition programs for the poor were similarly cut.[39]

One result of the welfare cuts was an increased demand for foster care. Indeed, the difference between AFDC and foster care payments is striking: while the national median AFDC payment was $377 per month in 1992, the median foster care payment (for children ages two and nine) was $604—a full 60 percent higher.[40] Lisa Johnson, an AFDC mother in Little Rock, Arkansas, who placed her son in foster care for several months in 1988, explained why she was considering it again five years later: "If I was alone, I could live above poverty level and with foster care my children would be better provided for economically. What is frustrating is that the system will pay a stranger more to take care of MY children than it will assist me."[41]

Another result of the cuts in cash assistance programs, especially general relief, was an alarming increase in homelessness. It is instructive that discussions of the supposedly undeserving poor rarely focus on homeless people—whether out of sympathy for their plight or fear of what they represent. People standing on street corners with signs saying that they "will work for food" became increasingly common throughout the 1980s and proliferated in the early 1990s. Although estimates of homelessness are notoriously unreliable, since they usually only count people who enter shelters, at least six million people were homeless by 1991; approximately one-third of these were in family groups. Increasing numbers of the homeless were formerly middle-class women who were divorced or widowed and little by little lost their savings and lived out of their cars.[42]

In spite of the harsh policies, AFDC rolls increased. There were three main reasons: recession-generated unemployment caused increasing numbers of people to lose their jobs and exhaust their resources, leading them onto welfare; cuts in unemployment compensation, particularly in length of time on the program, meant that more people were forced to turn to AFDC; and the steady increase in female-headed families in conjunction with the baby boomlet created more families who were potentially eligible for aid. In California, for example, AFDC rolls climbed from 659,000 families in July 1989 to 985,000 five years later, an almost 50 percent increase.[43] This trend was also seen across the nation, although not to as great a degree, as the number of families on AFDC rose from 3,800,000 in 1989 to slightly more than 5,000,000 by early 1994, an increase of almost one-third.[44] Approximately 7 percent of AFDC families consisted of two adults and one or more children; 93 percent were headed by a single parent, almost always a woman.[45]

Incentives: Increasing Asset Limits and Income Disregards
Eliminating the Maximum-Work-Hour Rule

Continuing the 1980s trend toward a "new federalism" and experimentation by individual states, many of the new policies and programs were set up in the wake of the 1988 Family Support Act through waivers obtained from the Department of Health and Human Services. While most of the programs were punitive, designed to modify behaviors, three important incentives were adopted by many states in the early 1990s: raising asset limits; increasing the "income disregard"; and eliminating the maximum work hour rule for AFDC-UP families.

Throughout the 1980s, AFDC recipients were allowed a maximum of one thousand dollars in savings and fifteen hundred dollars in automobile equity. This meant that people had to spend most of their savings before they became eligible for welfare, and cars, if they owned them, were often old and in need of repair. The savings limit also contributed to homelessness, since in many areas of the country one thousand dollars would not cover the first and last months' rent plus a deposit.

Recognizing these problems, several states obtained federal waivers to raise asset limits. California increased the savings amount to two thousand dollars and automobile equity to forty-five hundred, and allowed up to five thousand dollars to be placed in "special" savings accounts that could only be used for purchase of a home or business or for a child's education. Colorado permitted AFDC families with an employed adult to accumulate up to five thousand dollars in savings and removed the equity limit entirely for automobiles. Florida allowed savings of five thousand dollars and car equity of eighty-five hundred dollars. Many other states applied for similar increases.[46]

Another beneficial and very sensible change involved increasing the income disregard, or "work incentive bonus," which was established in 1967 when the WIN program began (see chapter 4). Of all the policies adopted by the Reagan administration, the evisceration of the income disregard (ending the one-third portion after four months and the basic portion after another eight months) made the least sense in light of the emphasis on wage labor, since it became more difficult to work for wages and remain on welfare (and thereby maintain Medicaid coverage). Making economically rational decisions, many women were in a sense forced back onto welfare.

Thus, by the early 1990s many states increased the income disregard. California extended the original thirty-dollar and one-third disregard indefinitely, Nebraska disregarded half of all earned income, Florida discounted the first two hundred dollars plus one-half of the remainder, and

Illinois continuously disregarded two-thirds of earned income. Even House Republicans, in their proposed welfare reform bill, recommended increasing the disregard to the first two hundred dollars plus half of the remaining earned income.[47]

Finally, several states eliminated the maximum-work-hour rule. This regulation terminates welfare payments in two-parent families if the primary wage earner works more than one hundred hours in a month. Getting rid of it removed one of the blocks to expanded wage labor for AFDC-UP families.[48]

"Welfare Fraud" Prosecutions

Incentives were the exception, however, and most of the policies developed in the 1990s were harsh and stigmatizing. Antiwelfare ideology was reinforced by and contributed to prosecutions for "welfare fraud." This term is purposely put in quotation marks since welfare rights advocates see these activities as an attempt to deal creatively with an untenable situation, supplementing insufficient grants in order to take care of children. As Elizabeth Briano, who received AFDC for four years, explained, "I was forced to do 'fraud' in order to survive."[49] "Welfare fraud" prosecutions were given a boost by the FRED (Fraud Early Detection) program in the 1988 Family Support Act. Beginning slowly in 1989 and expanding in the early 1990s, states throughout the country set up fraud units.

Both the method and purpose of "welfare fraud" prosecutions were reminiscent of the 1950s. In a return to the earlier ideological barrage about "relief chiselers," the media were full of stories about people on welfare receiving more money than they supposedly deserved. Special investigating units returned, often through district attorney's offices, to ferret out unreported income, as welfare recipients were charged with misdemeanors and felonies if they failed to report additional income. Welfare recipients were arrested even if eligibility workers made mistakes in their calculations and paid recipients more than they were entitled to receive. Due to the complexity of applications for AFDC and food stamps, as well as the inferior treatment (too many cases and low wages) of eligibility workers, this was a common occurrence—in fact, it accounted for more than half of all fraud cases in California.[50] As in the 1950s, these well-publicized investigations into "welfare fraud" further stigmatized and humiliated welfare recipients and discouraged eligible people from applying for aid. They also lent credence to the view that undeserving welfare recipients were cheating the government, and by extension, "hard-working taxpayers."

Contrary to popular belief, fraud prosecutions resulted in little if

any savings, since the cost of hiring investigators and prosecuting welfare recipients usually outweighed the amount of repaid welfare and
restitution payments. However, it did save tax dollars by increasing the
stigma of welfare and thereby deterring potential recipients from applying. In fact, this seems to have been a primary motivation for fraud
programs. There are few other explanations when mothers are arrested
and handcuffed in the welfare department in front of other recipients.
Furthermore, when welfare recipients were in jail their children were
sometimes turned over to child protective services departments for placement in foster homes, constituting both a disruption of the family and an
added expense for taxpayers.

The underlying punitive purpose of the prosecutions was clearly
revealed by a policy used in San Bernardino, California. Every month in
1991 AFDC recipients were sent the following notice along with their
income reporting (CA-7) forms:

> During 1990, 208 persons were convicted of Welfare Fraud in San Ber-
> nardino County. Collectively, these persons were sentenced to a total of:
> 32 years and 4 months in State Prison, 6,777 days in County Jail, 23,987
> hours of community service, fined $22,100, ordered to pay $559,536 in
> restitution. Please help us prevent Welfare Fraud by reporting *all income*
> and *all other changes* in your household or circumstances on your
> monthly CA-7 report. Don't become a statistic in 1991.

In case anyone doubted the true intent of these investigations, this
memo ended with the following statement:

> NOTE: You may report suspected Welfare Fraud by calling (714) 387–
> 2452 or 1–800 344–8477.[51]

The aim of the fraud prosecutions in Riverside County, California,
was similarly obvious. Throughout the early 1990s, the Riverside County
Department of Public Social Services took out weekly ads in the local
newspaper, the *Press-Enterprise,* publishing the names of all those con-
victed of fraud. Few questioned this use of taxpayers' dollars.

It is also telling that people hired in the special investigating units,
mostly men, invariably were paid more than the eligibility workers,
mostly women, who determined the amount of welfare payments. Some
welfare rights advocates argued that the money spent on "welfare fraud"
investigations and prosecutions should be used instead to hire more
eligibility workers so they could make more accurate and timely determi-
nations of welfare grants.

Beefing up "welfare fraud" prosecutions was a focus of some of the early 1990s programs. Again, California took the lead. A finger-imaging (fingerprinting) program was set up in 1993 in Los Angeles County for general assistance recipients. Claiming that this helped reduce fraud by detecting multiple applications for aid, as well as by generally deterring "welfare dependency," the Wilson administration proposed a Welfare Program Integrity Initiative the following year. In addition to expanded finger-imaging, including covering SSI recipients, it would increase verification procedures, for example by requiring eligibility workers to actually see all of the children named as dependents in a family applying for AFDC, and develop a "secret witness program" to reward people who report "welfare fraud." Sanctions would also be boosted. Unemployment Insurance and Disability Insurance payments would automatically be intercepted as restitution for AFDC overpayments, and AFDC payments would be suspended in cases of so-called Intentional Program Violations (IPVs)—for six months after the first offense, one year for the second, and the rest of someone's life for the third violation.[52]

While a great deal of attention was heaped on the supposed fraud committed by welfare mothers, others guilty of fraud got by with a slap on the wrist. The deregulation of the financial industry that was part of the 1980s economic policies encouraged speculation. Savings and loan (S&L) institutions were swept up in these changes, as regulations that had maintained them as relatively safe havens for investors' retirement income on the one hand and sources of funds for mortgages on the other, since the 1930s were removed.

As a result, those in charge of S&Ls invested the funds in often shaky ventures, including purchasing overinflated bonds (that is, junk bonds). The unstable and often illegal basis of these activities was revealed by 1990. Many small investors lost their savings, but few of those responsible faced consequences for their actions. And even though some of the most notorious figures in the S&L fiasco, for example Mike Milken and Ivan Boesky, spent time in jail, they still kept a good chunk of their fortunes. Instead, taxpayers will foot the bill. It's telling that although government bailouts of failed savings and loan institutions are estimated to cost more than $500 billion, the individuals responsible for this debacle are rarely portrayed as being "dependent" on the government and taking advantage of taxpayers' generosity.[53]

Behavioral Modification Programs

A great deal of attention in the early 1990s went into developing an array of programs designed to modify behavior. Viewing "welfare dependency" as a disease that could be cured if recipients learned to make responsible decisions, these programs infused a heightened paternalism into the welfare system. Set up in states throughout the country through federal waivers, they primarily used sanctions, along with a few incentives, and proliferated in spite of evidence showing them to be both punitive and counterproductive. New "fare" programs were developed, including "learnfare," "healthfare," and "wedfare." Other programs included a "teen pregnancy disincentive," "family cap" or "children's disallowance," child support enforcement, limiting aid to pregnant women, a residency requirement or "relocation grant," and cutting aid to legal immigrants. These, too, were intensified in early 1995. Many of these punitive policies were included in a welfare measure passed in February 1995 by the state of Massachusetts. And, not surprisingly, most are part of the Personal Responsibility Act.

Learnfare is theoretically intended to keep teenage recipients in school. It involves cutting AFDC payments for families of teenagers, and sometimes younger children as well, who have more than a specified number of unexcused absences from school; some learnfare programs also provide bonuses. One of the first programs was developed in Wisconsin, which reduces payments if teenagers have more than four unexcused absences in a month. Also using incentives, Cal Learn cuts payments by one hundred dollars for families of teen parents or pregnant teens who earn a grade of D or F, and pays a hundred-dollar bonus for a C or higher, as well as a five hundred dollar bonus for graduating from high school.[54]

Although learnfare sounds as though it could be beneficial, it has several serious flaws. First, it disregards valid reasons for school absences. By ignoring the reality that teenage welfare recipients often have to miss school or work to take care of their children or to attend welfare department appointments, it penalizes industrious students.[55] Second, cutting welfare payments for the entire family because of teenagers' school absences can lead to increased abuse of all children in the home. Indeed, studies have shown a correlation between poverty and child abuse—as family income falls, the likelihood of abuse and/or neglect increases.[56] Third, learnfare puts welfare departments in the position of truant officers, an unrealistic assignment given the already excessive workload of most eligibility workers.[57] And fourth, school attendance is already enforced through truancy laws, obviating the need for additional rules. Indeed, instead of monetary sanctions and rewards, studies show that teenage parents need support services to attend school successfully. As researchers in a study of Wisconsin learnfare concluded, "Resources spent on education rather than monitoring are more likely to move us toward that goal (of increased learning)."[58]

Healthfare programs are intended to prod welfare recipients to obtain medical checkups and/or immunizations for their children; failure to comply usually results in payment cuts. Yet common sense tells us that the best way to make sure that children get proper medical care is to make it more readily available. Setting up community health clinics in low-income neighborhoods (which was done in the 1960s as part of the War on Poverty), providing free vaccines, and even stationing public health aides in welfare offices would do more to ensure children's health than cutting a family's meager welfare check. Instead, the opposite has been happening, as government budget shortfalls led many communities to close some of their health clinics.

Wedfare programs are designed to "encourage family formation" by reducing financial disincentives to marry. Instead of counting the income earned by a stepparent if an AFDC recipient remarries, some or all of it is ignored, or deemed, resulting in higher total family income. Assuming that the biological father of the child(ren) already has an incentive to marry the mother, this applies only to nonbiological parents. The National Association of Social Workers criticized wedfare as "unduly coercive and intrusive." In contrast to the general view that two-parent (heterosexual) families provide the best living arrangements, they noted further that "there is no guarantee that the mere presence of an additional parent will lead to a healthier family life."[59]

The teen pregnancy disincentive is also described as a measure that encourages families to remain together, making AFDC payments to minor parents only if they live with their own parents. However, this is an extremely troubling measure, as it can force teenage mothers to remain in abusive situations. Indeed, the extent of abuse is much greater than commonly acknowledged. A study by the National Center on Child Abuse and Neglect found that 66 percent of women in the state of Washington who became pregnant as adolescents had been subjected to sexual abuse (molestation, attempted rape, or rape), most often by a family member.[60]

The family cap, or children's disallowance, is also explained as promoting responsible behavior—that is, deterring further pregnancies. Drawing on the widely held idea that welfare recipients have children for money, payments are not increased for additional children born to a woman already receiving AFDC. This measure was adopted in many states in spite of studies showing no correlation between the level of welfare payments and birth rates, either over time or among states. Instead, states such as Alabama and Mississippi, which have some of the lowest AFDC payments, also have some of the highest welfare birth rates, and states such as Vermont and Wisconsin, which make some of the highest payments, have some of the lowest fertility rates. This is true for teenagers as well as women age twenty or older.[61]

Contrary to popular belief, AFDC mothers have fewer babies than women in the general population. In a study of Wisconsin women age eighteen to forty-four conducted in the mid- to late 1980s, Mark R. Rank found that the fertility rate for welfare recipients was 40 percent below that of women in the overall population.[62] In fact, the average number of children in AFDC families had fallen slightly by the early 1990s. The average number of children in AFDC families was only 1.9 from 1979 through 1992, and by the following year it was down to 1.8.[63]

There are two additional considerations regarding family caps. First, they can lead women to have abortions, which are opposed by many conservatives who favor the punitive welfare policies. Second, proponents of family caps sometimes argue that since most people do not receive more income for additional children, AFDC recipients should not have their payments increased either. This argument is wrong, however, because it ignores the extra income tax exemptions people get for more dependents. In 1993, families in the 15 percent tax bracket in effect kept $307 per year, or $25.62 per month, for each child, while those in the 28 percent bracket were compensated $574 per year, or $47.83 per month.

Child support enforcement provisions were developed to establish paternity and compel fathers to pay for their children. In another negative characterization of the poor, the media were filled with stories of "deadbeat dads" when these measures were debated. Yet although child support enforcement is helpful when the father is working and has income, it is of little use if the father is unemployed.

The remaining programs found various ways to limit AFDC payments, thereby functioning as perverse incentives to avoid certain behaviors or sometimes were simply punishments. Some states repealed aid to pregnant women or, continuing a policy begun in the 1980s, confined aid to the third trimester of pregnancy. This provision did not even make sense in a cost-benefit evaluation, since study after study has shown that lack of proper nutrition and prenatal care increases the likelihood of babies having low birth weights and suffering other, often costly, medical problems.[64]

In an attempt to prevent poor people from moving to states with higher welfare payments, residency requirements or relocation grants limit AFDC for families living in a state less than a year to the amount they would have received in their previous state of residence. However, migration studies of the poor conducted in Connecticut and Vermont, which have the second and third highest AFDC payments, show that people move primarily to be closer to family and friends and secondarily in response to job prospects. Welfare payment levels have virtually no impact on the decision.[65]

Additional measures cut other cash assistance payments for certain categories of people. Some states, notably California, reduced SSI for legal immigrants in spite of the fact that they use public services less than the general U.S. population.[66] Yet these measures were not surprising given the racist, anti-immigrant sentiment stirred up in the 1980s and 1990s, as "illegal aliens" (actually immigrants without proper documentation) joined welfare recipients as targets of public wrath. Playing on the opprobrium heaped on addicts, some states limited SSI payments for disability due to drug and alcohol addiction. Building on the view that single male adults were among the most "undeserving" of all, many states reduced payments for general assistance. And simply ignoring the reality of homelessness, some states limited families to one instance of homeless assistance.[67]

Workfare and JOBS

By the 1990s mandatory work programs had become an accepted part of AFDC. There was no longer much discussion of the various programs' merits. Instead, debates concerned how to get recipients off welfare and into wage labor more effectively. Consistent with the emphasis on punitive policies instead of incentives, this was primarily done through sanctions.

Job Opportunities and Basic Skills Training (JOBS) programs were authorized through the Family Support Act. They began by October 1990, usually by states making permanent the WIN demonstration programs developed in the 1980s. Most states provided some funds for education, especially adult basic education (ABE), general high school equivalency degree (GED), and postsecondary education, as well as vocational training. Limited monies were available for support services, especially child care, both while recipients were in the program and for a transitional period, from three months to one year, after they left the welfare rolls. And CWEPs and job search assistance programs were common.

In contradiction to the earlier rhetoric (when the Family Support Act was passed) that JOBS would provide education, training, and support services to help get people out of poverty, these more beneficial components were seriously underfunded. As described in a report by the Washington, D.C., Center for Law and Social Policy, funds for on-the-job training and work supplementation, programs found to be most effective in leading to higher-wage jobs, were "almost nonexistent."[68] Instead, recipients often received only job search assistance, and if they failed to find a job, they were required to participate in CWEPs.

State budget deficits intensified punitive policies and led to low levels of funding for nearly all program components. Although Congress allocated one billion dollars in matching grants for JOBS programs in fiscal year 1991, the states used only 53 percent of this money.[69] By September 1991 only 10 to 13 percent of all AFDC recipients were involved in JOBS programs.[70] The paucity of child-care subsidies, in particular, meant that many people who should have been subject to the mandatory provisions were exempted.[71]

Greater Avenues for Independence

California's Greater Avenues for Independence (GAIN) program was important beyond the boundaries of the state, in part because it was one of the earliest and most widely studied of the 1980s WIN demonstration programs, and also because by the early 1990s California had more than twice as many AFDC recipients as any other state. GAIN was hailed as a success, an evaluation that was supported by a much heralded February 1993 report published by the Manpower Demonstration Research Corporation (MDRC). Front-page stories in one of the state's leading newspapers claimed that "[GAIN] not only moves recipients into jobs but, once employed, they steadily earn more, reducing the need for government assistance."[72] This could be seen in higher earnings for people who participated in GAIN compared to those in a control group. The GAIN program in Riverside County, in particular, was touted as the most successful of all. Lawrence Townsend, Jr., director of the Riverside County Department of Public Social Services, explained that this was due to a focus on job placements as opposed to education and training, as well the "aggressive" use of sanctions for people who failed to cooperate.[73]

The increased earnings were far below the amount needed to bring about the promised "independence" from wage labor, however. Two-year earnings for GAIN participants averaged only $5,883 in Riverside County, $5,965 in San Diego County, and a mere $2,998 in Los Angeles County. Although these amounts were higher than the two-year earnings of people in the control group, GAIN participants were still left deep in poverty, and often still on AFDC.[74] And when the transitional benefits ended, even more people were led back on the rolls. Thus, after two years, only 28.6 percent of the single-parent families in GAIN were still employed, and 61.3 percent were receiving AFDC.[75]

GAIN's alleged success in ending the need for welfare was further contradicted by the most recent results of the MDRC study. Its September 1994 report noted that 53 percent of the experimental group who participated in GAIN were receiving AFDC during the last quarter of a three-years follow-up period, only three percentage points less than the rate for the control group.[76] This meant two things. First, in spite of GAIN, more than half of the participants either were unemployed, or, if employed, earned so little that they continued to qualify for welfare. Second, most of those who participated in GAIN and were no longer on AFDC would have followed this course without the program. This, in turn, leads to two conclusions: the current education and training programs are not very effective in ending people's need for welfare; and there are far too few decent jobs available.

A core problem remains in the cohort of women who have been on AFDC for many years and have few job skills. As Judith Gueron, president of the MDRC, stated, "But the fact that, despite GAIN's success, many people still remain on welfare and in poverty after several years also reminds us that reducing long-term welfare receipt remains a major challenge that will likely require a mix of strategies."[77] Simply removing these women from the rolls is clearly not the answer.

As had been true in the 1980s, higher education was one of the most likely avenues out of poverty. Yet many obstacles remained in the paths of AFDC recipients trying to pursue college degrees, most importantly a limit on the number of years in the program. Many women tried to avoid JOBS programs and attend college on their own. Portia Craven, an AFDC recipient and a student at California State University, San Bernardino, explained why she was thankful that she was able to attend school through vocational rehabilitation: "I'm so relieved that I don't have to deal with GAIN. Having professors sign the attendance forms would be so humiliating. And GAIN doesn't let you have long-term plans. They just want you to finish school as quickly as possible and get a job."[78] Her sentiments were echoed by Lupe Rosas, another California State University student: "I've been very fortunate that I haven't had to deal with GAIN, since the Redlands office was too small to set up a program. I just want to finish my degree."[79]

Time Limits on AFDC

Limits on the amount of time people could receive AFDC became increasingly accepted during the early 1990s. Suggested in the late 1980s by David Ellwood, a policy analyst at Harvard University's Kennedy School of Government who was appointed cochair of the Clinton administration's committee to draft a welfare bill, it became the central plank of the administration's proposed legislation.[80] A time limit would accomplish Clinton's pledge to "end welfare as we know it"—terminating payments after a specified number of years on welfare, usually two. A "tough love" approach, it implemented age-old conservative calls for ending welfare and functioned as the ultimate "work incentive."

Time limits were first adopted in Wisconsin. Obtaining a federal waiver in early 1994, Wisconsin implemented its Work Not Welfare

(WNW) program in two demonstration counties. Families could receive AFDC payments—renamed WNW grants—for a total of twenty-four months in a four-year period, after which they became ineligible for three years. Payments were earned through participation in education and training programs (up to twelve months), and work in CWEPs for the remainder of the twenty-four months. Exemptions were limited. Women entering welfare while pregnant or with a child less than one year old were exempt, but women already on welfare were exempt only if their child was six months old or less.[81] WNW plays into the idea that welfare recipients need to be forced to work. Yet it is a cruel hoax, offering no assurances of services and no assistance to people wanting employment but unable to find jobs.[82]

Time limits were widely acclaimed even though most recipients remain on welfare a short time, using it as a safety net to tide them over during emergencies. Cohort studies show that among single-parent families on AFDC, about half leave the rolls within one year, almost two-thirds exit within two years, and fewer than 15 percent remain on AFDC for five continuous years without a break in aid. For two-parent families the length on time on AFDC is even less: 70 percent leave within a year, and fewer than 5 percent receive AFDC continuously for five years.[83] Furthermore, all studies show that long-term recipients need support services—not sanctions—to effectively move off welfare. Yet given the record of the 1980s and 1990s, this is not likely to be forthcoming.

Minimal Fair Work Programs

The Job Training Partnership Act (JTPA) continued in the early 1990s in a manner similar to the 1980s. Funding remained so low that only a small fraction of those eligible were served, training was time-limited and focused on immediate job placement, and on-the-job training (OJT) and job search assistance were emphasized at the expense of classroom training (CT) and support services. Again, women compared to men and people of color compared to whites were ill-served.

Problems with the JTPA

Problems with the JTPA were widely acknowledged. Continuing its 1980s policies, women and people of color were more likely to receive classroom training while men and whites were more readily placed in on-the-job training.[84] Yet OJT continued to lead to higher placement rates and higher wages, on average, compared to CT. Reports by the General

Accounting Office and the Department of Labor inspector general repeatedly documented the continuation of creaming, as the most job-ready workers were often chosen for the program. Abuses were even admitted by Representative William D. Ford, a Democrat from Michigan, and a key JTPA sponsor, who explained that some administrators used federal funds as "pure subsidies to local businesses, paying half the wages for a constant stream of new employees who train on the job as carwashers, dishwashers or broom pushers for six months until the subsidy runs out, their training ends, and a new trainee replaces them."[85] In contrast to the treatment of fair work programs in the 1930s and 1970s, however, the basic structure of the JTPA remained unchanged, as Private Industry Councils (PICs) in conjunction with local government officials continued to decide which programs to fund.

Secretary of Labor Robert Reich and others in the Clinton administration advocated training along the lines of fair work programs.[86] Initially insisting that retraining laid-off workers was necessary in order to maintain U.S. competitiveness, Reich became increasingly concerned about the erosion of the middle class, which he dubbed the "anxious class," of people who formerly had well-paying jobs. Yet results were minimal, and by autumn 1994 Reich acceded to conservative antigovernment rhetoric, calling for "a better way—voluntary commitments" from business. Incentives would include "awards or certificates for businesses that invest substantially in their workers," as well as changes in the tax codes, and they were bolstered by the threat that if businesses did not act on their own accord government would impose a "uniform requirement" for retraining.[87] The situation seemed bleak.

Job training remains small both in relation to employment and training in the 1960s and 1970s and to the numbers of people without jobs. And the question remains, retraining for what? As the *Los Angeles Times* reported in response to proposals for expanded training, "Politicians and economists have also voiced doubt that there will be jobs available for people once their training is done."[88]

In spite of the lack of jobs, public service employment similar to the WPA and CETA PSE was never seriously considered. Although community work programs were sometimes discussed in the early 1990s, and terminology evoking fair work programs was sometimes used, the reality was that the programs were workfare. Programs were not envisioned in which participation was voluntary, wages were related to market rates, and people were treated with some dignity. Rather, these were mandatory programs that usually set payments at or below the minimum wage or forced recipients to "work off" their welfare checks or food stamps. The underlying motivation was not to provide decent jobs but rather to teach welfare recipients the value of work.

A Neo-WPA?

Some policy analysts and government officials even suggested reviving the WPA. Yet their conception was a far cry from the 1930s program. An early, and most consistent, proponent was Mickey Kaus, senior editor of *The New Republic*. Originally proposed in 1986 in an article in *The New Republic* and elaborated in his 1992 book, *The End of Equality,* Kaus's WPA would offer payments slightly below the minimum wage.[89] Following Charles Murray, he urged ending cash assistance payments, as well as food stamps, for able-bodied workers. According to Kaus, this would "break the culture of poverty" and lead to a "transformation of the welfare state into the Work Ethic State."[90] His example of "Betsy Smith" was offered in the early article and repeated in his book, underscoring the punitive intent of his version of the WPA:

> If we want to end the underclass, remember, the issue is not so much whether working or getting two years of cash will best help Betsy Smith, teenage high-school dropout, acquire the skills to get a good private sector job *after* she's become a single mother. It is whether the prospect of having to work will deter Betsy Smith from having an out-of-wedlock child in the first place—or, failing that, whether the sight of Betsy Smith trying to work and raise a child without a husband will discourage her younger sisters and neighbors from doing as she did.[91]

Kaus admitted that a revived WPA would be "relatively inefficient" but defended it, since "at least the public would be getting *something* for its money" (emphasis in original).[92] Others disagreed. In a *Wall Street Journal* editorial, Martin Morse Wooster, Washington editor of *Harper's* magazine, excoriated the WPA, reiterating criticisms of fraud, high payments, and, especially, boondoggles. Calling the WPA a "pork barrel for the poor," he concluded, "The New Deal died some 40 years ago. Surely there are better ways to help the poor than by reanimating its corpse."[93]

Nevertheless, Kaus won some converts, and in 1992, and again in 1993, Senator David Boren (D-Oklahoma) introduced legislation that would create a Community Works Progress Administration (CWPA), as well as a Youth Civilian Community Corps (YCCC). But, like Kaus's proposal, Boren's measure was the WPA in name only—the content was workfare. AFDC recipients would be required to participate in JOBS for two years, as would unemployed noncustodial parents more than two months in arrears on child support payments. Furthermore, people could work no more than thirty-two hours a week, so they would have time to continue to look for jobs.[94]

It is instructive to note the selective use of quotes from the 1930s by

Boren and others advocating workfare. Most common was the reiteration of Roosevelt's 1935 condemnation of relief as "a narcotic, a subtle destroyer of the human spirit," a statement Boren recalled in his Introduction to the CWPA.[95] Whereas Roosevelt went on to advocate fair work for "employables" who would normally have jobs, as well as "[f]ederal aid to dependent children," 1990s critics simply called for workfare for everyone.

Welfare Reform in the Clinton Era

Welfare reform was high on the list of policy priorities for the Clinton administration. Playing on the negative public sentiment toward welfare recipients, Clinton honed his image as a "tough-minded New Democrat" through his 1992 campaign pledge to "end welfare as we know it" by terminating payments after two years on the rolls.[96] Proceeding to implement this promise shortly after he became President, he appointed a Working Group on Welfare Reform, Family Support, and Independence to hold hearings and draft a proposal. Cochaired by David Ellwood, an early advocate of time limits, Mary Jo Bane, like Ellwood a researcher from Harvard University, and Bruce Reed, and staffed with an additional thirty distinguished government officials and policy analysts, they discussed a range of measures.

Comprehensive welfare reform was not enacted at the federal level in 1994. However, at the time of this book's completion it remains high on the list of legislative priorities. Progressives have tried to counter the onslaught of puntive proposals with alternative prescriptions. It is therefore helpful to review the range of proposals generated in 1994, grouping them broadly into moderate, conservative, and progressive categories.

Moderate Proposals

The Clinton administration proposal was the best-developed example of a somewhat liberal position and shows just how far the political spectrum shifted to the right since the 1970s. Reflecting a change in focus from the 1960s and 1970s, David Ellwood expressed what he saw as the central dilemma of welfare reform: "Are we trying to reduce poverty or are we trying to reduce dependency?"[97] He went on to explain that in order to reduce poverty, benefits would need to be raised, but that higher payments lead to increased welfare use—that is, greater "welfare dependency." The Working Group chose dependency.

Its initial draft legislation, introduced in June 1994, followed the lines of welfare policies developed in the early 1990s. In sync with the dominant discourse and heightened paternalism, it concentrated on the need for the poor to learn "responsible behaviors." This would be accomplished by changing AFDC into a transitional program through a two-year limit on payments followed by a work requirement, preferably in the private sector, but if not, in temporary public-sector positions. Entry into the labor force would be aided by enhancing education, training, and support services, especially subsidies for child care, provided through JOBS programs. And job search assistance would remain of paramount importance. These work incentives and sanctions would be bolstered by other measures designed to promote "responsibility": behavioral modification programs set up by individual states; expanded "welfare fraud" programs; child support enforcement, including establishing paternity; and a national campaign, led by the President, to discourage teen pregnancy.[98]

This basic welfare legislation would be supported by other policies designed to "make work pay"—actually, to make low-wage labor a more rational choice for all of the working poor. Talk of raising the minimum wage was abandoned by most officials in the Clinton administration, an early casualty of the "realistic" proposals. Instead, "making work pay" would include the following strategies: expanding the Earned Income Tax Credit (EITC) to more effectively supplement low wages for adults with children—a nonintrusive strategy that does not interfere with low-wage labor markets, especially compared to raising the minimum wage; increasing child-care assistance, and enacting a national health care program, which would eliminate the need to stay on AFDC in order to remain eligible for Medicaid. And economic stimulus would create more private sector jobs. Indeed, jobs in what *Business Week* termed the "real economy" were the professed goal of the welfare reform legislation.[99]

There were many problems with the administration's welfare proposal. Most fundamental was its grounding in a "culture of poverty" analysis that "welfare dependency," not correcting the structural causes of poverty, was the main issue. This leads to "blaming the victims" for their poverty, and to the perverse work incentive of terminating welfare as well as to the paternalistic behavioral modification programs that treat adults like children.

Beyond this problematic orientation was a lack of adequate funds for helpful components, most importantly education, training, and child-care subsidies. The Clinton administration originally considered spending $15 to $18 billion over five years, but the amount quickly shrank to $9.5 billion.[100] If passed, the lack of adequate funds would have had a serious impact on the workfare program. In fact, the Congressional Budget Office estimated that day care would cost $3,000 a year for each child (based on a low appraisal of about $1.50 per hour) and that administering workfare would cost approximately $3,300 a year for each community service position. In a slightly more realistic approximation, *Business Week* figured on $4,000 a year for child care, although it noted that high-quality infant care can cost $900 per month, and $5,000 a year for each work slot.[101] Politicians admitted that the money needed to fund the program was not likely to be forthcoming. As a senior congressional budget expert explained, "The paradox is that ending welfare as we know it will cost much more than the existing system. . . . I think there is an increasing realization in Congress and in the public at large that it is cheaper to give people money and send them on their way than it is to give them money, give them a GED, give them child care and give them job training."[102]

Heidi I. Hartmann, director of the Institute for Women's Policy Research, put it more simply, "The real reason we have welfare is that it's cheaper to have poor mothers take care of their own children than to get them job-ready, create jobs for them, and pay someone else to look after their kids."[103]

The result of trying to cut costs, may well be terminating welfare payments without any supports, including the means to earn some income through a workfare position. *Business Week* warned that "imposing a cutoff would throw 1.5 million people into the labor market," increasing unemployment and depressing low wages even further. As a result more people would apply for other programs, such as food stamps, Medicaid, and unemployment insurance.[104] Logically, the state of the economy—whether enough private-sector jobs are being created—is seen as the key to the program's success.[105]

There also are problems with the administration's supplementary proposals and policies. National health care seems dead for the present time in spite of the constraints imposed on the proposal, especially by the insurance industry, and also by small businesses, as cost containment and universal coverage were sacrificed.[106] Economic stimulus has also been minimal. Although stimulating the economy through government expenditures would help create needed jobs, Clinton has been more interested in deficit reduction.[107] His 1993 proposal for a $16.3 billion two-year economic stimulus package would have done little.[108] Even so, this relatively small stimulus package was gutted by Congress.

Conservative Proposals

Presaging the 1995 Personal Responsibility Act, conservatives proposed their own welfare reform measures to counter the Clinton administration's proposal. In November 1993, 160 House Republicans introduced a comprehensive bill (H.R. 3500) offering what they termed "tough" responses to welfare.[109] Its centerpiece was an "AFDC Transition and Work Program" that would require participation in work-related activities—job search, education, and training for two years. But while the Clinton administration proposal stressed education and training—at least, rhetorically—the only JOBS component required under the Republican bill was job search assistance.[110] This would be followed by work for thirty-five hours per week, or, at a state's option, thirty hours of work and five hours of job search, in exchange for welfare payments. Given the 1994 median grant of $377 per month, this was comparable to a rate of pay of only $2.50 per hour, well below the minimum wage. And in Mississippi, where AFDC payments were $120 per month for a family of three, this was equivalent to a mere $0.80 per hour.

Following other policies of the early 1990s, the bill also contained a variety of behavioral modification programs and harsh sanctions, including terminating AFDC entirely, which could be done for the third violation of program rules, even if the violation was for "good cause," or after three years in the work program. Beefing up attempts to control "illegitimacy," aid would be denied for children whose paternity was not established (except in cases of rape, incest, or likely physical danger), as well as to parents under age eighteen.[111]

Even harsher measures were also introduced. Following Charles Murray's advocacy of ending welfare in order to end "illegitimacy," a 1994 proposal decreed that AFDC as well as food stamps and housing assistance would be denied to custodial parents under age twenty-one, and after four years, to parents under age twenty-six. The only way they could receive aid would be to marry someone who would assume paternity, legal guardianship, or adopt the child(ren). Monies would be made available for "Out-of-Wedlock" and "Abstinence Education" grants, some of which would be used for orphanages. And, of course, there would be time limits, work requirements, behavioral modification programs, and sanctions.[112]

The widely heralded Personal Responsibility Act (PRA), introduced into the House of Representatives on February 9, 1995, continues along these lines. Promising to save at least forty billion dollars during the first five years, it aims to end welfare as it has been construed since the 1930s. Time limits are central; recipients would be removed from the rolls after two years and would be allowed a lifetime maximum of five years of aid.

The PRA goes further in eviscerating AFDC and other social welfare programs. This would be done by collapsing approximately fifty programs into three block grants: for AFDC/cash assistance, food and nutrition, and child care. The block grants would allow a change in the status of the programs: instead of entitlements, in which the federal government is obligated to provide adequate funding so that anyone who qualifies can receive aid, the programs would be discretionary and subject to a spending cap. If the funds are not there the payments will not be provided.[113] Since the amount of appropriations would be frozen during a period of economic expansion, they would be sorely inadequate during the next recession when the need for aid increases.

The block grants would also devolve more authority from the federal government to the individual states. Indeed, the role of the federal government since the 1960s would be further changed; instead of providing some protections for the poor, it would prescribe constraining qualifications that would prevent many people from receiving aid. AFDC would be denied to children of unwed teenager mothers, to those without established paternity, and to additional children born to women already receiving welfare. Supplemental Security Income (SSI) would be ended for all disabled children with the exception of those who currentlt receive it and those who are so severly incapacitated that they would otherwise require institutional care. And legal immigrants would be barred from most federal aid. Positive federal oversight would be minimal, as states could set up behavioral modification programs without having to first obtain waivers.

The block grants are particularly troubling. One of them would incorporate the existing food and nutrition programs, including the school lunch program, and supplements for women, infants and children (WIC), which would be funded at significantly reduced levels. This was proposed in spite of the knowledge that hunger causes children to have a difficult time concentrating and learning and leads to increased likelihood of school failure and a range of problems in the future. Yet it corresponds to the harm that will be done to children if AFDC is terminated for their parents. Indeed, Secretary of Health and Human Services Donna Shalala estimated that at least five million children, more than half of those currently receiving aid, would lose their AFDC benefits if the PRA is enacted.[114]

Yet this seems to be of little concern; indeed, these proposals reflect the current generally accepted view of children. Instead of seeing children as subjects in their own right whom society has a responsibility to protect, they seem to have become objects, the property of their parents. In the case of poor children, they are most clearly seen as the property of their mothers. Since their mothers chose to have them, so the argument goes, they must take full responsibility for the care of their property—that is, they must provide for their own children without societal help.

Relatively Progressive Proposals

Some relatively progressive measures were also proposed. During the summer of 1993, principles underlying constructive welfare reform emphasizing incentives instead of penalties were delineated by the Coalition on Human Needs, an alliance of more than one hundred civil rights, labor, religious, and professional organizations, including the Children's Defense Fund, Catholic Charities USA, the Council of Jewish Federations, National Association of Social Workers, National Organization for Women Legal Defense Fund, and United Way of America.[115] The Coalition's *Principles* were later endorsed by eighty-nine members of the House of Representatives in a letter to President Clinton.[116] Some of these ideas were incorporated into the Working Off Welfare Act (H.R. 4318), co-sponsored by Lynn Woolsey (D-California), a former welfare recipient, and Ralph Regula (R-Ohio). As Woolsey explained, "The key to welfare reform is not to reduce the **availability** of assistance, it is to reduce the **need** for assistance (emphasis in original)."[117] This would be accomplished through five strategies: strengthening support services; improving education and training by preparing people for jobs at "living wages," in part by tripling the JOBS program and eliminating restrictions on education; encouraging work by increasing child-care assistance, expanding the Earned Income Tax Credit (EITC), and promoting "fill-the-gap" budgeting (in which families receive partial welfare payments up to the state's standard of need); and improving child support collections.[118] Child support was also addressed through Woolsey's Secure Assurance for Families Everywhere (SAFE) (H.R. 4051), which would create a child support *assurance* program.[119]

Job creation was discussed by the Coalition for Human Needs, as well as some of the member groups. Denouncing mandatory work in exchange for welfare payments, they advocated some fair work principles. According to the Coalition, "Any public service employment for people leaving the AFDC system must provide pay and benefits equal to other workers doing the same work, without displacing current workers and jobs."[120] This was important, but not sufficient.

Conclusion

Punitive and paternalistic policies marked the early 1990s. Aimed at ending "welfare dependency" instead of addressing the structural causes of poverty, they focused on reducing payments, terminating welfare entirely after a specified amount of time on the rolls, prosecutions for "welfare fraud," and programs to modify "irresponsible" behaviors. As in the 1980s, fair work programs were almost nonexistent.

Not only were fair work education and training programs negligible, but in spite of the continual insistence that welfare recipients should work there was virtually no discussion of job creation. Indeed, even Ellwood backed off from his earlier advocacy that the government should serve as "employer of last resort." Instead, he only equivocated that providing job opportunities was "a compelling mission" and "a tough problem."[121] And although welfare rights advocates explained that welfare recipients are already engaged in caretaking work in the home, real work that should be compensated, nothing in congressional bills recognized this reality.

However, there are alternatives to the punitive policies that blame the poor for their poverty. We turn to these next.

Conclusion: Replace Workfare with Fair Work

The analysis of government work programs in this study shows that the United States has an alternative tradition to punitive welfare policies and mandatory work programs. In light of the increasingly draconian nature of the proposals, it is even more important to put forward a progressive alternative. It's time to replace workfare with fair work and related policies that respect the dignity of the individual and give women and men choices about combining caretaking work in the home with wage labor while maintaining an adequate standard of living.

New policies could build on proposals from the past—Employment Assurance from the Social Security Act, the National Resources Planning Board's "new bill of rights," the 1945 Full Employment Bill, and the original Humphrey-Hawkins Bill in the mid-1970s. Their visions—that everyone has the right to socially useful work and freedom from poverty—should be recaptured and reinterpreted through a feminist analysis to develop a set of policies that focuses on women as well as men and on people of color as well as whites.

We can see from history that policies should incorporate three basic guidelines. First, programs should be universal so that welfare recipients are not singled out and stigmatized. This helps create cross-class alliances to push for these policies and to maintain them after they are enacted. In fact, universalized benefits explain the successful resistance to the Reagan administration's attempts in the early 1980s to cut social security along with the other social welfare programs. Second, programs should be federalized. History shows that direct provision by the federal government leads to relatively more progressive policies, in contrast to leaving more discretion to states. Third, programs should be funded by the government instead of by individual employers. Requiring employers to pay for programs for their workers fosters a reluctance to hire new full-time employees, since benefits as well as wages must be paid; it also exacerbates the current situation in which those already employed full-time are required to work overtime while millions of others are hired for only part-time work or fail to secure any job at all.[1]

Most fundamentally, alternative policies would recognize the value of caretaking work in the home and compensate women and men for this work. This involves countering the generally accepted view that only paid labor is "real work" and reinterpreting work in the home as critically important, socially necessary labor. In fact, this argument is not new, but was forcefully made in the 1960s and 1970s by the National Welfare Rights Organization, as well as by welfare rights advocates today. Further, it is not only work in women's own homes that is important, but also work in the community. Welfare mothers often function as a type of social glue that holds low-income communities together; their presence in the schools and in the projects is critically important. This needs to be recognized as socially useful work, much more valuable than flipping hamburgers or entering data in a computer.

In order to enable women and men to balance work for wages with work in the home while maintaining an adequate standard of living, three overlapping types of policies are needed—family, labor market, and fair work. Although the proposals regarding labor market and family policies may sound like a laundry list to readers familiar with a feminist analysis of social welfare policy, they are very briefly described in order to paint a complete picture. Most of the discussion focuses on proposals for a fair work program and to responses to the criticisms that are likely to arise.

Family policy would be founded on a recognition of the value of currently unpaid caretaking work in the home. Financial compensation would be provided in the form of a family allowance or caretaker allowance that is not means-tested for work in the home. In conjunction with a truly progressive income tax, people with higher incomes would, in effect, repay this money back to the government. This could be accomplished by expanding the Earned Income Tax Credit (EITC) to include work in the home as well as wage labor, and disbursing the payments each month instead of only once a year. A minimum payment would be guaranteed by the federal government, based on bringing families up to a realistically defined poverty line.[2] In fact, the idea of a minimum federal AFDC payment is not new; it was seriously considered in the 1960s and 1970s and was included in both of the comprehensive welfare reform proposals made in those decades, Nixon's Family Assistance

Plan and Carter's Program for Better Jobs and Income. It is currently supported by many policy analysts and organizations, from Richard Nathan, who developed Nixon's welfare reform plan, to poverty policy analysts Sheldon H. Danziger, Robert H. Haveman, and Robert D. Plotnick, to the National Association of Social Workers.[3]

Other policies are also needed to support the work of care and facilitate work outside the home. All we have to do is to copy programs that are already in effect in Canada and western European countries. A paid six-month family leave would make it easier for both women and men to take care of infants as well as family members who are ill. Flexible work hours would allow women and men to reduce hours of wage labor in order to spend more time working in the home. Universal federal health care would enable everyone to obtain high-quality health care regardless of their welfare or labor market status and would obviate the economic rationality of remaining on AFDC in order to retain Medicaid eligibility. The U.S. could simply copy Canada, funding the program by a single payer, the federal government, thereby eliminating the insurance companies, which siphon off billions of dollars that could be used instead to provide health care services. Federally supported high-quality child care, including subsidies for child-care workers, would recognize the social responsibility for children and similarly eliminate this expense as a barrier to wage labor. And an adequate supply of low-cost housing would help provide shelter for all people.

Policies focusing on the labor market are needed to boost income from wage-labor, close income gaps between women and men and between people of color and whites, and thereby make wage work a more rational economic choice. This would be part of "making work pay," a concept endorsed by the Clinton administration as well as several Washington, D.C., policy institutes.[4] One step involves raising the minimum wage and indexing future annual increases to the rate of inflation.[5] Further expanding the EITC to include adults without children and to provide a larger subsidy would similarly help all the working poor. A pay equity policy, in which women and people of color design the evaluations and assess the work, as well as invigorated affirmative action policies, are necessary to combat discrimination based on race and gender and to help ensure that women and people of color receive compensation for their wage labor commensurate with that of white men. Through incentives such as tax credits as well as sanctions such as fines, affirmative action should address institutional barriers that limit job opportunities and wages for women and people of color. Finally, undoing some of the damage inflicted on labor unions since the early 1980s and creating an atmosphere conducive to union organizing would help all workers obtain higher wages and better working conditions.

Other policies targeting the poor would recognize the current reality that approximately 40 percent of all AFDC recipients combine work in the home with wage labor, either "cycling" between the two or doing both simultaneously.[6] Policies that would make it easier for people to combine welfare and wage labor include waiving the hundred-hour rule (in which a family loses eligibility if a member works for wages more than one hundred hours in a month) and "fill-the-gap" budgeting (in which families receive partial welfare payments up to the state's standard of need).

Finally, a comprehensive fair work program is needed. In designing such a program, lessons can be learned from their history so they can better meet the needs of women and people of color. There are four main factors to consider with respect to education and training programs. First, decent stipends need to be offered in order to enable those with no other source of income to participate. Second, training women for male-dominated occupations can help them obtain higher-wage jobs, but this needs to be supplemented by pay equity and affirmative action policies to enable women to obtain and keep these jobs and receive wages equal to those of male workers. Similarly, training for people of color needs to be broadened beyond racially stereotyped, lower-wage jobs and buttressed with pay equity and affirmative action enforcement. Third, successfully targeting groups of women who have been relatively marginal to the labor market—for example, welfare recipients, teenage parents, and "displaced homemakers"—needs to include well-funded support services. In addition to reimbursing work-related expenses, most importantly child care and transportation, it is helpful to offer couseling, especially peer counseling and support groups, which are effective and relatively easy and inexpensive to implement. Fourth, the limitations of the JTPA in the 1980s and 1990s shows not only that spending for support services should be increased in order to facilitate women's participation but also that performance standards should be changed to encourage more extensive, longer-term education and training that would give people skills to obtain higher-wage jobs.

At the center of fair work policies would be a public-sector job creation program. The federal government would be the employer of last resort, providing jobs when the private sector fails to do so. Participation would be clearly voluntary and wages would be based on labor market rates, which would be boosted through the policies just described. We can see from the massive and innovative programs of the 1930s that large-scale programs providing a range of work are indeed possible. Especially in light of the 1980s cutbacks in both services and publicly funded construction, there is much that needs to be done, and it could easily provide work for millions of people. A partial list of projects includes repair of crumbling infrastructure (such as repairing roads and bridges), other construction projects (including low-cost housing and public transportation systems), public-sector projects (for example, teacher's aides in public schools, public health projects, programs for school dropouts, and conservation), and increased public support for the arts.

History also suggests that timeworn criticisms are likely to resurface in response to a massive federal job creation program. How could we respond to these criticisms of fraud and abuse, overly high payments, and inefficient and unnecessary make-work?

Charges of fraud and corruption can be dismissed as red herrings. Although routinely made toward federal agencies and programs, they have been far more constraining when directed at job creation, since these programs expose the inability of capitalist economic systems to create enough jobs for everyone who wants to work for wages.

Criticisms that payments are too high simply reflect capitalists' worries that people will have attractive alternatives to private-sector jobs and that women will have alternatives to marriage. Yet allegations that people refuse other jobs because they are participating in work programs are usually baseless. Investigations in the 1930s of several hundred such cases found that 97 percent of the time people had valid reasons for refusal, primarily that they were already employed.[7] The other side of the job issue concerns the potential replacement of public-sector union members with work program participants. This could be countered by adopting measures developed in the 1970s in cities such as Philadelphia and New York, as CETA workers were required to join the union and/or were paid the same amount as union workers.

The second alternative—that women would have more attractive choices than marriage—is real. In fact, this independence effect is, in a sense, the flip side to "welfare dependency," and needs to be defended as a legitimate choice.

The most problematic criticisms historically—surfacing during the 1930s and the 1970s—concern inefficiency and unnecessary make-work. These can be countered by clarifying the contradictions that cause them. In both periods, charges of make-work resulted from measures designed to avoid substituting work program participants for normal government workers or normal government operations. These mandates made the work easily appear unnecessary—otherwise it was assumed that the government would already be doing it.

However, much of the work done in the job creation programs was socially useful. In fact, many of the 1930s projects still stand, especially the construction projects, testimony to the possibilities of fair work programs. And the work done through PSE, from setting up recreation programs for young people to staffing women's health clinics, clearly enhanced the lives of both the workers and the people receiving the services. Indeed, if program administrators were free to develop projects based on peoples' needs instead of constrained by capitalists' profits, an increased range of activities would be possible.

Criticisms of inefficiency and make-work have also been exacerbated by contradictory regulations. This was especially clear in the 1930s when charges of inefficiency followed inevitably from requirements to use a maximum amount of labor and a minimum of capital goods—that is, to *make work*. Additional constraints on the 1930s' programs were caused by regulations designed to ensure that the programs would not interfere with production-for-profit, and limited the production of clearly useful consumer goods.

An additional argument needs to be made in favor of job creation programs: they make good economic sense. Economic policies in the 1980s and 1990s were based on trickle-down theories, as tax breaks were given to the rich under the premise that they would increase investment and create private-sector jobs. However, instead of investing in productive plant and equipment, much of the increased wealth was used for luxury consumption and for speculation, especially in stocks and junk bonds. Instead of trickle-down economics, we need bubble-up policies that get money into the hands of people who will quickly spend it. This percolator effect increases demand for goods and services and induces capitalists to increase production, hire more workers, and revive the economy. Instead of high unemployment to keep a lid on wages and maintain profits, we need policies that create jobs—in the private sector as well as the government. In fact, as was argued in the 1960s and 1970s, unemployment has costs—lost production and lost human potential, as well as increased payments for unemployment insurance and other assistance programs.

A comprehensive fair work program would be expensive, but the money can easily be found. It can come from rescinding the 1980s tax cuts for the wealthy and for corporations, from substantially reducing the military budget, from forcing those responsible for the savings and loan crisis and bank failures to end their dependency on the government and to pay for the bailouts themselves, and from a tax on the sale of assets held less than one year (which would also discourage speculation). Furthermore, a more equitable tax system would fuel the percolator effect, thereby creating more jobs and providing additional tax revenues.

Although job creation programs are generally dismissed as unrealistic, they continue to find supporters. Sar Levitan, who has written extensively on government work programs, recently in conjunction with Frank Gallo, recommends their revival.[8] Noted sociologist William Julius Wilson, writing with Loic J. D. Wacquant, similarly advocates their reinstatement.[9] And in its current proposals for welfare reform, the National Association of Social Workers advocates public service employment jobs that "pay adequate wages and provide the same benefits and protections provided to other workers."[10] In making these proposals, it is important to be clear that fair work programs are different from workfare. The Clinton administration's community service programs as well as proposals for a neo-WPA (for example, from Mickey Kaus and Senator David Boren) are mandatory programs for welfare recipients—workfare—not fair work.

Bringing these ideas into the mainstream discourse involves expanding the boundaries of what is now considered feasible. In place of the constricted vision that dominates current debates, we need to recapture the sense of possibility that pervaded the 1930s, 1960s, and 1970s. A social-structural analysis that sees poverty and unemployment as endemic to capitalist economic systems needs to replace current notions that "welfare dependency" is an individual, psychological problem that destroys a person's moral fiber. Widely accepted antiwelfare rhetoric needs to be challenged and exposed as ideology that helps justify punitive and stigmatizing policies that increase the vulnerability of poor women, helping maintain a more than adequate supply of low-wage labor and pushing women into often abusive relationships.[11] Given the appalling increase in destitution engendered by more than a decade of right-wing economic and social policies, a politics that revives the idea of "human reclamation" should be counterposed. The narrow politics of greed and emphasis on the bottom line must be replaced by a politics grounded in people's needs—in ways that make women central—and workfare must be replaced by policies grounded in principles of fair work.

Notes

CHAPTER 1 *Women, Welfare, and Work Programs*

1. This difference is consistent with the "two-channel welfare state" posited by Barbara J. Nelson, who describes its origins in the cash assistance programs of Mothers' Aid and Workmen's Compensation. She shows how Workmen's Compensation, designed for white, industrial workingmen, was socially legitimate, with standardized decision-making criteria for eligibility and payments, while Mothers' Aid, intended primarily for workingmen's widows with young children, was connected to poor-law tradition and consequently gave caseworkers a great deal of discretion in determining eligibility and payments. In a similar vein, Theda Skocpol discusses the maternalist origins of the U.S. welfare state. According to Skocpol, in contrast to western European countries, whose stronger labor movements and different state configurations led to more comprehensive "paternalist" social insurance programs primarily for workingmen, the relatively weak U.S. labor movement and obstructionist tactics of southern congressmen meant that these programs were not as fully developed. Instead, women social reformers advocated policies such as Mothers' Aid pensions to assist mothers and children. Barbara J. Nelson, "The Origins of the Two-Channel Welfare State: Workmen's Compensation and Mothers' Aid," in Linda Gordon, ed., *Women, the State, and Welfare* (Madison: University of Wisconsin Press, 1990); and Theda Skocpol, *Protecting Soldiers and Mothers: The Political Origins of Social Policy in the United States* (Cambridge, Mass.: Harvard University Press, 1993). See also Margaret Weir, Ann Shola Orloff, and Theda Skocpol, eds., *The Politics of Social Policy in the United States* (Princeton, N.J.: Princeton University Press, 1988).

2. For a discussion of the evolution of feminist theory to incorporate a series of "lenses," see Alison M. Jaggar and Paula S. Rothenberg, *Feminist Frameworks: Alternative Theoretical Accounts of the Relations between Women and Men,* 3rd ed. (New York: McGraw-Hill, 1993). See also Nancy Folbre, *Who Pays for the Kids? Gender and the Structures of Constraint* (New York: Routledge, 1994).

3. Mimi Abramovitz, *Regulating the Lives of Women: Social Welfare Policy from Colonial Times to the Present* (Boston: South End Press, 1988).

4. The term "feminization of poverty" has been widely accepted since it was coined in 1978 by Diana Pearce. Diana Pearce, "The Feminization of Poverty: Women, Work and Welfare," *Urban and Social Change Review* 11 (1978): 28–36.

5. These were developed through a 1939 amendment to the Social Security Act.

6. The term "families" was added to the program name in 1962. "Undeserving poor" women, and men without dependent children, are eligible for general assistance (which provides even less than AFDC), and Supplemental Security Income (depending on their circumstances), as well as some food stamps.

7. See Daniel P. Moynihan, U.S. Department of Labor, Office of Policy and Planning Research, *The Negro Family: The Case for National Action* (Washington, D.C.: U.S. Government Printing Office, 1965), for an early and widely read elaboration of these ideas, and William Julius Wilson, *The Truly Disadvantaged: The Inner City, the Underclass, and Public Policy* (Chicago: University of Chicago Press, 1987), for a later, more liberal version.

8. Throughout this book the term "people of color" is used when discussing people of racial-ethnic groups that have been colonized and oppressed by whites of European descent. Thus, it refers primarily to African-Americans, people of Mexican and other Latin American heritage, and Native American Indians. Yet I am not totally comfortable using this term, and it should be understood as a shorthand and the current generally preferred term. Furthermore, problems with the available data sometimes lead to generalizations about all people of color based on the experiences of blacks, since much of the data on race compiled through the mid-1970s had only two categories, "white" and "nonwhite." Even the term "white" is not clearly defined. While people of European descent were classified as "white," and blacks and Native American Indians were categorized as "nonwhite," people of Mexican and Spanish descent were sometimes classified as white and sometimes as nonwhite, reflecting the ongoing process of the social construction of racial categories. For a thoughtful discussion of this process, see Evelyn Nakano Glenn, "White Women/Women of Color: The Social Construction of Racialized Gender, 1900–1940," paper presented at "The Feminist Future: A Transnational Perspective from California," University of California Council of Women's Programs, Lake Arrowhead Conference Center, November 19–21, 1993).

9. A descriptive book about slavery in the U.S. is Eugene Genovese, *Roll, Jordan, Roll: The World the Slaves Made* (New York: Vintage Books, 1976). For helpful discussions of the histories of different people of color in the U.S., see Teresa Amott and Julie Matthaei, *Race, Gender, and Work: A Multicultural Economic History of Women in the United States* (Boston: South End Press, 1991).

10. June Axinn and Herman Levin, *Social Welfare: A History of the American Response to Need, Second Edition* 2nd. ed. (New York: Longman, 1982), 42.

11. Frances Fox Piven and Richard A. Cloward, *Regulating the Poor: The*

Functions of Public Welfare (New York: Pantheon Books, 1971). They also argue that work programs are instituted as the system becomes more restrictive. However, they gloss over the differences between work programs, especially in their discussion of the 1930s, leading to their assertion that the WPA, which began in September 1935, reinforced work norms, and they do not sufficiently address the earlier New Deal programs, the FERA and the CWA.

12. Before the 1900s, people of color rarely received any relief at all. Those who managed to receive aid were treated in the most stigmatized manner. For example, during the 1700s and 1800s free blacks in New York City were placed in a filthy, damp cellar in the city poorhouse. Raymond A. Mohl, *Poverty in New York, 1783–1825* (New York: Oxford University Press, 1971), 93; and Winifred Bell, Aid to Dependent Children (New York: Columbia University Press, 1965), 46.

13. General Accounting Office, *Work and Welfare: Current AFDC Work Programs and Implication for Federal Policy* (Washington, D.C.: Government Printing Office, 1987), 69–71.

14. Robert F. Cook, Charles F. Adams, Jr., V. Lane Rawlins, and Associates, *Public Service Employment: The Experience of a Decade* (Kalamazoo, Mich.: W. E. Upjohn Institute for Employment Research, 1985). See chapter 5 of this book for a more extensive discussion of that study.

15. Abundant land, taken at the expense of Native American Indians who had been living there for centuries prior to the European invasion, served as a safety valve for some people. However, survival as a pioneer required both the skills necessary to function as a farmer and enough money to buy the needed seed, oxen, and implements to set up a homestead.

16. Abramovitz, *Regulating the Lives of Women,* 78.

17. England's harsher poor laws in the eighteenth and nineteenth centuries resulted primarily from the need to discipline potential workers to enter the newly developing factories. The enclosure movement had removed the means of livelihood for many peasants as the gentry claimed ownership of land that had been farmed for generations, fenced it in, and raised sheep and grew grain for sale on the market. See, for example, Karl deSchweinitz, *England's Road to Social Security: From the Statute of Laborers in 1349 to the Beveridge Report of 1942* (Philadelphia: University of Pennsylvania Press, 1943), for a history of England's system of relief.

18. Abramovitz, *Regulating the Lives of Women,* 79–82; Walter I. Trattner, From *Poor Law to Welfare State: A History of Social Welfare in America,* 4th ed. (New York: The Free Press, 1989), 18–21; Axinn and Levin, Social Welfare, p. 24.

19. Abramovitz, *Regulating the Lives of Women,* 80–81.

20. Eleanor Parkhurst, "Poor Relief in a Massachusetts Village in the Eighteenth Century," *Social Service Review* 11 (September 1937): 446–464, reprinted in Frank R. Breul and Steven J. Diner, eds., *Compassion and Responsibility: Readings in the History of Social Welfare Policy in the United States* (Chicago: University of Chicago Press, 1980), 97.

21. Abramovitz, *Regulating the Lives of Women,* 81–82; Josephine Chapin Brown, *Public Relief 1929–1939* (New York: Holt, Rinehart and Winston, 1940; New York: Octagon Books, 1971), 13.

22. For example, a 1824 New York report on the Relief and Settlement of the Poor, chaired by Secretary of State John V. N. Yates, found that one-ninth of all taxes raised for poor relief were spent on fees for determining and administering issues of settlement. Michael B. Katz, *In the Shadow of the Poorhouse: A Social History of Welfare in America* (New York: Basic Books, 1986), 21.

23. Ibid., 17.

24. These quotes are taken from documents of the early 1800s, cited in Benjamin Joseph Klebaner, *Public Poor Relief in America, 1790–1860* (New York: Arno Press, 1976), 12.

25. Katz, *In the Shadow of the Poorhouse*, 18. As with the Yates Report, this *Report of the Committee on the Pauper Laws of this Commonwealth [1821]*, chaired by Josiah Quincy, was also an important component of the 1820s attack on relief.

26. Abramovitz, *Regulating the Lives of Women*, 90–91.

27. Quoted in deSchweinitz, *England's Road to Social Security*, 123.

28. Frances Fox Piven and Richard A. Cloward, "The Historical Sources of the Contemporary Relief Debate," in Fred Block, Richard A. Cloward, Barbara Ehrenreich, and Frances Fox Piven, eds. *The Mean Season: The Attack on the Welfare State* (New York: Pantheon Books, 1987), 12.

29. Axinn and Levin, *Social Welfare*, 23.

30. Abramovitz, *Regulating the Lives of Women*, 86; Edward A. Williams, *Federal Aid for Relief* (New York: Columbia University Press, 1939), 9.

31. Brown, *Public Relief*, 10.

32. Leah Hannah Feder, *Unemployment Relief in Periods of Depression: A Study of Measures Adopted in Certain American Cities, 1857 through 1922* (New York: Russell Sage Foundation, 1936; New York: Arno Press, 1971), 184. For a discussion of Charity Organization Societies see Katz, *In the Shadow of the Poorhouse*, chap. 3.

33. Quoted in Brown, *Public Relief*, 9.

34. The New York Association for Improving the Condition of the Poor, 32nd annual report, October 1875, 33, quoted in Feder, *Unemployment Relief*, 41.

35. The first poorhouse was built in Boston in 1664, followed by Portsmouth, New Hampshire in 1716, Salem in 1719, Newport, Rhode Island, in 1723, Philadelphia in 1732, New York City in 1736, Charlestown in 1736, Providence in 1753, and Baltimore in 1773. Katz, *In the Shadow of the Poorhouse*, 14.

36. The 1800s also saw the development of the "cult of domesticity," the ideology that women's place was in the home as caretaker of the family. However, many women, especially women of color and recent immigrants, also worked for wages to support their families.

37. Mohl, *Poverty in New York*, 81–82; Axinn and Levin, *Social Welfare*, 62; and Katz, *In the Shadow of the Poorhouse*, 91.

38. David M. Schneider, "The Patchwork of Relief in Provincial New York, 1664–1775," *Social Service Review* 12 (September 1938): 464–494, reprinted in Breuhl and Diner, eds., *Compassion and Responsibility*, 77. Since few cities created separate institutions, poorhouses and workhouses were often combined in the same establishment, and at times they were merged with houses of

correction. For example, in 1736 Manhattan opened a combined "House of Correction, Workhouse, and Poorhouse" to care for people who had previously been put out to private families. See also Abramovitz, *Regulating the Lives of Women*, 88; Katz, *In the Shadow of the Poorhouse*, 33; David J. Rothman, *The Discovery of the Asylum: Social Order and Disorder in the New Republic* (Boston: Little Brown, 1971), 293.

39. Klebaner, *Public Poor Relief*, 109–110; and Katz, *In the Shadow of the Poorhouse*, 25–26. A New York State legislative committee wrote of rural poorhouses during the 1850s: "Common domestic animals are usually more humanely provided for than paupers in some of these institutions." Trattner, *From Poor Law to Welfare State*, 62.

40. Katz, *In the Shadow of the Poorhouse*, 33–34.

41. Quoted in Edith Abbott, *Women in Industry: A Study in American Economic History* (New York: D. Appleton and Company, 1910; reprint, New York: Arno Press, 1969), 20–21.

42. Ibid., 37–39.

43. Katz, *In the Shadow of the Poorhouse*, 14; Abramovitz, *Regulating the Lives of Women*, 92–93; Trattner, *From Poor Law to Welfare State*, 23; and Axinn and Levin, *Social Welfare*, 20–21.

44. The poor were often boarded in homes of other members of the community, who were paid a small amount for taking care of them, a practice that continued into the nineteenth century in small towns and rural areas. Geoffrey Guest, "The Boarding of the Dependent Poor in Colonial America," *Social Service Review* 63, no. 1 (March 1989): 92–112.

45. Abramovitz, *Regulating the Lives of Women*, 85; Katz, *In the Shadow of the Poorhouse*, 37.

46. Bell, *Aid to Dependent Children*, chap. 1; and Nelson, "The Origins of the Two-Channel Welfare State."

47. See Piven and Cloward, "The Historical Sources of the Contemporary Relief Debate," for an in-depth discussion of early arguments that were repeated in the 1980s attack on welfare.

48. This statement, made by George Arnold, minister-at-large to the poor in New York; is quoted in Katz, *In the Shadow of the Poorhouse*, 40.

49. In 1899, Frederic Almy published an extensive survey of the relationship between private charity and the amount of relief provided in the forty largest U.S. cities. Katz notes that although Almy wanted to show that private charity would increase when outdoor relief was decreased, many cities did not evidence this correlation. Ibid., 42–44.

50. Michael Katz gathered data on the number of people receiving outdoor and indoor relief and the cost of both types of relief in New York from 1840 to 1890. Poorhouse costs per person were approximately two to three times higher than outdoor relief per person. Ibid., 37.

51. Lucy Komisar, *Down and Out in the USA: A History of Public Welfare*, 2nd ed. (New York: New Viewpoints, 1977), 9; Trattner, *From Poor Law to Welfare State*, 48.

52. One of the most outspoken critics of relief was Benjamin Franklin, better known historically as a statesman and inventor. Katz, *In the Shadow of the*

Poorhouse, 22; and Howell V. Williams, "Benjamin Franklin and the Poor Laws," in Ira C. Colby, ed., *Social Welfare Policy: Perspectives, Patterns, and Insights* (Chicago: Dorsey Press, 1989).

53. See Abramovitz, *Regulating the Lives of Women,* 148–149.

54. Ibid., 149; Katz, *In the Shadow of the Poorhouse,* 46–47; and Brown, Public Relief, 40.

55. Food rations were also distributed. Mohl, *Poverty in New York,* 111–112.

56. Feder, *Unemployment Relief;* Joanna C. Colcord, *Community Planning in Unemployment Emergencies* (New York: Russell Sage Foundation, 1930). Public works had been an integral part of relief in Europe as early as the first quarter of the sixteenth century. They were extensively used three centuries later during the Irish potato famine. In 1845, the first year of the famine, approximately 750,000 people—of a total population of 8,000,000—were given jobs on public works projects. By the following year, however, the situation had worsened so dramatically that public works were stopped and more than 3,000,000 people were given free soup. Despite this, more than a million people died of starvation and fever. Many emigrated to the United States during this time. Piven and Cloward, *Regulating the Poor,* 23–26.

57. Feder, *Unemployment Relief,* 31, 67, 123, 187, 217, 288, 324; Klebaner, *Public Poor Relief,* 381–384, 667–676; Joanna C. Colcord, *Emergency Work Relief,* 13; Frances Cahn and Valeska Bary, *Welfare Activities of Federal, State, and Local Governments in California, 1850–1934* (Berkeley: University of California, 1936), 202–205. The most helpful study of the use of public works is Feder's extensive survey of relief during the depressions between 1857 and 1922.

58. Feder, *Unemployment Relief,* 69–70, 108, 173–176.

59. They were paid piece rates for their work. Ibid., 123, 173, 283, 284.

60. Ibid., 35, 175, 285, 286.

61. Ibid., 180.

62. Feder mentions only separate classes in needlework and domestic service that were set up for black women during the 1893–1897 depression. However, given the segregation evidenced in most New Deal work relief, and, indeed, in most New Deal programs, it can be assumed that other projects for blacks before the 1930s were similarly segregated. Ibid., 286.

63. Philip W. Ayres, "Is Emergency Relief by Work Wise?," *Proceedings of the National Conference of Charities and Corrections,* 1895, 100, quoted in Feder, *Unemployment Relief,* 179.

64. Mohl, *Poverty in New York,* 225; Klebaner, Public Poor Relief, p. 138; and Katz, *In the Shadow of the Poorhouse,* 31.

65. Feder, *Unemployment Relief,* 67, 182, 183; and Katz, *In the Shadow of the Poorhouse,* 31–32, 41.

66. In fact, in some places, poorhouses were known as "poor farms," since farming was the main type of work carried out.

67. Mohl, *Poverty in New York,* 95; and Katz, *In the Shadow of the Poorhouse,* 28. Katz reports that poorhouses in some large cities were virtually run by the inmates.

68. Klebaner, *Public Poor Relief,* 195.

69. Piven and Cloward, "Historical Sources of the Contemporary Relief Debate," 12.

70. Livingston was apparently influenced by the writings of Jeremy Bentham and Alexander Hamilton. In Hamilton's *Report on Manufactures* he recommended providing the poor with work instead of alms. Mohl, *Poverty in New York,* 222–237.

71. Klebaner, *Public Poor Relief,* 157; Katz, *In the Shadow of the Poorhouse,* 30.

72. Feder, *Unemployment Relief,* 170 and 178.

73. Ibid., 67, 182, 324; Cahn and Barry, *Welfare Activities,* 202.

74. Feder, *Unemployment Relief,* 32–33, 179–182; Cahn and Bary, *Welfare Activities,* 204.

75. Feder, *Unemployment Relief,* 123, 158–160, 177, 215.

CHAPTER 2 *Job Creation Programs in the Depression*

1. Although disaster relief had been provided by the federal government in response to calamities such as hurricanes and cyclones, this was the first time that the federal government provided relief for unemployment caused by a depression. Thus the FERA reversed the denial of federal aid for relief, which had been accepted policy since President Pierce's 1854 veto of federal land grants for states to build insane asylums. Frances Fox Piven and Richard A. Cloward, *Regulating the Poor: The Functions of Public Welfare* (New York: Vintage Books, 1971), 47.

2. "WPA" originally stood for "Works Progress Administration." In July 1939, as part of the growing reaction following the election of many conservatives to Congress the previous November, the name was changed to the Work Projects Administration and the program was henceforth housed under the Federal Works Agency. See James T. Patterson, *Congressional Conservatism and the New Deal: The Growth of the Conservative Coalition in Congress* (Lexington: University of Kentucky Press, 1967).

3. Although the Depression was set off by the October 1929 stock market crash, its primary underlying causes included a decade of very little regulation of financial institutions that left the banking system and the securities markets unstable and open to collapse, a sustained attack on labor that led to an increasingly inequitable distribution of income, and the lack of a hegemonic country that created instability in the international monetary and trade systems. Helpful discussions of the causes of the depression can be found in Robert A. Gordon, *Economic Instability and Growth: The American Record* (New York: Harper and Row, 1974), chap. 2; and Richard B. DuBoff, *Accumulation & Power: An Economic History of the United States* (New York: M. E. Sharpe, 1989), chap. 5.

4. U.S. Bureau of the Census, *Historical Statistics of the United States, Colonial Times to 1970* (Washington: U.S. Government Printing Office, 1975), 126.

5. Lester V. Chandler, *America's Greatest Depression 1929–1941* (New York: Harper and Row, 1970), 6.

6. Average hourly wages in manufacturing fell 21 percent, and average weekly hours of work decreased from 44.4 in 1929 to 38.1 in 1933 and then to 34.6 in 1934. Bureau of the Census, *Historical Statistics of the United States,* 170. The severity of the Depression was reflected in other statistics as well. In March 1933, gross national product (GNP), which measures the total production of goods and services, stood at 69 percent of its 1929 level; iron and steel production was at only 41 percent of its 1929 level; prices had fallen 25 percent; and investment in new plant and equipment was a dismal 12 percent of its corresponding amount four years earlier. Chandler, *America's Greatest Depression,* 4, 7, 21, 23.

7. Mary Elizabeth Pidgeon, U.S. Women's Bureau Bulletin, no. 155, *Women in the Economy of the United States of America: A Summary Report* (Washington D.C.: U.S. Government Printing Office, 1937; New York: DaCapo Press, 1975), 7. A 1937 WPA study of two thousand women workers in Philadelphia found that although 90 percent of them were married, only 15 percent were living with their husbands. Donald S. Howard, *The WPA and Federal Relief Policy* (New York: Russell Sage Foundation, 1943; New York: DaCapo Press, 1973), 283. For an examination of the effects of Depression-generated unemployment on families see E. Wight Bakke, *Citizens Without Work: A Study of the Effects of Unemployment Upon the Workers' Social Relations and Practices* (New Haven: Yale University Press, 1940), and Ruth Cavan and Katherine Ranck, *The Family and the Depression: A Study of One Hundred Chicago Families* (Chicago: University of Chicago Press, 1938).

8. About 29 percent of all black families were headed by women in 1930; the figure increased to 31 percent by 1940. Jacqueline Jones, *Labor of Love, Labor of Sorrow: Black Women, Work, and the Family from Slavery to the Present* (New York: Basic Books, 1985), 225.

9. Ruth Milkman, "Women's Work and the Economic Crisis: Some Lessons from the Great Depression," *Review of Radical Political Economics* 8, no. 1 (Spring 1976): 76–77; National Industrial Conference Board Studies, no. 220, *Women Workers and Labor Supply* (New York: National Industrial Conference Board, 1936), 36, 42.

10. U.S. Bureau of the Census, *Historical Statistics,* 172.

11. Susan Ware, *Holding Their Own: American Women in the 1930s* (Boston: Twayne, 1982), 27.

12. State relief administrations found a 20 percent unemployment rate for women compared to 19 percent for men in Massachusetts (which included new entrants into the labor force), and 31 percent for women compared to 27 percent for men in Pennsylvania. The Bureau of Labor Statistics found rates of 18 to 23 percent for women and of 18 to 21 percent for men in Lancaster, Pennsylvania; Springfield, Ohio; and Bridgeport, Connecticut. National Industrial Conference Board, *Women Workers and Labor Supply,* 30–36.

13. Winifred D. Wandersee, *Women's Work and Family Values, 1920–1940* (Cambridge, Mass.: Harvard University Press, 1981), 91.

14. Cited in ibid., 91–92.

15. This could be seen in the increased sales of glass jars for preserving foods; sales were higher in 1931 than in any of the preceding eleven years. Dixon

Wecter, *The Age of the Great Depression 1929–1941* (New York: MacMillan, 1948), 26.

16. Mimi Abramovitz, *Regulating the Lives of Women: Social Welfare Policy from Colonial Times to the Present* (Boston: South End Press, 1988), 224.

17. Ibid.; Wandersee, *Women's Work and Family Values*, 67–69, 99–100; Ware, *Holding Their Own*, 27.

18. "Pin Money or 'Coupling Pin'?" *Life and Labor Bulletin* 10 (January 1932): 3; cited in Lois Scharf, *To Work and to Wed: Female Employment, Feminism, and the Great Depression* (Westport, Conn.: Greenwood Press, 1980), xiii.

19. National Industrial Conference Board, *Women Workers and Labor Supply*, 33.

20. Jones, *Labor of Love*, 197.

21. Ibid.

22. Ibid., 205–206; Abramovitz, *Regulating the Lives of Women*, 280; Scharf, *To Work and to Wed*, 116; and Jean Collier Brown, U.S. Women's Bureau Bulletin, no. 165, *The Negro Woman Worker* (Washington D.C.: U.S. Government Printing Office, 1938), 1. African-American men were similarly fired from a variety of low-wage jobs traditionally reserved for them, for example, elevator operators, sanitary wagon drivers, waiters, and bellboys. Methods used to replace black men with white men included racist groups intimidating employers who hired blacks, and municipal ordinances (for example, in Tulsa, Oklahoma and West Palm Beach, Florida) prohibiting "Negro competition" in certain types of work. Raymond Wolters, *Negroes and the Great Depression: The Problem of Economic Recovery* (Westport, Conn.: Greenwood Publishing, 1970), 113–116.

23. Jones, *Labor of Love*, 205.

24. Julia Kirk Blackwelder, *Women of the Depression: Caste and Culture in San Antonio, 1929–1939* (College Station: Texas A&M University Press, 1984), 152–157.

25. Sarah Deutsch, *No Separate Refuge: Culture, Class, and Gender on an Anglo-Hispanic Frontier in the American Southwest, 1880–1940* (New York: Oxford University Press, 1987), 65. However, there were relatively few deportations in cities such as San Antonio that had large concentrations of Mexican-Americans and a continually high demand for their low-wage marginal labor. Blackwelder, Women of the Depression, 14.

26. Deutsch, *No Separate Refuge*, 165. As early as 1929, when the Depression was just beginning, the Border Patrol was created to enforce a new law making immigration from Mexico illegal. Teresa L. Amott and Julie A. Matthaei, *Race, Gender and Work: A Multicultural Economic History of Women in the United States* (Boston: South End Press, 1991), 77.

27. Furthermore, approximately half of the African-American recipients lived in Ohio and Pennsylvania. North Carolina and Florida each had one black family on Mother's Aid. Winifred Bell, *Aid to Dependent Children* (New York: Columbia University Press, 1965), 9–10.

28. William E. Leuchtenburg, *Franklin D. Roosevelt and the New Deal, 1932–1940* (New York: Harper Colophon, 1963), 26; Ware, *Holding Their Own*, 32–33; Louis Adamic, *My America, 1928–1938* (London: Hamish Hamilton,

1939), 263–309; David A. Shannon, *The Great Depression* (Englewood Cliffs, N.J.: Prentice-Hall, 1960), 55–71; *The Nation*, August 9, 1933, 143. The situation of the Okies who left the Midwest dustbowl to travel to California was described most vividly in John Steinbeck's classic, *The Grapes of Wrath* (New York: Viking, 1939).

29. Bernard Karsh and Philip L. Garman, "The Impact of the Political Left," in Milton Derber and Edwin Young, eds. *Labor and the New Deal* (Madison: University of Wisconsin Press, 1957); Frances Fox Piven and Richard A. Cloward, *Poor People's Movements: Why They Succeed, How They Fail* (New York: Vintage Books, 1979), chap. 2; Roy Rosensweig, "Radicals and the Jobless: The Musteites and the Unemployed Leagues, 1932–1936," *Labor History* 16 (Winter 1975): 52–77.

30. See John L. Shover, *Cornbelt Rebellion: The Farmers' Holiday Association* (Urbana: University of Illinois Press, 1965).

31. Annelise Orleck, " 'We Are That Mythical Thing Called the Public': Militant Housewives during the Great Depression," *Feminist Studies* 19, no. 1 (Spring 1993): 147–172; Irving Bernstein, *The Lean Years: A History of the American Worker 1920–1933* (Baltimore: Penguin Books, 1960), 416–419; and Clark Kerr and Paul S. Taylor, "The Self-Help Cooperatives in California," in *Essays in Social Economics in Honor of Jessica Blanche Peixotto* (Freeport, N.Y.: Books for Libraries Press, 1935; reprint ed. 1967).

32. Bernstein, *The Lean Years*, 423–425; Adamic, *My America*, 316–324.

33. Bernstein, *The Lean Years*, chap. 13; Arthur M. Schlesinger, Jr. *The Crisis of the Old Order, 1919–1933*, vol. 1 of *The Age of Roosevelt* (Boston: Houghton Mifflin, 1957), 256–265.

34. In response to pressure for federal aid, Congress enacted the Reconstruction Finance Corporation (RFC) in 1932. It made loans, not grants, for public works, and most of the money was given to banks. Edward Ainsworth Williams, *Federal Aid for Relief* (New York: Columbia University Press, 1939), 43–45; Josephine Chapin Brown, *Public Relief 1929–1939* (New York: Holt, Rinehart and Winston, 1940; New York: Octagon Books, 1971), 124–128; and Schlesinger, *The Crisis of the Old Order*, 236–238.

35. Although most localities, especially the large cities, substantially increased their public relief expenditures during the early years of the Depression, they were never sufficient to meet the need. Ann E. Geddes, Works Progress Administration Division of Social Research, Research Monograph X, *Trends in Relief Expenditures, 1910–1935* (Washington, D.C.: Government Printing Office, 1937; New York: DaCapo Press, 1971), 6–47.

36. Brown, *Public Relief,* 138–139; Schlesinger, *The Crisis of the Old Order,* 249; and Piven and Cloward, *Regulating the Poor,* 60.

37. Work Projects Administration, *Final Statistical Report of the Federal Emergency Relief Administration* (Washington D.C.: U.S. Government Printing Office, 1942), 46.

38. Joanna C. Colcord, *Emergency Work Relief: As Carried Out in Twenty-Six American Communities, 1930–1931, With Suggestions for Setting Up a Program* (New York: Russell Sage Foundation, 1932), 11–223. See also Henrietta

Leibman, "Work Relief in Certain States, 1930–1933," *Monthly Report of the Federal Emergency Relief Administration* (May 1936), 34–43.

39. Colcord, *Emergency Work Relief,* 29.

40. Shover, *Cornbelt Rebellion,* 112–113; Leuchtenburg, *Franklin D. Roosevelt,* 49–52; Schlesinger, *The Coming of the New Deal,* vol. 2 of *The Age of Roosevelt* (Boston: Houghton Mifflin, 1959), 40–49.

41. The FSRC was established in October 1933 and was the center of a great deal of controversy, much of it related to its relief activities. Janet Poppendieck, *Breadlines Knee-Deep in Wheat: Food Assistance in the Great Depression* (New Brunswick, N.J.: Rutgers University Press, 1986), especially chaps. 8 and 9.

42. Schlesinger, *The Coming of the New Deal,* 87–102; Leuchtenburg, *Franklin D. Roosevelt,* 53–58; Wecter, *The Age of the Great Depression,* 82–87.

43. The PWA reached its maximum during the summer 1934, when five hundred thousand people were given work. Theodore E. Whiting and T. J. Woofter, Jr., Work Projects Administration, Division of Statistics and Division of Research, *Summary of Relief and Federal Work Program Statistics, 1933–1940* (Washington, D.C.: Government Printing Office, 1941), 46, 48. See also B. W. Thoron, "The Federal Emergency Administration of Public Works," in Clarence E. Ridley and Orin F. Nolting, eds., *The Municipal Yearbook 1937: The authoritative resume of activities and statistical data of American cities* (Chicago: The International City Managers' Association, 1937), 455–472; Schlesinger, *The Coming of the New Deal,* 109, 282–288; Leuchtenburg, *Franklin D. Roosevelt,* 70–71; Wecter, *The Age of the Great Depression,* 76–78.

44. Schlesinger, *The Coming of the New Deal,* 323–333; Leuchtenburg, *Franklin D. Roosevelt,* 54–55.

45. Studs Terkel, *Hard Times: An Oral History of the Great Depression* (New York: Pantheon Books, 1970), 76–77; James Lasswell, "Shovels and Guns: the CCC in Action," *Social Work Today* (April 1935): 9–13; Leuchtenburg, *Franklin D. Roosevelt,* 52–53; Schlesinger, *The Coming of the New Deal,* 336–341.

46. At the program's height in August 1935, there were 265 CCC camps for African-American men. Richard Sterner, *The Negro's Share: A Study of Income, Consumption, Housing and Public Assistance* (New York: Harper and Brothers, 1943), 255.

47. Leuchtenburg, *Franklin D. Roosevelt,* 185.

48. Ibid.; Wolters, *Negroes and the Great Depression,* 27–34, 113–135; Jones, *Labor of Love,* 200; Walter I. Trattner, *From Poor Law to Welfare State: A History of Social Welfare in America* (New York: The Free Press, 1982), 257.

49. Harry L. Hopkins, *Spending to Save: The Complete Story of Relief* (New York: W. W. Norton, 1936), 99.

50. If the states did not follow federal regulations, grants could be suspended or the relief administration could be taken over, or federalized, by the federal administration.

51. House Committee on Appropriations, *Deficiency Appropriations for the CWA: Hearing before the Subcommittee* in charge of Deficiency Appropriations on H. R. 7527, January 30, 1934, 37–38; House Committee on Expenditures

in Executive Departments, *Hearings on H.R. 7527*, 73rd Cong., 2nd sess., February 13, 1934, 14–15; "Johnson Hits CWA Pay," *New York Times, December 23, 1933, 6; Time,* January 1, 1934, 10; Corrington Gill, "The Civil Works Administration," in Ridley and Nolting, *The Municipal Year Book 1937,* 431; Florida Emergency Relief Administration, *Unemployment Relief in Florida, July, 1932–March, 1934* (October 1935), 130–131; and Harry A. Millis and Royal E. Montgomery, *The Economics of Labor,* vol. 2, *Labor's Risks and Social Insurance* (New York: McGraw-Hill, 1938), 95.

52. Federal Works Agency, *Final Report on the WPA Program, 1935–1943* (Washington, D.C.: Government Printing Office, 1947; Westport, Conn.: Greenwood Press, 1976), 106–109.

53. *Monthly Report of the Federal Emergency Relief Administration* (May 22–June 30, 1933), 11–12.

54. Brown, *Public Relief,* 231–237; Howard, *The WPA,* 359–372.

55. Howard, *The WPA,* 278.

56. Ibid., 279.

57. Federal Works Agency, *Final Report on the WPA Program* (Washington D.C.: U.S. Government Printing Office, 1947; Westport, Conn.: Greenwood Press, 1976), 17.

58. Howard, *The WPA,* 279.

59. Federal Works Agency, *Report on Progress of the WPA Program* (June 30, 1941), 51.

60. Federal Works Agency, *Final Report on the WPA Program,* 44.

61. Howard, *The WPA,* 279–280.

62. Hilda W. Smith, "Educational Camps for Unemployed Women," *Monthly Report of the Federal Emergency Relief Administration* (May 1936), 27–33.

63. Whiting and Woofter, *Summary,* 46.

64. Howard, *The WPA,* 291.

65. Ibid.; and National Archives, Record Group 69, WPA General Subject Series 11 [hereafter RG 69, WPA Series 11], no. 102: Public Relations. In February 1935 a decimal classification system was adopted for FERA records in the National Archives. Documents obtained before this time were included in the CWA Series 2 and the FERA Old General Subject Series 8 (hereafter FERA Series 8), while documents gathered after this date were filed in FERA New General Subject Series 9 (hereafter FERA Series 9) and FERA State Series (for each state) 10. The decimal classification system was continued in the WPA in the General Subject Series 11 and in the State Series 12. These numbers will be used whenever references are made to series 9, 10, 11, and 12.

66. National Archives, RG 69, FERA Series 8, Interracial Correspondence, and FERA Series 9, no. 360, Transient Program.

67. The lack of data about African-Americans was periodically decried by Alfred Edgar Smith. In a 1936 report on the WPA he complained: "There has been no accurate census of Negro workers, and late year (1936) estimates range from 300,000 to 500,000." Alfred Edgar Smith, *Negro Project Workers: An Annual Report of Matters Incident to the Administration of Race Relations in Federal Unemployment Relief for the Year 1936* (January 1937), 3, in National

Archives, RG 69, WPA Series 11. A wealth of information about African-Americans in the WPA can be found in the reports by Alfred Edgar Smith, WPA assistant administrator, Labor Relations staff advisor. These include monthly *Highlights of Activities,* weekly *Negro Press Digests,* and a 1936 report on *Negro Project Workers,* and can be found in the National Archives, RG 69, WPA Series 11, no. 102: Public Relations.

Donald Howard tries to explain that the decision not to include data about race, as well as religion and politics, was intended to prevent discrimination. He adds, however, that the lack of official data did not prevent local officials from including symbols or codes denoting a person's race "in order to guide them in making assignments." Howard, *The WPA,* 286.

68. Federal Works Agency, *Final Report on the WPA Program,* 45.

69. A. Smith, Negro *Project Workers,* 9.

70. Phyllis Palmer, *Domesticity and Dirt: Housewives and Domestic Servants in the United States, 1920–1945* (Philadelphia: Temple University Press, 1989), 102–110. The Housekeeping Aide projects were much larger than the Home Demonstration projects. For example, a January 1936 survey found that of all the women on the WPA, 4.4 percent were in the former and only 0.1 percent were in the latter. Housekeeping projects were also developed through the National Youth Administration (NYA), established to provide work for young women and men. Marie Dresden Lane and Francis Steegmuller, *America on Relief* (New York: Harcourt, Brace, 1938), 69.

71. This was true, for example, in San Antonio, where Mexican-American women were also found with Anglo women as clerical workers on the relief programs. Blackwelder, *Women of the Depression,* 109–110, 176.

72. Brown, *Public Relief,* 235; See also "White Collar Relief Planned by Hopkins," *New York Times,* April 7, 1934, 5.

73. Work Division Series-9, in Doris Carothers, Works Progress Administration, Division of Social Research, Research Monograph 6, *Chronology of the Federal Emergency Relief Administration, May 12, 1933, to December 31, 1935* (Washington D.C.: Government Printing Office, 1937; New York: DaCapo Press, 1971), 61.

74. A. Smith, *Highlights of Activities* (September 1938), 3.

75. A. Smith, *Highlights of Activities* (December 1937), 8.

76. A. Smith, *Negro Project Workers,* 4–7; Alfred E. Smith, "The Negro and Relief," *Monthly Report of the Federal Emergency Relief Administration* (March 1936), 14; National Archives, RG 69, CWA Series 2, Interracial Correspondence; and Howard, *The WPA,* 292.

77. Sterner, *The Negro's Share,* 252.

78. By February 1935 approximately three hundred thousand people received transient services. Ellery F. Reed, *Federal Transient Program: An Evaluative Survey May to July, 1934* (New York City: The Committee on Care of Transient and Homeless, 1934); *Social Work Today* 1, no. 1 (March-April, 1934): 7; Whiting and Woofter, *Summary,* 70–74.

79. These programs were expanded during the winter months, providing work for a maximum of thirty-three thousand teachers in February 1934, and reaching another maximum of forty-four thousand teachers in March 1935.

Eunice Langdon, "The Teacher Faces the Depression," *The Nation,* August 16, 1933, 182–185; Office of Education, U.S. Department of the Interior, Leaflet no. 44, *The Deepening Crisis in Education* (Washington, D.C.: Government Printing Office, 1933); "Emergency Education Program," *Monthly Report of the Federal Emergency Relief Administration* (June 1935), 16–19; "Rural School Continuation Program," *Monthly Report of the Federal Emergency Relief Administration* (October 1935), 21–24.

80. Federal Emergency Relief Administration, *Proceedings of the Conference on Emergency Needs of Women* (Washington, D.C.: Government Printing Office, November 20, 1933), 5–38.

81. Whiting and Woofter, *Summary,* 46–49.

82. The persistence of employers complaints led to a 1935 FERA survey of 943 cases of alleged job refusals, which found that only 3 percent of them could be attributed to "unjustified" causes perhaps related to work relief. "Alleged Refusal by Relief Clients to Accept Employment," *Monthly Report of the Federal Emergency Relief Administration* (June 1935), 1–8; "Summary Study of Alleged Job Refusals by Relief Persons," *Monthly Report of the Federal Emergency Relief Administration* (November 1935), 6–10.

83. There was debate concerning the private-sector wage that people on the work programs were required to accept—whether this would be the prevailing wage, even if it were lower than the rate they received on the work program, or whether the industry wage had to be greater than or equal to the work program rate. Initially, workers were required to accept employment even if the wage rate were lower than the amount they earned on the WPA. In 1937, in response to pressure from organized labor, workers had to accept employment only if the wage rate were greater than or equal to the WPA rate. In 1939, as part of the conservative turn in social policies, the initial policy was reinstated. Millis and Montgomery, *Labor's Risks and Social Insurance,* 106; Federal Works Agency, *Final Report on the WPA Program,* 23–25; Arthur W. Macmahon, John D. Millett, and Gladys Ogden, *The Administration of Federal Work Relief* (New York: DaCapo Press, 1971), 151–157; and Howard, *The WPA,* chap. 6.

84. Thus in addition to setting industry level rates, work relief was primarily paid in cash, as opposed to direct relief which continued to be paid mostly in kind. Work Projects Administration, *Final Statistical Report of the Federal Emergency Relief Administration,* 21.

85. For example, if a family's budgetary deficiency was thirty dollars per month and the project worker was classified as earning fifty cents per hour, then she or he could work sixty hours a month on the program.

86. FERA Rules and Regulations no. 3, in Carothers, *Chronology of the Federal Emergency Relief Administration,* 9. In addition, some workers, usually skilled or supervisory personnel, could be hired through the labor market, and therefore paid the going wage and work normal hours. In the WPA, this was set at a maximum of 10 percent of project workers. Executive Order 7046, in ibid., 80.

87. FERA Rules and Regulations no. 4, in ibid., 12; Arthur E. Burns, "Work Relief Wage Policies" *Monthly Report of the Federal Emergency Relief Administration* (June 1936), 32.

88. States were classified into three zones, with minimum hourly rates set for each. In the southern zone the minimum for skilled workers was set at $1.00 and for unskilled workers at 40 cents; in the central zone the corresponding rates were $1.10 and 45 cents; and in the northern zone rates were $1.20 and 50 cents. Wage rates for semiskilled labor were set between those for skilled and unskilled. FCWA Rules and Regulations no. 1, in Carothers, *Chronology of the Federal Emergency Relief Administration,* 28–30.

89. Telegram from Hopkins on Civil Works Service Projects, in ibid., 33.

90. This was a form of wage cutting: total payments fell 25 percent the following week. Burns, "Work Relief Wage Policies," 37.

91. Night letter, mimeo, 1283, in Carothers, *Chronology of the Federal Emergency Relief Administration,* 45.

92. "Minimum Pay Rate Ends on Relief Jobs; Local Scales Replace FERA's 30-Cent Rule," *New York Times,* November 23, 1934, 2.

93. "Survey of Common Labor Rates Paid on the Work Program," *Monthly Report of the Federal Emergency Relief Administration* (January 1935), 5 and 7.

94. Debates about wage rate policy in the WPA primarily concerned use of the "prevailing wage." At issue was whether hours of work would be set, generally between 120 and 140 per month, or whether the total payment would be divided by the prevailing wage to determine the hours of work. Although skilled workers' hours were greatly reduced when the prevailing wage was used, leading some people to work only one or two days each week, this policy was strongly supported by organized labor in order to help maintain private-sector wage rates. Burns, "Work Relief Wage Policies," 43–54; Federal Works Agency, *Final Report on the WPA Program,* 23–25.

95. By 1939, employer complaints that work program participants were too attached to their temporary government jobs and were not sufficiently motivated to accept private sector employment led to the "eighteen-month ruling" as part of the conservative changes that year. This policy mandated that people who had been working on the WPA for eighteen continuous months had to be removed from the rolls and wait thirty days before they could be reassigned. However, there were always more workers waiting for assignments than available placements, and people often had to wait several months before again obtaining WPA work, that is, if they were lucky enough to get back on the rolls at all. Federal Works Agency, *Final Report on the WPA Program,* 21; and Howard, *The WPA,* 519–522.

96. "Removal From Relief Rolls to Meet Labor Shortages," *Monthly Report of the Federal Emergency Relief Administration* (July 1935), 49.

97. Deutsch, *No Separate Refuge,* 176–177.

98. Thad Holt to Harry Hopkins, September 21, 1934, National Archives, RG 69, FERA Series 8, Cotton Reports.

99. "Removal from Relief Rolls to Meet Labor Shortages," 49.

100. Smith, *Highlights* (January 16, 1937), 1-A. See also Howard, *The WPA,* 486–492; and A. Smith, *Negro Project Workers,* as well as A. Smith's monthly *Highlights of Activities* and weekly *Negro Press Digest* reports.

101. A. Smith, *Highlights of Activities* (May 1937), 6.

102. Ibid.

103. A. Smith, *Highlights of Activities* (August 1937), 8.

104. National Archives, RG 69, CWA Series 2, Interracial Correspondence; A. Smith, "The Negro and Relief," 14; National Archives, RG 69, CWA Series 2, Interracial Correspondence; Howard, *The WPA*, 292.

105. National Archives, RG 69, CWA Series 2, Interracial Correspondence.

106. Three methods were used to follow dual wage scales. First, in some cases industries that primarily employed men paid higher wages than industries dominated by women workers. Thus, in all of the major industries employing mostly women (such as textiles, boot and shoe manufacture, canning, hotels and restaurants, retail trade, and laundries), the minimum wage rate was set at thirty (or sometimes at twenty-five) cents per hour. Second, although almost three-fourths of the codes set the same rates for workers of both genders, the preceding industries, along with others such as automobile manufacture and pottery making, set higher minimum rates for men. Third, women were sometimes classified as "learners," industrial homeworkers, or as doing "light repetitive work," and consequently paid 20 percent below the minimum code rate. Mary Elizabeth Pidgeon, Bulletin of the Women's Bureau, no. 130, *Employed Women Under N.R.A. Codes* (Washington D.C.: U.S. Government Printing Office, 1935; New York: DaCapo Press, 1975), 9–25.

107. Ibid., p. 13.

108. Work Projects Administration, *Final Report on the WPA Program*, 27.

109. Work Division Series-16, in Carothers, *Chronology of the Federal Emergency Relief Administration*, 63.

110. Construction absorbed 70 percent of the funds in the FERA, almost 90 percent in the CWA, and 77 percent in the WPA. Federal Works Agency, *Final Statistical Report of the Federal Emergency Relief Administration*, 54; Federal Works Agency, *Final Report on the WPA Program*, 122; and Gill, "The Civil Works Administration," 424–425.

111. WPA, *Final Statistical Report of the FERA*, 57; Gill, "The Civil Works Administration," 424–425; and Federal Works Agency, *Final Report on the WPA Program*, 131–132.

112. For example, in the week ending May 17, 1934, women made up 0.7 percent of those working on all public property projects. "Emergency Work Program," *Monthly Report of the Federal Emergency Relief Administration* (May 1934), 12.

113. A. Smith, *Highlights of Activities* (June 1936 through November 1936); and Jones, *Labor of Love*, 219.

114. "Relief for White-Collar Workers," *Monthly Report of the Federal Emergency Relief Administration* (December 1935), 59–64; Federal Works Agency, *Final Report on the WPA Program*, 59–67.

115. "Emergency Work Program," *Monthly Report of the Federal Emergency Relief Administration* (May 1934), 11–12; Federal Works Agency, *Final Report on the WPA Program*, 44.

116. "Relief for White-Collar Workers," 60.

117. P. A. Kerr, "Production-for-Use and Distribution in Work Relief Activities," *Monthly Report of the Federal Emergency Relief Administration* (Sep-

tember 1935), 2 and 5; and Federal Works Agency, *Final Report on the WPA Program*, 44.

118. This bind was described by a high-level work program official: "If a project is useful it is sure to be criticized because it is competitive, while if it is noncompetitive it is just as likely to be condemned by the same critics as not being useful." Nels Anderson, *The Right to Work* (New York: Modern Age Books, 1938), 65.

119. P. A. Kerr, "Production-for-Use," 3. Some observers described the workrooms as sweatshops. North Carolina Emergency Relief Commission, *Emergency Relief in North Carolina: A Record of the Development and the Activities of the North Carolina Emergency Relief Administration, 1932–1935* (Raleigh, N.C.: Edwards and Broughton, 1936), 159.

120. *Trend of Developments in the Sewing and Mattress Program*, 2–3, in National Archives, RG 69, WPA Series 11, no. 218.1, Sewing and Mattress Projects, 1940.

121. P. A. Kerr, "Production-for-Use," p. 3.

122. Division of Self-Help Cooperatives, Federal Emergency Relief Administration, *Self-Help Cooperatives: An Introductory Study* (Washington, D.C.: Government Printing Office, 1934); C. Kerr and Taylor, "The Self-Help Cooperatives in California"; and P. A. Kerr, "Production-for-Use," 12–16.

123. Senate Committee on Agriculture and Forestry, *Hearings on S. 2500, A bill to aid in relieving the existing national emergency through the free distribution to the needy of cotton and cotton products*, 73rd Cong., 2nd sess., February 9, 1934; Press releases, National Archives, RG 69, FERA Series 9, no. 371, Production of Goods; and Poppendieck, *Breadlines Knee-Deep in Wheat*, chap. 7.

124. P. A. Kerr, "Production-for-Use," 7–9; Poppendieck, *Breadlines Knee-Deep in Wheat*, 144–145.

125. Factories for production of clothing (long underwear and knitted goods) were also leased in Michigan and Massachusetts. P. A. Kerr, "Production-for-Use," 12; State Relief Commission of Ohio, *The State Relief Commission of Ohio and Its Activities, April 1932 to January 1, 1935* (Columbus, Ohio: Carroll Press, 1935), 53; Joanna C. Colcord, "Ohio Produces for Ohioans," *The Survey* 70, no. 12 (1934): 371–373; Raymond G. Swing, "EPIC and the Ohio Plan," *The Nation*, October 3, 1934, 379–381; and "Operation of Idle Factories," *Monthly Labor Review* (December 1934): 1311–1319.

126. Two full boxes of letters under the heading "Production-for-Use Complaints" can be found in the National Archives. National Archives, Record Group 69, Series 8, Boxes 16 and 17.

127. "Organized Business Presents Its Recovery Program," *Congressional Digest* (January 1935): 26–29.

128. For further discussion of these issues see Nancy E. Rose, "Production-for-Use or Production-for-Profit?: The Contradictions of Consumer Goods Production in 1930s Work Relief," *Review of Radical Political Economics* 20, no. 1 (1988): 46–61.

129. Federal Works Agency, *Final Report on the WPA Program*, 122 and 133.

130. *Trend of Developments in the Sewing and Mattress Program*, 2.

131. Federal Works Agency, *Final Report on the WPA Program*, 68.

132. Ibid., 68, 122, 133; and Bureau of Agricultural Economics, *The School Lunch Program and Agricultural Surplus Disposal* (October 1941), in National Archives, WPA Series 11, no. 212.2, School Lunch Program.

133. Federal Works Agency, *Final Report on the WPA Program*, 69–70; Palmer, *Domesticity and Dirt*, 102–110; and National Archives, WPA Series 11, no. 212.2, Welfare Projects, WPA; no. 218.2, Women's Projects WPA; and no. 230, Women's Work.

134. Federal Works Agency, *Final Report on the WPA Program*, 91–92; and National Archives, WPA Series 11, no. 045, WPA In Plant Training; In Plant Training for Women; and WPA In Plant Training, Lack of for Negroes.

135. Quoted in Leuchtenburg, *Franklin D. Roosevelt*, 124; and Macmahon et al., *The Administration of Federal Work Relief*, 42.

136. Quoted in National Conference on Social Welfare, *50th Anniversary Edition: The Report of the Committee on Economic Security of 1935: And Other Basic Documents Relating to the Development of the Social Security Act* (Washington, D.C.: National Conference on Social Welfare, 1985), 142.

137. For further discussion about the exclusion of Employment Assurance from the permanent system of relief, see Nancy E. Rose, "Work Relief in the 1930s and the Origins of the Social Security Act," *Social Service Review* 63, no. 1 (March 1989): 63–91.

138. House Committee on Ways and Means, *Economic Security Act: Hearings on H.R. 4120*, 74th Cong., 1st sess., January 21–Feabuary 12, 1935, 25.

139. It was generally acknowledged that national health care was eliminated as a result of fierce opposition from the American Medical Association, for example by Frances Perkins, who was secretary of labor in the Roosevelt administration. Frances Perkins, "Introduction," in Edwin Witte, *The Development of the Social Security Act* (Madison: University of Wisconsin Press, 1962), viii.

140. See Ann Shola Orloff, "The Political Origins of America's Belated Welfare State," in Margaret Weir, Ann Shola Orloff, and Theda Skocpol, eds., *The Politics of Social Policy in the United States* (Princeton: Princeton University Press, 1988).

141. The "reasonable subsistence" phrase was also struck from the ADC program. Paul H. Douglas, *Social Security in the United States: An Analysis and Appraisal of the Federal Social Security Act* (New York: McGraw-Hill, 1936), 100–101. See also Jill Quadagno, "From Old-Age Assistance to Supplemental Security Income: The Political Economy of Relief in the South, 1935–1972," in Weir, Orloff, and Skocpol, *The Politics of Social Policy*.

142. A. Smith, *Highlights of Activities* (March 1937); and Sterner, *The Negro's Share*, 272–277.

143. "Unemployables" made up approximately 20 percent of the FERA rolls. Arthur E. Burns, "Federal Emergency Relief Administration," in *The Municipal Yearbook 1937*, 397.

144. Lincoln Fairley, "Survey of Former Emergency Relief Administration Cases in New Jersey," *Monthly Report of the Federal Emergency Relief Administration* (June 1936), 100–108; and Brown, *Public Relief*, 385–389.

145. Howard, *The WPA*, 99.

146. Corrington Gill, "Local Work for Relief," *Survey Midmonthly* (May 1940); Brown, *Public Relief,* 378–379.

147. This discussion draws on Nancy E. Rose, "From the WPA to Workfare: It's Time for a Truly Progressive Government Work Program," *Journal of Progressive Human Services,* 1, no. 2 (1990): 17–42; and Nancy E. Rose, *Put to Work: Relief Programs in the Great Depression* (New York: Monthly Review Press, 1994).

148. J. C. Lindsey to Perry A. Fellows, Administrative Officer, FERA, December 10, 1934, National Archives, FERA Series 8, Goods, Production of for Unemployed.

149. Anderson, *The Right to Work,* 92.

CHAPTER 3 *Return to the Dark Ages*

1. From the end of World War II through 1960 the economy (that is, GNP adjusted for inflation) grew 52 percent. It increased another 65 percent from 1960 through the peak year of 1973, so that by 1973 it was two and one half times its 1946 size. Council of Economic Advisors, *Economic Report of the President, 1991* (Washington D.C.: U.S. Government Printing Office, 1991), table B-2: Gross national product in 1982 dollars, 1929–90.

2. This hegemonic position allowed the U.S. to exert disproportionate influence over the international monetary and trade system, enthroning the dollar as the basis of world trade and effectively forcing other countries to borrow dollars for many international transactions. This was implemented through the Treaty of Bretton Woods, which established the International Monetary Fund and the World Bank, both largely controlled by the U.S. Some of the clearest explanations of the postwar boom, as well as the subsequent decline, can be found in Samuel Bowles, David M. Gordon, and Thomas E. Weisskopf, *After the Wasteland: A Democratic Economics for the Year 2000* (Armonk, N.Y.: M. E. Sharpe, 1990).

3. For a discussion of the political and economic importance of anticommunism in the postwar period, see Marty Jezer, *The Dark Ages: Life in the United States, 1945–1960* (Boston: South End Press, 1982).

4. Inflation-adjusted earnings grew a full 60 percent from 1947 to the peak years of 1972 and 1973. Council of Economic Advisors, *Economic Report of the President, 1991,* table B-44: Average weekly hours and hourly and weekly earnings in private nonagricultural industries, 1947–90.

5. The capital-labor accord was an important component of the post-War economic prosperity. See Bowles, Gordon, and Weisskopf, *After the Wasteland.*

6. Council of Economic Advisors, *Economic Report of the President,* table B-40: Civilian unemployment rate by demographic characteristic, 1948–90; and Richard B. DuBoff, *Accumulation & Power: An Economic History of the United States* (London: M. E. Sharpe, 1989), 94.

7. For example, only 1 percent, or 4,000 of those employed in the air industry in April 1941 were women, but eighteen months later these numbers

had jumped to 39 percent, or 310,000 of the total. William Henry Chafe, *The American Woman: Her Changing Social, Economic, and Political Roles, 1920–1970* (London: Oxford University Press, 1972), 140.

8. Three-fourths of the women who obtained jobs during World War II had worked for wages before the war and were drawn back into the labor force. Alice Kessler-Harris, *Out to Work: A History of Wage-Earning Women in the United States* (New York: Oxford University Press, 1982), 276. For a spirited description of women working during World War II see Miriam Frank, Marilyn Ziebarth, and Connie Field, *The Life and Times of Rosie the Riveter: The Story of Three Million Working Women During World War II* (Emeryville, Calif.: Clarity Education Productions, 1982), as well as the film of the same title.

9. Chafe, *The American Woman*, 161–171; and Frank et al., *Rosie the Riveter*, 83–87.

10. Jacqueline Jones, *Labor of Love, Labor of Sorrow: Black Women, Work, and the Family from Slavery to the Present* (New York: Basic Books, 1985), 235–256; and Frank et al., *Rosie the Riveter*, 49–56.

11. Between 1945 and 1947 approximately 2.7 million women lost their industrial jobs. John Ehrenreich, *The Altruistic Imagination: A History of Social Work and Social Policy in the United States* (Ithaca, N.Y.: Cornell University Press, 1985), p. 147.

12. In contrast to women, men's labor force participation rate steadily fell—from 86.6 percent in 1948 to 83.3 percent in 1960. Council of Economic Advisors, *Economic Report of the President*, table B-36: Labor force participation rate and employment/population ratio, 1948–90.

13. Ibid., table B-37: Civilian labor force participation rate by demographic characteristic, 1954–90. Labor force participation rates for African-American women outpaced those for Native American Indian and Hispanic women but were eclipsed by rates for Asian-American women. In 1960 women's labor force participation rates were as follows: African-Americans, 42.2 percent; American Indians, 25.5 percent; Mexican-Americans, 28.8 percent; Chinese-Americans, 44.2 percent; Japanese-Americans, 44.1 percent; and European-Americans, 33.6 percent. Teresa L. Amott and Julie A. Matthaei, *Race, Gender, and Work: A Multicultural Economic History of Women in the United States* (Boston: South End Press, 1991), 403, table C-1.

14. See Frances Fox Piven and Richard A. Cloward, *Regulating the Poor: The Functions of Public Welfare* (New York: Vintage Books, 1971), chap. 7.

15. The Bracero Program lasted from 1942 through 1964, when it was replaced by the maquiladora program, which set up "free trade zones" in Mexico along the U.S. border. Amott and Matthaei, *Race, Gender, and Work*, 79.

16. Ibid., 271–273.

17. Council of Economic Advisors, *Economic Report of the President*, table B-40.

18. Although the NRPB had four different incarnations during its ten-year history, usually changing because of different authorizing legislation, it was essentially the same agency throughout. Its names were: the National Planning Board, from July 20, 1933, to June 30, 1934; the National Resources Board, from July 1, 1934, to June 7, 1935; the National Resources Committee, from

June 8, 1935, to June 30, 1939; and finally the National Resources Planning Board, from July 1, 1939, to August 31, 1943. Marion Clawson, *New Deal Planning: The National Resources Planning Board* (Baltimore: Johns Hopkins University Press, 1981), chap. 4.

19. Ibid.; and Philip W. Warken, *A History of the National Resources Planning Board, 1933–1943* (New York: Garland Publishing, 1979).

20. National Resources Planning Board [hereafter NRPB], *Security, Work, and Relief Policies* (Washington D.C.: U.S. Government Printing Office, 1942); and NRPB, *National Resources Development Report for 1943,* part 1, *Post-War Plan and Program* (Washington D.C.: U.S. Government Printing Office, January 1943).

21. NRPB, *Security, Work, and Relief Policies,* 1.

22. NRPB, *Post-War Plan and Program,* 3.

23. Ibid., 17; and NRPB, *Security, Work, and Relief Policies,* 457–460.

24. NRPB, *Security, Work, and Relief Policies,* 463.

25. Ibid., 464–466.

26. NRPB, *Post-War Plan and Program,* 17.

27. Senate Special Committee on Unemployment Problems, *Readings in Unemployment,* 86th Cong., 1st sess. (Washington D.C.: U.S. Government Printing Office, 1960), 1–2. In fact, although *Security, Work, and Relief Policies* was given to Roosevelt in December 1941 (three days before Pearl Harbor), it was not released until March 1943.

28. *Full Employment Bill of 1945,* S. 380, 79th Cong., 1st sess., reprinted in House Committee on Education and Labor, *Hearing before the Subcommittee on Equal Opportunities of the Committee on Education and Labor on H.R. 15476,* 93rd. Cong., 2nd sess., October 8, 1974, 70–73.

29. This echoed the recommendations of Alvin H. Hansen, perhaps the most articulate proponent of the stagnationist version of Keynesianism in the U.S. In his 1942 pamphlet published by the NRPB, *After the War—Full Employment,* he advocated that the federal government use public debt to increase demand for goods and services and maintain full employment. Alvin H. Hansen, *After the War—Full Employment* (Washington D.C.: U.S. Government Printing Office, 1942).

30. See, for example, Helen Ginsburg, *Full Employment and Public Policy: The United States and Sweden* (Lexington, Mass.: Lexington Books, 1983), 16–17, in which she cites the Conference Report explaining the difference between the two terms. See also Herbert Stein, *The Fiscal Revolution in America* (Chicago: University of Chicago Press, 1969), 201.

31. As stated in the act, the federal government would "coordinate and utilize all its plans, functions, and resources for the purpose of creating and maintaining, in a manner calculated to foster and promote free competitive enterprise and the general welfare, conditions under which there will be afforded useful employment opportunities, including self-employment, for those able, willing, and seeking to work, and to promote maximum employment, production, and purchasing power." Ibid., 12.

32. Quoted in Russell A. Nixon, "The Historical Development of the Conception and Implementation of Full Employment as Economic Policy," in

Alan Gartner, Russell A. Nixon, and Frank Riessman, eds., *Public Service Employment: An Analysis of Its History, Problems, and Prospects* (New York: Praeger, 1973), 27.

33. Helpful discussions of the failure to enact the Full Employment Bill of 1945 can be found in: ibid., 26–27; Ginsburg, *Full Employment and Public Policy*, 13–17; Stephen K. Bailey, *Congress Makes a Law: The Story Behind the Employment Act of 1946* (New York: Columbia University Press, 1950), 129–149; Stein, *The Fiscal Revolution in America*, 198–204; Clawson, *New Deal Planning*, 270; Robert M. Collins, *The Business Response to Keynes, 1929–1964* (New York: Columbia University Press, 1981), 100–112; Philip Harvey, *Securing the Right to Employment Social Welfare Policy and the Unemployed in the United States* (Princeton: Princeton University Press, 1989), 107–110; Edwin Amenta and Theda Skocpol, "Redefining the New Deal: World War II and the Development of Social Provision in the United States," in Margaret Weir, Ann Shola Orloff, and Theda Skocpol, eds., *The Politics of Social Policy in the United States* (Princeton: Princeton University Press, 1988), 88; and Margaret Weir, "The Federal Government and Unemployment: The Frustration of Policy Innovation from the New Deal to the Great Society," in Weir, Orloff, and Skocpol, *The Politics of Social Policy*, 160–167.

34. Both the Chamber of Commerce and the Farm Bureau opposed the Full Employment Bill and the NRPB's reports. Weir, "The Federal Government and Unemployment," 160–161.

35. The National Manpower Council lasted from 1951 to 1965 and was based at Columbia University under the direction of Eli Ginzberg. Ibid., 170; and Henry David, National Manpower Council, *Manpower Policies for a Democratic Society: The Final Statement of the Council* (New York: Columbia University Press, 1965), Introduction.

36. Although employers and unions were urged to "take additional steps to apply the principle of equal pay for equal work," the government was not admonished to do so. National Manpower Council, *Womanpower* (New York: Columbia University Press, 1957), especially 7–39.

37. The Council's final statement, written in 1965, also discussed the problems faced by African-Americans, primarily discrimination and failure to "take advantage of educational opportunities . . . because they are victims of cultural isolation, ignorance, and preoccupation with immediate economic needs." David, *Manpower Policies for a Democracy*, 58.

38. The actual amounts (not adjusted for inflation) were $31.98 in 1940, $48.18 in 1945, $71.33 in 1950, and $105.75 in 1960. Social Security Administration, *Social Security Bulletin Annual Statistical Supplement, 1994* (Washington D.C.: U.S. Government Printing Office, 1994), table 9.G1: AFDC and Emergency Assistance: Average monthly number of recipients, total amount of cash payments, and average monthly payment, 1936–92.

39. Ibid.

40. Numbers of total recipients grew from 1,182,000 in 1940 to 2,205,000 in 1950, and to 3,005,000 in 1960. Ibid.

41. In 1930, 53.5 percent of African-American women who were employed worked in domestic service, a figure that slowly fell to 39.3 percent by

1960. Furthermore, the percentage of African-American workers in domestic service remained well above the rates for all other women of color. See Amott and Matthaei, *Race, Gender, and Work,* 324, table 10–3.

42. Mimi Abramovitz, *Regulating the Lives of Women: Social Welfare Policy from Colonial Times to the Present* (Boston: South End Press, 1988), 319–321.

43. Social Security Administration, *Social Security Bulletin, 1994,* table 3.E2. Number and percent of poor persons, by age, at end of 1959–92.

44. These efforts to limit ADC to the "deserving poor" were applauded in the 1940s and 1950s by most professional social work organizations, who wanted to protect the new program from criticism, as well as to raise the standards of home care. Winifred Bell, *Aid to Dependent Children* (New York: Columbia University Press, 1965), 29–30.

45. See Piven and Cloward, *Regulating the Poor, chap. 5.*

46. Abramovitz, *Regulating the Lives of Women,* 327–328.

47. Bell, *Aid to Dependent Children,* 50.

48. Ibid., 55.

49. Piven and Cloward, *Regulating the Poor,* appendix, source table 4: Percentage of Black Families on AFDC Rolls. This data is given for all states except Alaska and Hawaii for the years 1948, 1953, 1961, and 1967.

50. See Bureau of Public Assistance, *Illegitimacy and its Impact on the Aid to Dependent Children Program* (Washington D.C.: U.S. Government Printing Office, 1960), 61–66, for a list.

51. Ibid., 2.

52. Ibid., 36.

53. See Rickie Solinger, *Wake Up Little Susie: Single Pregnancy and Race before Roe v. Wade* (New York: Routledge, 1992).

54. Bureau of Public Assistance, *Illegitimacy,* 36.

55. The 1950 amendments to the Social Security Act included the Notification of Law Enforcement Officers (NOLEO) provision, which required relief departments to notify law enforcement agencies whenever aid was granted to a family with a deserted or abandoned child, which served to endorse the focus on "illegitimacy." Bell, *Aid to Dependent Children,* 80; and Abramovitz, *Regulating the Lives of Women,* 322.

56. Bell, *Aid to Dependent Children,* 87.

57. Ibid., 214. For a federal study of absent fathers and ADC, see Saul Kaplan, Public Assistance Report no. 41, *Support from Absent Fathers of Children Receiving ADC 1955* (Washington D.C.: U.S. Government Printing Office, 1955).

58. Virginia Franks, "Shall We Sneak Up on Our Clients?" *Public Welfare* 9, no. 5 (May 1951): 106–110.

59. "Midnight raids" and other punitive policies are vividly described in Bell, *Aid to Dependent Children,* chaps. 4–9; and Piven and Cloward, *Regulating the Poor,* chaps. 4 and 5.

60. Bell, *Aid to Dependent Children,* 88.

61. Ibid., chap. 9.

62. Lucy Komisar, *Down and Out in the USA: A History of Public Welfare* (New York: New Viewpoints, 1977), 84–86.

63. Cited in ibid., 84.

64. Cited in ibid., 85.

65. As with all statistics, the average amounts of the payments obscure the differences among groups of people.

66. Richard A. Cloward and Frances Fox Piven, "Mississippi: Starving by the Rule Book," *The Nation,* April 3, 1967, 429–431.

67. Bell, *Aid to Dependent Children,* 46.

68. Ibid.

69. Ibid., 82.

70. Ibid., 107.

71. This was well below the minimum wage of $1.25 per hour (in 1965). Social Security Administration, *Annual Statistical Supplement, 1994,* table 3.B3: Federal minimum wage rates under the Fair Labor Standards Act and average hourly earnings and average weekly hours for production workers in manufacturing, 1938–94; Piven and Cloward, *Regulating the Poor,* 141–143.

72. Piven and Cloward, *Regulating the Poor,* 143.

73. Bell, *Aid to Dependent Children,* 82.

74. The Newburgh plan also proposed denying relief to "able-bodied" men who refused a job, but no one fit this category.

CHAPTER 4   *The Flowering of Government Work Programs*

1. The phrase "human reclamation" was sometimes used to refer to these programs, for example, in the 1967 *Manpower Report of the President.* Department of Labor and Department of Health, Education, and Welfare, *Manpower Report of the President* (Washington, D.C.: Government Printing Office, 1967), 51.

2. Council of Economic Advisors, *Economic Report of the President, 1994* (Washington, D.C.: Government Printing Office, 1994), table B-2: Gross domestic product in 1987 dollars, 1959–93; and table B-41: Civilian unemployment rate by demographic characteristic, 1950–93.

3. Ibid., table B-45: Hours and earnings in private nonagricultural industries, 1959–93. Steadily rising wages, in turn, began to squeeze profit rates, which increased until 1966 and fell thereafter, causing stagnation by the mid-1970s. For a clear and accessible analysis of the post–World War II decline of the U.S. economy, the crisis beginning in the 1960s, and attempted solutions since the 1970s, see Samuel Bowles, David M. Gordon, and Thomas E. Weisskopf, *After the Wasteland: A Democratic Economics for the Year 2000* (Armonk, N.Y.: M. E. Sharpe, 1990).

4. Council of Economic Advisors, *Economic Report of the President, 1985* (Washington, D.C.: Government Printing Office, 1985), table B-27: Number and median income (in 1983 dollars) of families and persons, and poverty status, by race, selected years, 1947–83.

5. Bureau of the Census, *Statistical Abstract of the United States, 1992,* table 700: Money income of families—Median family income in current and constant dollars, by race and Hispanic origin of householder.

6. Council of Economic Advisors, *Economic Report of the President, 1994,* table B-41: Civilian unemployment rate by demographic characteristic, 1954–93.

7. Teresa Amott and Julie Matthaei, *Race, Gender, and Work: A Multicultural Economic History of Women in the United States* (Boston: South End Press, 1991), 404.

8. In comparison, men of all races saw slight decreases in their labor force participation rates. Rates for white men fell steadily from 83.4 percent in 1960 to 80.0 percent by 1970, while rates for African-Americans and other men of color decreased more markedly, from 83.0 percent to 76.5 percent. Council of Economic Advisors, *Economic Report of the President, 1994,* table B-38: Civilian labor force participation rate by demographic characteristic, 1954–93.

9. Several reports expressed the belief that manpower programs were a permanent component of federal policy, which simply needed to be altered in order to be more effective. See, for example, the Introductions to the *Manpower Reports of the President* written in the 1960s and 1970s; and Henry David, National Manpower Council, *Manpower Policies for a Democratic Society: The Final Statement of the Council* (New York: Columbia University Press, 1965).

10. Richard B. DuBoff, *Accumulation & Power: An Economic History of the United States* (Armonk, N.Y.: M. E. Sharpe, 1989), 94.

11. Senate Special Committee on Unemployment Problems, *Readings in Unemployment,* 86th Cong., 1st sess. (Washington, D.C.: U.S. Government Printing Office, 1960).

12. The ARA was first passed in 1955. See Garth L. Mangum, *MDTA: Foundation of Federal Manpower Policy* (Baltimore: The Johns Hopkins Press, 1968), 10–12.

13. Ibid., chaps. 2 and 3. In 1962 the minimum wage was $1.15 per hour, or $46 per week for a forty-hour workweek. This disparity increased further when the minimum wage was raised to $1.25 per hour in September 1963.

14. Ibid., 62.

15. See ibid., 12–19.

16. Department of Labor and Department of Health, Education, and Welfare, *Manpower Report of the President, 1967,* 51. Jill Quadagno explains how the types of training allowed were constrained by the objections of craft unions to government programs that increased the supply of workers, especially of African-Americans, in some fields, primarily construction. The unions wanted to maintain control over who was admitted to the trade and thereby both help preserve craft jobs for their sons and other community members and keep supply restricted in order to maintain wages. Jill Quadagno, "Social Movements and State Transformation: Labor Unions and Racial Conflict in the War on Poverty," *American Sociological Review* 57 (October 1992): 616–634.

17. Grace A. Franklin and Randall B. Ripley, *CETA: Politics and Policy, 1973–1982* (Knoxville: University of Tennessee Press, 1984), 8–9.

18. Charles R. Perry, Richard L. Rowan, Bernard E. Anderson, and Herbert R. Northrup, The Wharton School Industrial Research Unit, *The Impact of Government Manpower Programs: In General, and on Minorities and Women* (Philadelphia: University of Pennsylvania Press, 1975), 22.

19. Ibid., 111–114; Sharon L. Harlan, "Women and Federal Job Training Policy," in Sharon L. Harlan and Ronnie J. Steinberg, eds., *Job Training for Women: The Promise and Limits of Public Policies* (Philadelphia: Temple University Press, 1989), 67–70; and Sharon L. Harlan, "Federal Job Training Policy and Economically Disadvantaged Women," in Laurie Larwood, Ann H. Stromberg, and Barbara A. Gutek, eds., *Women and Work: An Annual Review,* vol. 1 (Beverly Hills: Sage Publications, 1985), 293–295.

20. Mangum, *MDTA,* 98.

21. See Frances Fox Piven and Richard A. Cloward, *Poor People's Movements: Why They Succeed, How They Fail* (New York: Vintage Books: 1977), chaps. 4 and 5; and Taylor Branch, *Parting the Waters: America in the King Years, 1954–1963* (New York: Simon and Schuster, 1988). Other protest movements emanated from the civil rights movement, which was the "borning struggle" for all of the movements of the 1960s. Many leaders of the student movement, particularly those in Students for a Democratic Society (SDS), had participated in earlier civil rights struggles. As the 1960s progressed, concerns of SDS shifted to the escalating Vietnam War and led to the antiwar movement. The treatment of women, who were generally relegated to "copying leaflets and making coffee" in left organizations, led in turn to the formation of the radical, or collectivist, branch of the women's movement. See Dick Cluster, ed., *They Should Have Served That Cup of Coffee: Seven Radicals Remember the 1960s* (Boston: South End Press, 1979), chap. 1; Sara Evans, *Personal Politics: The Origins of the Women's Movement in the New Left* (New York: Vintage Books, 1979); and Myra Marx Feree and Beth Hess, *Controversy and Coalition: The New Feminist Movement* (Boston: Twayne, 1985).

The more liberal branch of the women's movement had its origins elsewhere. Important to this movement was Betty Friedan's *The Feminine Mystique,* which gave voice to the frustrations of white middle-class women who dutifully had children and worked (unpaid) in the home. Important, too, were the federal recognition and national platform for demands for change provided by President Kennedy's Commission on the Status of Women, which documented some of the pervasive economic inequality. See Betty Friedan, *The Feminine Mystique* (New York: W. W. Norton, 1963); and Ferree and Hess, *Controversy and Coalition,* chap. 3.

Labor organizing and actions also intensified during the 1960s. As the economic expansion continued and unemployment fell, workers' increased bargaining power was reflected in a rise in strike activity; in 1970 almost 53 million days were lost to work stoppages involving almost 2.5 million workers. U.S. Bureau of the Census, *Statistical Abstract of the United States, 1992,* table 669. Work Stoppages.

22. This process was most clearly described in Frances Fox Piven and Richard A. Cloward, *Regulating the Poor: The Functions of Public Welfare* (New York: Vintage Books, 1971), chaps. 7 and 8.

23. Cited in Sar A. Levitan, *The Great Society's Poor Law: A New Approach to Poverty* (Baltimore: The Johns Hopkins University Press, 1969), 3.

24. Piven and Cloward argue that the Great Society programs were designed to circumvent much of the existing state and local bureaucratic appara-

tus in order to funnel resources directly to the growing African-American electoral constituency in the cities. Piven and Cloward, *Regulating the Poor,* chap. 9.

25. A helpful discussion of the origins of the War on Poverty can be found in Hugh Heclo, "The Political Foundations of Antipoverty Policy," in Sheldon H. Danziger and Daniel H. Weinberg, eds., *Fighting Poverty: What Works and What Doesn't* (Cambridge, Mass.: Harvard University Press, 1986).

26. In fact, tax cuts became a strategy preferred by many, since they were less intrusive and less direct than government spending.

27. For helpful discussions of these issues, see William J. Spring, "Congress and Public Service Employment," in Harold L. Sheppard, Bennett Harrison, and William J. Spring, eds., *The Political Economy of Public Service Employment* (Lexington, Mass.: D. C. Heath, 1972), 129–139; Margaret Weir, "The Federal Government and Unemployment: The Frustration of Policy Innovation from the New Deal to the Great Society," in Margaret Weir, Ann Shola Orloff, and Theda Skocpol, eds., *The Politics of Social Policy in the United States* (Princeton, N.J.: Princeton University Press, 1988), 172–179; and Charles V. Hamilton and Dona C. Hamilton, "Social Policies, Civil Rights, and Poverty," in Danziger and Weinberg, eds., *Fighting Poverty,* 299–303.

28. This rate was documented in November 1966. Spring, "Congress and Public Service Employment," 134.

29. From a 1966 statement to Congress, quoted in Hamilton and Hamilton, "Social Policies, Civil Rights, and Poverty," 303.

30. Senator Gaylord Nelson of Wisconsin, who introduced the initial ARA in 1955, advocated "massive funding of public employment" in the mid-1960s. Perry et. al., *The Impact of Government Manpower Programs,* 256; and Spring, "Congress and Public Service Employment," 139.

31. Weir, "The Federal Government and Unemployment," 183; and Hamilton and Hamilton, "Social Policies, Civil Rights, and Poverty," 299.

32. Spring, "Congress and Public Service Employment," 129.

33. Ibid., 137.

34. Ibid., 137, see also, 136–141; and Perry et al., *The Impact of Government Manpower Programs,* 256.

35. Daniel P. Moynihan, U.S. Department of Labor, Office of Policy and Planning Research, *The Negro Family: The Case for National Action* (Washington, D.C.: U.S. Government Printing Office, 1965), reprinted in Lee Rainwater and William L. Yancey, *The Moynihan Report and the Politics of Controversy* (Cambridge, Mass.: Massachusetts Institute of Technology Press, 1967), 41–124.

36. Other programs construed as part of the Great Society included the 1961 Juvenile Delinquency and Youth Offenders Control Act, the 1963 Community Mental Health Centers Act, the 1966 Demonstration Cities and Metropolitan Development Act (model cities), and the 1967 Neighborhood Service Program. See Piven and Cloward, *Regulating the Poor,* chap. 9.

37. Nancy A. Naples, "Contradictions in the Gender Subtext of the War on Poverty: The Community Work and Resistance of Women from Low Income Communities," *Social Problems* 38, no. 3 (August 1991): 316–332; Nancy A. Naples, "Women Against Poverty: Community Workers in Anti-Poverty

Programs, 1964–1984" (Ph.D. diss., City University of New York, 1988), chap. 3; and Levitan, *The Great Society's Poor Law,* chap. 3.

38. Quoted in Naples, "Women Against Poverty," 268.

39. Thus it remained small, serving slightly more than one hundred thousand people through 1972, approximately two-thirds of whom were women. Perry et al., *The Impact of Government Manpower Programs,* chap. 9; Department of Labor and Department of Health, Education, and Welfare, *Manpower Report of the President, 1979,* 73–74; and Naples, "Women Against Poverty," 76–78.

40. Perry et al., *The Impact of Government Manpower Programs,* 425.

41. Department of Labor and Department of Health, Education, and Welfare, *Manpower Report of the President, 1969,* 98.

42. Perry et al., *The Impact of Government Manpower Programs,* chap. 16; Sar A. Levitan, *Antipoverty Work and Training Efforts: Goals and Realities* (Ann Arbor: University of Michigan Institute of Labor and Industrial Relations and the National Manpower Policy Task Force, January 1970), chap. 3.

43. Diana Pearce, "Welfare Is Not *for* Women: Why the War on Poverty Cannot Conquer the Feminization of Poverty," in Linda Gordon, ed., *Women, the State, and Welfare* (Madison: University of Wisconsin Press, 1990), 272. The Job Corps provided counseling, basic education, high school equivalency degrees (GED), skill training, work experience, and placement assistance.

44. Through 1972, only 27 percent of those in the program were women, and 60 percent of the total participants were black. Perry et al., *The Impact of Government Manpower Programs,* 22–23.

45. Ibid., chap. 15; Levitan, *Antipoverty Work and Training Efforts,* chap. 2.

46. See Perry et al., *The Impact of Government Manpower Programs,* chaps. 10 and 12, for discussions of these programs.

47. Quoted in ibid., 256.

48. Ibid., chap. 17.

49. Ibid., chap. 13.

50. Ibid., 9–10, chap. 8.

51. Ibid.; and Spring, "Congress and Public Service Employment," 138.

52. Piven and Cloward, *Poor People's Movements,* 275–276.

53. Guida West, *The National Welfare Rights Organization: The Social Protest of Poor Women* (New York: Praeger, 1981).

54. Johnnie Tillmon, "Welfare Is a Women's Issue," *Liberation News Service,* no. 415, February 26, 1972; reprinted in Rosalyn Baxandall, Linda Gordon, and Susan Reverby, eds., *America's Working Women: A Documentary History—1600 to the Present* (New York: Vintage Books, 1976), 355–358.

55. See Piven and Cloward, *Poor People's Movements,* chap. 5.

56. The total number of recipients increased from 3,005,000 in 1960, to 8,466,000 in 1970. Social Security Administration, *Annual Statistical Supplement, 1994,* table 9.G1: AFDC and Emergency Assistance: Average monthly number of recipients, total amount of cash payments, and average monthly payment.

57. See Martha F. Davis, *Brutal Need: Lawyers and the Welfare Rights Movement, 1960–1973* (New Haven, Conn.: Yale University Press, 1994), for a

helpful discussion of the role of Legal Aid lawyers in conjunction with welfare rights organizing in ending these punitive rules.

58. Cited in Levitan, *Antipoverty Work and Training Efforts,* 77.

59. Ibid., 83; Mimi Abramovitz, *Regulating the Lives of Women: Social Welfare Policy from Colonial Times to the Present* (Boston: South End Press, 1988), 333.

60. Levitan, *Antipoverty Work and Training Efforts,* 77–80; Abramovitz, *Regulating the Lives of Women,* 331–332; and Leonard Goodwin and Pauline Milius, "Forty Years of Work Training," in Charles D. Garvin, Audrey D. Smith, and William J. Reid, eds., *The Work Incentive Experience* (Montclair, N.J.: Allanheld, Osmun, 1978), 16.

61. Cited in Levitan, *Antipoverty Work and Training Efforts,* 82.

62. Ibid., 82–83.

63. Ibid., 83–89, 97; Abramovitz, *Regulating the Lives of Women,* 347 n.

64. Richard A. Cloward and Frances Fox Piven, "Mississippi: Starving by the Rule Book," *The Nation,* April 3, 1967, 429–431.

65. Piven and Cloward, *Regulating the Poor,* 129.

66. Levitan, *Antipoverty Work and Training Efforts,* 96–99; Abramovitz, *Regulating the Lives of Women,* 347, n. 81.

67. For example, before WIN's enactment, if a family received $155 per month (the average AFDC payment in 1967) and a family member obtained a job paying $90 per month, their welfare payment would have been reduced by the full $90, to $65 per month, still leaving them with a total monthly income of $155. After WIN, their AFDC payment would only have been reduced to $115 per month (disregarding $50 of their earnings, that is, the first $30 plus one-third of the remaining $60). They would now have a total income of $205 per month and would also be reimbursed for work-related expenses.

68. In fact, an April 1967 White House report, which was given much attention by the media, suggested that mothers should be encouraged to remain home taking care of their children rather than participate in work and training programs. Levitan, *Antipoverty Work and Training Efforts,* 83.

69. "Aid to Families with Dependent Children: History of Provisions: Work Incentive," *Social Security Bulletin, Annual Statistical Supplement, 1994.*

70. Many analysts who wrote about WIN in the 1960s and 1970s noted that the program was a response to the rising costs of the rolls. See, for example, Goodwin and Milius, "Forty Years of Work Training," 17; and George Mink, "The Organization of WIN and Its Impact on Participants," in Garvin et al., *The Work Incentive Experience,* 111.

71. This is yet another instance of trends being recognized as such only when white middle-class people are affected.

72. The years are fiscal years. Department of Labor and Department of Health, Education, and Welfare, *Manpower Report of the President, 1974,* 358; and Perry et al., *The Impact of Government Manpower Programs,* 22.

73. Goodwin and Milius, "Forty Years of Work Training," 18.

74. Piven and Cloward, *Poor People's Movements,* 319.

75. These studies were published in 1972. Perry et al., *The Impact of Government Manpower Programs,* 374.

76. Full-time, year-round work at $2.12 per hour (the higher wage for women) yields an annual income of $4,409.60, slightly above the $3,968 poverty line for a family of four in 1970.

77. Perry et. al., *The Impact of Government Manpower Programs,* 378.

78. Testimony of L. V. Jones, reprinted in Piven and Cloward, *Regulating the Poor,* 143.

CHAPTER 5   *The Revival of Job Creation Programs*

1. The 1973–1975 recession is sometimes attributed to the Organization of Petroleum Exporting Countries (OPEC), which raised the price of oil and thereby set off high inflation. However, OPEC was composed of Third World countries and was only able to coalesce because of the U.S. loss in Vietnam and the subsequent perceived inability of the U.S. to defend its empire. Instead, the crisis needs to be understood in terms of the breakdown of the post–World War II institutional structure, most importantly the "capital-labor accord" that gave mostly white, male workers higher wages in exchange for relinquishing some control over the production process; increased challenges to corporate decisions vis-à-vis the environment and health and safety; the growth of rivalries among capitalists; and the demise of an international system based on "Pax Americana." See Samuel Bowles, David M. Gordon, and Thomas E. Weisskopf, *After the Wasteland: A Democratic Economics for the Year 2000* (Armonk, N.Y.: M. E. Sharpe, 1990), esp. chap. 5.

2. Council of Economic Advisors, *Economic Report of the President, 1994* (Washington D.C.: U.S. Government Printing Office, 1994), table B-2: Gross domestic product in 1987 dollars, 1959–93; and Richard B. DuBoff, *Accumulation & Power: An Economic History of the United States* (Armonk, N.Y.: M. E. Sharpe, 1989), 94.

3. Council of Economic Advisors, *Economic Report of the President, 1994,* table B-45: Hours and earnings in private nonagricultural industries, 1959–93.

4. Inflation, as measured by the Consumer Price Index (CPI-U), remained below 3.3 percent from the end of the Korean War through 1966. Indeed, it was between 0.7 and 1.7 percent from 1959 through 1965. It slowly rose in the late 1960s, to 5.4 percent by 1969, and fell to 3.2 percent in 1972 before its somewhat precipitous climbs, to 11.0 percent in 1974, and after another decline, to 11.3 percent in 1979 (and to 13.5 percent in 1980), as the OPEC oil-price increases led to higher prices throughout the economy. Council of Economic Advisors, *Economic Report of the President, 1994,* table B-59: Consumer price indexes for major expenditure classes, 1950–93.

5. Fiscal policy deals with government spending and taxation, and monetary policy is carried out by the Federal Reserve Board and concerns the level of interest rates and the supply of money and credit.

6. At the same time, the aging of the population and decreasing employment opportunities led to lower labor force participation rates for men—from 80 percent to 78.6 percent for white men and a troublesome drop from 76.5 percent

to 71.3 percent for men of color. Council of Economic Advisors, *Economic Report of the President, 1994,* table B-38: Civilian labor force participation rate by demographic characteristic, 1954–93.

7. During this decade, the ratio of earnings between all women and all men narrowed slightly, from 33 percent in 1970 to 37 percent by 1979, reflecting women's increased working time, both more hours per week and more weeks per year. Council of Economic Advisors, *Economic Report of the President, 1985,* table B-27: Number and median income (in 1983 dollars) of families and persons, and poverty status, by race, selected years, 1947–83.

8. Council of Economic Advisors, *Economic Report of the President, 1994,* table B-38.

9. Council of Economic Advisors, *Economic Report of the President, 1985,* table B-27.

10. These measure median earnings for year-round, full-time workers. Ibid.

11. Teresa Amott and Julie Matthaei, *Race, Gender, and Work: A Multicultural Economic History of Women in the United States* (Boston: South End Press, 1991), 404.

12. Nancy Naples, "Women Against Poverty: Community Workers in Anti-Poverty Programs, 1964–1984" (Ph.D. diss., City University of New York, 1988), 79; and Frances Fox Piven and Richard A. Cloward, *Poor People's Movements: Why They Succeed, How They Fail* (New York: Vintage Books: 1977) 332.

13. Social Security Administration, *Social Security Bulletin Annual Statistical Supplement, 1994,* (Washington, D.C. Government Printing Office, 1994), table 9.G1: AFDC & Emergency Assistance: Average monthly number of recipients, total amount of cash payments, and average monthly payment, 1936–92.

14. The average size of AFDC families fell very gradually through the 1980s and early 1990s, although when rounded to the nearest tenth it remained at 2.9 members per family. By 1993, however, it had fallen to 2.8 members per family. Ibid.

15. This first version of FAP was never brought out of committee and a similar bill was debated, and defeated, the following year. Descriptions of FAP can be found in Piven and Cloward, *Poor People's Movements,* 335–343; Department of Labor, *Manpower Report of the President, 1970* (Washington, D.C.: Government Printing Office, 1971), 155–158; Vincent J. Burke and Vee Burke, *Nixon's Good Deed: Welfare Reform* (New York: Columbia University Press, 1974); Daniel P. Moynihan, *The Politics of a Guaranteed Income: The Nixon Administration and the Family Assistance Plan* (New York: Random House, 1973); Milwaukee County Welfare Rights Organization, *Welfare Mothers Speak Out: We Ain't Gonna Shuffle Anymore* (New York: W. W. Norton, 1972), chaps. 10 and 11; Timothy J. Sampson, *Welfare: A Handbook for Friend and Foe* (Philadelphia: Pilgrim Press Book, 1972), chap. 6; and Charles V. Hamilton and Dona C. Hamilton, "Social Policies, Civil Rights, and Poverty," in Sheldon H. Danziger and Daniel H. Weinberg, eds. *Fighting Poverty: What Works and What Doesn't* (Cambridge, Mass.: Harvard University Press, 1986), 303–305.

16. Moynihan, *The Politics of a Guaranteed Income,* 76.

17. Full-time work was considered to be twenty-four hours per week, or one hundred hours per month.

18. Social Security Administration, *Social Security Bulletin Annual Statistical Supplement, 1994,* table 3.E1: Poverty: Weighted average poverty thresholds for nonfarm families of specified size, 1959–93.

19. National Welfare Rights Organization, *$6500 Now! The NWRO Adequate Income Plan* (June 25, 1971); reprinted in Sampson, *Welfare,* 181–195.

20. Although the FAP was defeated, the other categorical assistance programs—Old Age Assistance (OAA), Aid to the Blind (AB), and Aid to the Totally and Permanently Disabled (ATPD)—were federalized in 1972 as Supplemental Security Income (SSI). Jill Quadagno examines the federalization of OAA. She contends that although in 1935 when the Social Security Act was enacted southerners bitterly opposed federal payments for the aged poor, believing that they would be used to support other African-Americans and offer an alternative to low-wage labor, the migration of young blacks out of the rural South in the intervening years left many older blacks as a financial burden. Thus, by 1972 southern states welcomed federal payments. Jill Quadagno, "From Old-Age Assistance to Supplemental Security Income: The Political Economy of Relief in the South, 1935–1972," in Margaret Weir, Ann Shola Orloff, and Theda Skocpol, eds., *The Politics of Social Policy in the United States* (Princeton, N.J.: Princeton University Press, 1988).

21. National Welfare Rights Organization, *$6500 Now!,* 6, reprinted in Sampson, *Welfare,* 186.

22. Milwaukee County Welfare Rights Organization, *Welfare Mothers Speak Out,* 79.

23. Hamilton and Hamilton, "Social Policies, Civil Rights, and Poverty," 304–305.

24. Social Security Administration, *Social Security Bulletin Annual Statistical Supplement, 1994,* "Aid to Families with Dependent Children: History of Provisions: Work Incentive."

25. George Mink, "The Organization of WIN and Its Impact on Participants," in Charles D. Garvin, Audrey D. Smith, and William J. Reid, eds., *The Work Incentive Experience* (Montclair, N.J.: Allanheld, Osmun, 1978), 116.

26. Jesse E. Gordon, "WIN Research: A Review of the Findings," in Garvin et al., *The Work Incentive Experience.*

27. Department of Labor, Employment and Training Administration, R&D Monograph 49, *The Work Incentive (WIN) Program and Related Experiences: A Review of Research With Policy Implications* (Washington, D.C.: U.S. Government Printing Office, 1977), 1–2, cited in Department of Labor and Department of Health, Education, and Welfare, *Employment and Training Report of the President, 1978* (Washington, D.C. Government Printing Office, 1978), 64. With the exception of the year, the publication data is the same for all issues of the *Manpower Report of the President* and the *Employment and Training Report of the President.*

28. Throughout the 1970s, between 36 and 45 percent of WIN participants were African-American, 10 to 20 percent were Hispanic, and 32 to 45 percent were white. Department of Labor and Department of Health, Education, and

Welfare, *Employment and Training Report of the President, 1971,* 310; ibid., *1972,* 59; ibid., *1974,* 367; ibid., *1975,* 326; ibid., *1977,* 59; Department of Labor and Department of Health and Human Services, *Employment and Training Report of the President, 1980,* 52; and ibid., *1982,* 44.

29. Gordon, "WIN Research," 45–46.

30. Department of Labor and Department of Health, Education, and Welfare, *Employment and Training Report of the President, 1977,* 59; ibid., *1978,* 55; ibid., *1979,* 54; Department of Labor and Department of Health and Human Services, *Employment and Training Report of the President, 1980,* 52; and ibid., *1982,* 44.

31. Department of Labor and Department of Health, Education, and Welfare, *Employment and Training Report of the President, 1977,* 61.

32. Ibid., *1978,* 55. Different statistics are included in different reports.

33. A helpful description and analysis of the Supported Work Demonstration (SWD) project can be found in Robinson G. Hollister, Jr., Peter Kemper, and Rebecca A. Maynard, *The National Supported Work Demonstration* (Madison: University of Wisconsin Press, 1984).

34. All participants were followed for twenty-seven months, and some were surveyed forty-five months after they left the program. Significant employment effects continued through the entire time period. Ibid., chap. 4.

35. This differed from WIN, which considered mothers employable if their youngest child was five years of age or older.

36. State of California Employment Development Department, *Third Year and Final Report on the Community Work Experience Program* (Sacramento, Calif.: Government Printing Office, April 1976), 2.

37. Of the 182,735 people available for CWEP, only 4,760 were enrolled in the program. Placement was also complicated by the requirement that a specified level of WIN slots had to be filled before people could be put in CWEP. Ibid., 3.

38. Ibid., 4.

39. Ibid., 3.

40. Ibid., 9–10.

41. Ibid., 17.

42. Cited in Department of Labor and Department of Health, Education, and Welfare, *Employment and Training Report of the President, 1978,* 56.

43. Ibid., *1979,* 56, 196–197.

44. The issues involved in these debates, as well as the PBJI and alternative proposals, are described in Gordon L. Weil, *The Welfare Debate of 1978* (White Plains, N.Y.: Institute for Socioeconomic Studies, 1978).

45. Ibid.

46. Interview with Sue Hamlin, Redlands, California, November 24, 1993.

47. Carol Brightman, "The CETA Factor," *Working Papers* (May-June 1978): 34–42.

48. This was emphasized in hearings on bills to expand PSE. For example, Alan Gartner, secretary of the National Conference on Public Service Employment, claimed that such a program "can provide additional *quality services* to the

community while creating *quality jobs* [emphasis in original]." Subcommittee on Employment, Poverty, and Migratory Labor of the Senate Committee on Labor and Public Welfare, *Hearings on S. 4079*, 93rd Cong., 2nd sess., September 16, October 16 and 17, 1974, 141. [Hereafter *PSE Hearings.*]

49. While most of the changes in the 1930s programs were made by work program administrators, in the 1970s they were primarily made by Congress. This was done when PEP and CETA were first passed, as well as through later acts affecting CETA: the 1974 Emergency Jobs and Employment Assistance Act (PL 93–567); the 1976 Emergency Jobs Programs Extension Act (PL 94–444); and the 1978 Comprehensive Employment and Training Act Amendments (PL 95–524).

50. A helpful discussion can be found in William J. Spring, "Congress and Public Service Employment," in Harold L. Shepard, Bennett Harrison, and William J. Spring, eds., *The Political Economy of Public Service Employment* (Lexington, Mass.: D. C. Heath, 1972), 138.

51. Quoted in ibid., 138–140. This article contains an extremely helpful discussion of the politics of job creation programs in the 1960s and early 1970s.

52. Ibid., 141.

53. Ibid., 142–146; Sar A. Levitan and Frank Gallo, *A Second Chance: Training for Jobs* (Kalamazoo, Mich.: The W. E. Upjohn Institute for Employment Research, 1988), 7; and Grace A. Franklin and Randall B. Ripley, *CETA: Politics and Policy, 1973–1982* (Knoxville: University of Tennessee Press, 1984), 14.

54. Franklin and Ripley, *CETA*, 10–11.

55. Ibid., 18.

56. As a result, CETA expenditures increased from $5.6 billion in (fiscal year) 1977 to $9.5 billion in 1978 and $9.4 billion in 1979. Department of Labor and Department of Health, Education, and Welfare, *Employment and Training Report of the President, 1979*, 32; and Department of Labor and Department of Health and Human Services, *Employment and Training Report of the President, 1980*, 24.

57. Department of Labor and Department of Health and Human Services, *Employment and Training Report of the President, 1981*, table F-3: Number of participants in activity and percent of annual plans accomplished under selected CETA youth employment and training programs: Fiscal 1980.

58. This buildup was also related to the Carter administration's welfare reform proposal, PBJI, which recommended placing several hundred thousand AFDC recipients in a PSE program that would be further expanded to 1.4 million jobs.

59. William Mirengoff, Lester Rindler, Harry Greenspan, and Scott Seablom, *CETA: Assessment of Public Service Employment Programs* (Washington, D.C.: National Academy of Sciences, 1980), 40.

60. This was reflected in total CETA expenditures, which fell to $8.9 billion in 1980 and $7.7 billion in 1981. Department of Labor and Department of Health and Human Services, *Employment and Training Report of the President, 1981*, 23; and ibid., *1982*, 28.

61. These figures are for fiscal years and include the carryover from the

previous year. Department of Labor and Department of Health, Education, and Welfare, *Employment and Training Report of the President, 1979*, 369; Department of Labor and Department of Health and Human Services, *Employment and Training Report of the President, 1980*, 354; and ibid., *1981*, 258.

62. Charles R. Perry, Richard L. Rowan, Bernard E. Anderson, and Herbert R. Northrup, The Wharton School Industrial Research Unit, *The Impact of Government Manpower Programs: In General, and on Minorities and Women* (Philadelphia: University of Pennsylvania Press, 1975), 259.

63. Ibid., 100–101.

64. Ibid., 101.

65. Quoted in ibid., 131. See also National Commission for Manpower Policy, Special Report no. 23, *CETA: An Analysis of the Issues (Washington D.C.: U.S. Government Printing Office, May 1978)*, 8.

66. Isabel Sawhill, "Introduction and Summary," in National Commission for Manpower Policy, *CETA*; Robert F. Cook, Charles F. Adams, Jr., V. Lane Rawlins, and Associates, *Public Service Employment: The Experience of a Decade* (Kalamazoo, Mich.: The W. E. Upjohn Institute for Employment Research, 1985), 46; and Mirengoff et al., *CETA*, 49.

67. These regulations were applied to the new positions created as part of the expansion of Title VI (termed nonsustainment) and to half of the vacancies in existing Title VI positions (sustainment).

68. In 1976, when these regulations were implemented, 70 percent of the lower living standard was $6,712 for a family of four, compared to a poverty line of $5,815. However, the poverty line was sometimes higher than the lower living standard for smaller families. Mirengoff et al., *CETA*, 20–21 and 77.

69. Ibid., 23.

70. Ibid., 117.

71. Ibid., 19.

72. Through the decade, participation rates for Hispanics showed no trend, varying between 10 percent and 14 percent, and rates for other people of color ranged from 3 percent to 9 percent. Statistics simultaneously breaking down participation by both gender and race are not available. Department of Labor and Department of Health, Education, and Welfare, *Employment and Training Report of the President, 1974*, 367; ibid., *1975*, 326; ibid., *1976*, 344; ibid., *1977*, 267; ibid., *1978*, 313; ibid., *1979*, 369; Department of Labor and Department of Health and Human Services, *Employment and Training Report of the President, 1980*, 354; ibid., *1981*, 276; and ibid., *1982*, 291.

73. Mirengoff et al., *CETA*, 107–113.

74. Cook et al., *Public Service Employment*, 27; and Mirengoff et al., *CETA*, 165–168.

75. The figure for national average earnings, $9,828, was calculated from the data for average weekly earnings. Mirengoff et al., *CETA*, 31; Council of Economic Advisors, *Economic Report of the President, 1994*, table B-45: Hours and earnings in private nonagricultural industries.

76. No supplementation was allowed for Title II. Ibid., 169–170.

77. Department of Labor and Department of Health and Human Services, *Employment and Training Report of the President, 1981*, 28.

78. Mirengoff et al., *CETA*, 173–174.

79. "Implementation of the Comprehensive Employment and Training Act," AFSCME (American Federation of State, County, and Municipal Employees) Research Department, Lot 10, Box 5 (unprocessed), Archives of Labor and Urban Affairs, Wayne State University, Detroit; and memo from Llew Toulmin and Marilyn DePoy to Nanine Meiklejohn, April 4, 1978, AFSCME Research Department, Lot 10, Box 6 (unprocessed), Archives of Labor and Urban Affairs, Wayne State University.

80. Mirengoff et al., *CETA*, 170.

81. Ibid., chap. 8.

82. Statement of William Welsh, assistant to the President for Legislative Affairs, AFSCME, in *PSE Hearings*, 188.

83. AFSCME Research Department, Lot 10, Box 5 (unprocessed), Archives of Labor and Urban Affairs, Wayne State University.

84. *PSE Hearings*, 60–61.

85. Memo from Sheldon Mann to Don Wasserman, April 21, 1976, and memo from Don Wasserman to Jerry Wurf, April 23, 1976, AFSCME President's Office: Jerry Wurf (unprocessed), Box 89, Archives of Labor and Urban Affairs, Wayne State University.

86. Mirengoff et al., *CETA*, 125–126.

87. Ibid., 126–128.

88. Helpful discussions of women in CETA's training programs can be found in Sharon L. Harlan and Ronnie J. Steinberg, eds., *Job Training for Women: The Promise and Limits of Public Policies* (Philadelphia: Temple University Press, 1989). In particular, see Sharon L. Harlan and Ronnie J. Steinberg, "Job Training for Women: The Problem in a Policy Context"; Sharon L. Harlan, "Women and Federal Job Training Policy"; Jill Miller, "Displaced Homemakers in the Employment and Training System"; Denise F. Polit, "Employment Services for Teenage Mothers"; Elizabeth Durbin and Roger J. O'Brien, "Women and Public Service Employment: A Case Study in Connecticut"; Leslie Lilly, "Training Women for Jobs in Rural Economies: A Southern Experience"; and Lois Hagnere and Ronnie J. Steinberg, "Nontraditional Training for Women: Effective Programs, Structural Barriers, and Political Hurdles."

89. Subcommittee on Employment Opportunities of the House Committee on Education and Labor, *Hearings on H.R. 28*, 95th Cong., 1st sess., July 14, 1977, 98–99, testimony of Rose House.

90. Paraphrasing Tish Sommers, who organized the Alliance for Displaced Homemakers with Laurie Shields, in Miller, "Displaced Homemakers," 146.

91. Interview with Chani Beeman, Riverside, California, October 28, 1993.

92. Ibid.

93. Studies found statistically significant gains of five hundred to thirteen hundred dollars a year. Cited in Harlan, "Women and Federal Job Training Policy," 76.

94. Harlan, "Women and Federal Job Training Policy"; Lynn C. Burbridge, "Black Women in Employment and Training Programs," in Margaret Simms and Julianne Malveaux, eds., *Slipping Through the Cracks: The Status of Black*

Women (New Brunswick, N.J.: Transactions Books, 1987); and Linda J. Waite and Sue E. Berryman, "Occupational Desegregation in CETA Programs," in Barbara F. Reskin, ed., *Sex Segregation in the Workplace: Trends, Explanations, Remedies* (Washington, D.C.: National Academy Press, 1984).

95. Harlan, "Women and Federal Job Training Policy," 74.

96. See ibid.

97. Burbridge, "Black Women in Employment and Training Programs," 97–114.

98. The PSIP was not the first CETA program to involve the private sector; Carter's 1977 economic stimulus package included two small programs to provide training in the private sector. The Skills Training Improvement Program (STIP) offered training for long-term unemployed skilled workers and was well received by the private sector. The Help through Industry Retraining and Employment (HIRE) program developed both training and jobs for veterans, but met with less success than the STIP. Franklin and Ripley, *CETA, 121–125; and Department of Labor and Department of Health, Education, and Welfare, Employment and Training Report of the President, 1979,* 46–47.

99. Department of Labor and Department of Health and Human Services, *Employment and Training Report of the President, 1982,* 30; and Franklin and Ripley, *CETA,* 193.

100. Statistics from Franklin and Ripley, *CETA,* 129.

101. Helpful discussions of the Full Employment and Balanced Growth Act can be found in Elliott Currie, "The Politics of Jobs: Humphrey-Hawkins and the Dilemmas of Full Employment," *Socialist Review* 7, no. 2 (March-April 1977): 93–114; Helen Ginsburg, *Full Employment and Public Policy: The United States and Sweden* (Lexington, Mass.: Lexington Books, 1983); Harvey L. Schantz and Richard H. Schmidt, "Politics and Policy: The Humphrey-Hawkins Story," in Charles Bulmer and John L. Carmichael, eds., *Employment and Labor Relations Policy* (Lexington, Mass.: Lexington Books, 1980); and Hamilton and Hamilton, "Social Policies, Civil Rights, and Poverty," 305–306.

102. Subcommittee on Equal Opportunities of the House Committee on Education and Labor, *Hearings on H.R. 50,* 94th Cong., 1st sess., March 18, 1975, Part 2, 1. [Hereafter *1975 Hawkins Hearings.*] Senate Committee on Banking, Housing, and Urban Affairs, *Hearings on S. 50,* 94th Cong., 2nd sess., May 20, 21, and 25, 1976, 6. [Hereafter *1976 Humphrey-Hawkins Hearings.*]

103. *1975 Hawkins Hearings,* 3.

104. Ibid., 2. By 1976 this had become the "Full Employment and Balanced Growth Plan."

105. For example, *1976 Humphrey-Hawkins Hearings,* 9 and 12.

106. Ibid., 11–12; *1975 Hawkins Hearings,* 2.

107. *1976 Humphrey-Hawkins Hearings,* 3–4.

108. Ibid., 3, 221, 222.

109. 95th Cong., 2nd sess., *Full Employment and Balanced Growth Act of 1978,* Public Law No. 95–523, Title 1, sec. 102, 92 Stat. 1887, 1890.

110. Ibid., sec. 201.

111. Ibid., sec. 102.

112. DuBoff, *Accumulation and Power,* 94.

113. See, for example, "Why CETA Is in Trouble," *Business Week,* October 2, 1978, 124–126; and "Favoritism, Kickbacks Found in Public Jobs Program," *The Washington Post,* April 19, 1978, A2.

114. Department of Labor and Department of Health, Education, and Welfare, *Manpower Report of the President* (Washington D.C.: U.S. Government Printing Office, 1975), 40.

115. The National Planning Association estimated displacement at 46 percent in PEP; George Johnson and James Tomola found displacement increasing from 29 percent to 67 percent after one year of PEP; the National Academy of Sciences estimated a displacement rate of 35 percent in the first ten quarters of CETA; and Alan Fechter found rates between 50 and 90 percent after one year. Mirengoff et al., *CETA,* 125 n.

116. For example, if the rate of growth of government jobs was greater than the past rate of growth of state and local government expenditures, the difference was attributed to fiscal substitution of federal CETA funds for state and local tax revenues. Cook et al., *Public Service Employment,* 51–52.

117. Job creation was defined in the following way: "*New programs and services*: Cases in which additional programs or services were provided with PSE funding that would not otherwise have been undertaken; *Special projects:* New, one-time projects lasting one year or less that were undertaken with PSE funds; *Program expansion*: Cases in which the level of services was raised or services were improved under existing programs by using PSE funds beyond what they would be with local funds; *Program maintenance*: Cases in which PSE employees were used to maintain existing services that would have been curtailed without PSE funding." Job displacement was defined as: "*Transfers*: Cases involving the transfer of existing state and local government positions to PSE funding; *Rehires*: Cases in which state or local employees were laid off and then rehired with PSE funding; *Contract reduction*: Cases in which PSE participants were used to provide services or to work on projects that had been, or normally would have been, contracted to an outside organization or private firm; and *Potential hires*: Cases in which PSE participants were hired to fill positions that otherwise would have been funded with other revenue." Ibid., 52–53.

118. Ibid., chap. 3.

119. Mirengoff et al., *CETA,* 42.

CHAPTER 6   *Workfare for the "Truly Needy"*

1. The 1981–1982 recession was caused by tight monetary policy, initially implemented in October 1979 by the Federal Reserve Board. Reagan was politically able to allow this policy to remain in place through October 1982, as sustained high interest rates (in 1981 the prime interest rate, which banks charge their best customers, averaged 18.87 percent) choked off borrowing, causing investment and production to fall, unemployment to rise, and wages and inflation to fall. Council of Economic Advisers, *Economic Report of the President, 1994,* (Washington D.C.: U.S. Government Printing Office, 1994), table B-72: Bond yields and interest rates, 1929–93, and table B-41: Civilian unemployment

rate by demographic characteristic, 1950–93; and Richard B. DuBoff, *Accumulation & Power: An Economic History of the United States* (London: M. E. Sharpe, 1989), 94.

2. The Reagan administration's position toward unions became clear in the summer of 1981 when the Professional Air Traffic Controllers (PATCO) strikers were fired. Other antilabor policies included appointing to the National Labor Relations Board people who were opposed to unions and maintaining the minimum wage at $3.35 per hour throughout the decade. Furthermore, in the name of "getting government off the backs of the people," an era of deregulation was ushered in, as businesses were given much freer rein in employment and the production process (for example, gutting the Occupational Safety and Health Administration). The results of deregulating the financial industry will be felt for years to come in the collapses of banks and savings and loan institutions.

3. Council of Economic Advisors, *Economic Report of the President, 1994,* table B-45: Hours and earnings in private nanagricultural industries, 1959–93.

There is a serious problem with restraining wages. Capitalists invest in plant and equipment only when they can sell what they produce, and declining incomes caused middle- and lower-income people to reduce their purchases of goods and services, which leads capitalists to cut the level of production and to lower rates of investment. Thus the orgy of financial speculation in the 1980s was not a surprising result—the rich had to do something with their money.

4. These data are from the Congressional Budget Office. The income gains for the middle quintiles were as follows: 0.2 percent for the second lowest quintile; 2.7 percent for the third quintile; and 8.6 percent for the fourth quintile. Robert Greenstein and Scott Barancik, "Drifting Apart: New Findings on Growing Income Disparities Between the Rich, the Poor, and the Middle Class" (Washington, D.C.: Center on Budget and Policy Priorities, July 1990), 17.

5. David Stockman, head of the Office of Management and the Budget in the early years of the Reagan administration, admitted that the term "safety net" was coined prior to a news conference and was "just a spur-of-the-moment thing that the press office wanted to put out." Reported in the *Washington Post,* December 4, 1983, 1, quoted in Robert Greenstein, "End Results: The Impact of Federal Policies Since 1980 on Low-Income Americans" (Washington D.C.: Center on Budget and Policy Priorities 1984), 3.

6. For example, the number of people receiving food stamps, which had steadily increased from 4,340,000 in 1970 to 22,430,000 in 1981, fell throughout the 1980s so that by 1989 only 18,766,000 got them. Social Security Administration, *Annual Statistical Supplement, 1994* (Washington D.C.: U.S. Government Printing Office, December 1994), table 9.H1: Food stamps: Number of persons participating, value of bonus coupons, and average bonus per person, fiscal years 1962–93. For discussions of the cuts in all social programs, see Greenstein, "End Results"; and Coalition on Women and the Budget, "Inequality of Sacrifice: The Impact of the Reagan Budget on Women" (Washington, D.C.: Coalition on Women and the Budget, 1984), 1–2.

7. Council of Economic Advisers, *Economic Report of the President, 1994,* table B-2: Gross domestic product in 1987 dollars, 1959–93.

8. See the following articles for enlightening discussions about the development of the term "dependent" to connote individual moral and psychological defectiveness. Nancy Fraser and Linda Gordon, "Dependency' Demystified: Inscriptions of Power in a Keyword of the Welfare State," *Social Politics* 1, no. 1 (Spring 1994): 4–31; and Nancy Fraser and Linda Gordon, "A Genealogy of *Dependency*: Tracing a Keyword of the U.S. Welfare State," *Signs,* 19, no. 2 (Winter 1994): 309–336.

9. George Gilder, *Wealth and Poverty* (Toronto: Bantam Books, 1981), 148.

10. Ibid., 143.

11. Ibid., 150.

12. Ibid., 162.

13. Charles Murray, *Losing Ground: American Social Policy, 1950–1980* (New York: Basic Books, 1984). Other widely read books and articles claiming that higher welfare payments led to increased poverty include: Ken Auletta, *The Underclass* (New York: Random House, 1982); Lawrence Mead, *Beyond Entitlement: The Social Obligations of Citizenship* (New York: Free Press, 1985); Mickey Kaus, "The Work Ethic State," *The New Republic,* July 7, 1986, 22–33; and Nicholas Lemann, "The Origins of the Underclass," *The Atlantic Monthly,* July 1986, 54–68. In addition, economists Lowell Gallaway, Richard Vedder, and Therese Foster developed a "poverty-welfare curve," taking off from the Laffer curve to show allegedly that higher welfare payments led to higher rates of poverty. Richard Vedder and Lowell Gallaway, "AFDC and the Laffer Principle," *Wall Street Journal,* March 26, 1986; Lowell Gallaway, Richard Vedder, and Therese Foster, "The 'New' Structural Poverty: A Quantitative Analysis," and Lowell Gallaway and Richard Vedder, " 'Suffer Little Children': The True Casualties of the War on Poverty," both in *War on Poverty—Victory or Defeat? Hearings before the Subcommittee on Monetary and Fiscal Policy of the Joint Economic Committee,* 99th Cong., 1st sess., June 20, 1985.

14. U.S. Department of Labor, Women's Bureau, *20 Facts on Women Workers* (Washington, D.C.: U.S. Department of Labor, September 1990), no. 90–2. Some of the apparent increase in female-headed families resulted from different methods of counting them. Prior to the mid-1960s teenage mothers living at home with their mothers were not counted as a separate family; after the mid-1960s they were enumerated separately.

15. William Julius Wilson and Kathryn M. Neckerman explain that the rise in black births outside marriage was caused by declines in both the rate of marital fertility and in marriage itself. Among white women, the rise in female-headed families was primarily due to increased economic independence. William Julius Wilson and Kathryn M. Neckerman, "Poverty and Family Structure: The Widening Gap between Evidence and Public Policy Issues," in Sheldon H. Danziger and Daniel H. Weinberg, eds., *Fighting Poverty: What Works and What Doesn't* (Cambridge, Mass.: Harvard University Press, 1986), 232–259.

16. Illustrating the confluence of antiwelfare and antilabor policies, the OBRA also prohibited workers on strike from receiving AFDC.

17. Social Security Administration, *Social Security Bulletin Annual Statistical Supplement, 1994,* table 9.G1: AFDC and emergency assistance: Average

monthly number of recipients, total amount of cash payments, and average monthly payment, 1936–90.

18. This phrase was used by welfare rights activists.

19. As will be discussed in the following chapter, the poverty rate remained high in the early 1990s. Social Security, Administration, *Annual Statistical Supplement, 1994,* table 3.E2: Number and percent of poor persons, by age, at end of 1959–92.

20. The corresponding figures for children in households headed by men with or without a women present are 8.5 percent in 1979, 13.5 percent in 1983, 10.0 percent in 1988, and 10.7 percent in 1990. Ibid.; Bureau of the Census, *Statistical Abstract of the United States, 1992* (Washington D.C.: U.S. Government Printing Office, 1992), table 714: Persons below poverty level and below 125 percent of poverty level, by race of householder and family status; and Department of Labor, *20 Facts on Women Workers.*

21. Bureau of the Census, *Statistical Abstract of the United States, 1992,* table 719: Distribution of all children and of poor children, by family type and race: 1990.

22. Council of Economic Advisors, *Economic Report of the President, 1994, table B-31: Median money income (in 1992 dollars) and poverty status of families and persons, by race, selected years, 1971–92.*

23. See Bennett Harrison and Barry Bluestone, *The Great U-Turn: Corporate Restructuring and the Polarizing of America* (New York: Basic Books, 1988).

24. Council of Economic Advisors, *Economic Report of the President, 1994,* Table B-31.

25. Ibid.

26. Ibid., table B-38: Civilian labor force participation rate by demographic characteristic, 1954–93.

27. California Department of Social Services, *GAIN Guidebook* (Sacramento: State of California Health and Welfare Agency, Department of Social Services, 1990), 3.

28. In addition, gross income could not exceed 150 percent of the state's need standard.

29. Some slight increases were made throughout the 1980s. In 1984, the $30 portion of the disregard was extended for another eight months, the work expense disregard was raised to $90 per month, and the amount of gross income was raised to 185 percent of the state's need standard. Four years later the expenses for child-care deductions were raised to $175 per month for incapacitated adults and children age two and over and to $200 per month for children under age two. Social Security Administration, *Annual Statistical Supplement, 1994,* 2.E: "Aid to Families with Dependent Children: History of Provisions: Income and Resources Considered and Disregarded."

30. Robert Moffitt and Douglas A. Wolf, "The Effect of the 1981 Omnibus Budget Reconciliation Act on Welfare Recipients and Work Incentives," *Social Service Review* 61, no. 2 (June 1987): 247–260.

31. See Fred Block and John Noakes, "The Politics of New-Style Workfare," *Socialist Review* 88, no. 3 (July–September, 1988): 31–58; and Teresa Amott and Jean Kluver, *ET: A Model for the Nation? An Evaluation of the*

Massachusetts Employment and Training Choices Program (Philadelphia: American Friends Service Committee, 1986).

32. General Accounting Office [hereafter GAO], *Work and Welfare: Current AFDC Work Programs and Implications for Federal Policy* (Washington, D.C.: U.S. Government Printing Office, 1987), 69–70.

33. James Riccio, Barbara Goldman, Gayle Hamilton, Karin Martinson, and Alan Orenstein, *GAIN: Early Implementation Experiences and Lessons* (New York: Manpower Demonstration Research Corporation, 1989), 193.

34. See Marilyn Gittell and Sally Covington, Report to the Ford Foundation, *Higher Education in JOBS: An Option or an Opportunity? A Comparison of Nine States* (New York: Howard Samuels State Management and Policy Center, City University of New York, September 1993); and Marilyn Gittell, Jill Gross, and Jennifer Holdaway, Report to the Ford Foundation, *Building Human Capital: The Impact of Post-Secondary Education on AFDC Recipients in Five States* (New York: Howard Samuels State Management and Policy Center, City University of New York, September 1993).

35. When I called a GAIN supervisor in San Bernardino to complain that the attendance cards further stigmatized those on AFDC and were inappropriate for college, I was told that the GAIN program had to make sure that participants went to school instead of to the beach.

36. Interview with Lori Richard, San Bernardino, California, January 18, 1994.

37. GAO, *Work and Welfare*, 69. The remaining 3.3 percent, of the 10.4 percent total, received education and training services that could not be classified into a narrower category.

38. Amott and Kluver, *ET*, 21.

39. GAO, *Work and Welfare*, 84.

40. Ibid.

41. Ibid., 90.

42. Ibid., 74.

43. Ibid., 16.

44. Ibid., 29.

45. Kaus, "The Work Ethic State," 31.

46. GAO, *Work and Welfare*, 29.

47. Riccio et al., *GAIN*, 3.

48. Mimi Abramovitz, "Social Disservices: Why Welfare Reform is a Sham," *The Nation*, September 26, 1988, 221, 238–241.

49. Judith M. Gueron, "Work Programs for Welfare Recipients," in Sharon L. Harlan and Ronnie J. Steinberg, eds., *Job Training for Women: The Promise and Limits of Public Policies* (Philadelphia: Temple University Press, 1989), 374–375.

50. Nanine Meiklejohn, "Work and Training Opportunities for Welfare Recipients" (statement before the Subcommittee on Public Assistance and Unemployment Compensation of the House Ways and Means Committee, June 17, 1987, 4–5), cited in GAO, *Work and Welfare*, 110.

51. Ibid.

52. Lisa Schiff, "Unions see 'workfare' as hidden exploitation," *Economic Justice Speakout!* 3, no. 1 (March 1989): 12.

53. GAO, *Work and Welfare,* 109–110.

54. Gueron, *Work Initiatives for Welfare Recipients* (New York: Manpower Development Research Corporation, 1986), 13.

55. See Riccio et al., *GAIN*; Gueron, *Work Initiatives for Welfare Recipients*; and Gueron, "Work Programs for Welfare Recipients." A helpful criticism of the MDRC studies can be found in Block and Noakes, "New-Style Workfare."

56. Barbara Goldman, Daniel Friedlander, and David Long, *Final Report on the San Diego Job Search and Work Experience Demonstration* (New York: Manpower Demonstration Research Corporation, February 1986), 15. See also Colleen Fahey Fearn, "The Final Word: Workfare in San Diego: Findings from the Manpower Demonstration Research Corporation Third Study, Released February 1986" (San Diego: Legal Aid Society of San Diego, 1986); and Block and Noakes, "New-Style Workfare."

57. Fearn, "The Final Word," 2.

58. Block and Noakes, "New-Style Workfare," 33.

59. Cited in ibid., 36.

60. In California this was called "money management."

61. GAO, *Work and Welfare,* 62; and Riccio et al., *GAIN,* 11.

62. In California, it was also caused by the elimination of "money management," which was difficult to oversee, and by the immediate use of suspending the grant. As a result there was a twelvefold increase in sanctions—from 0.2 percent of those who registered for GAIN before October 1987 to 2.5 percent in 1989. Casey McKeever, "The More Things Change . . . GAIN Revisited" (Sacramento, Calif.: Western Center on Law and Poverty, February 1990), 2.

63. GAO, *Work and Welfare,* 105.

64. Cited in Jack Kemp, "Liberate America's Other Economy," *The Wall Street Journal,* June 12, 1990.

65. GAO, *Work and Welfare,* 112.

66. Indeed, during the deliberations on the 1988 Family Support Act, MDRC studies were often cited in support of the cost effectiveness of workfare and WIN demonstration programs.

67. Nancy A. Naples, "Deconstructing Consensus in the Legislative Hearings on Welfare Reform, 1986–1988" (paper presented at the annual meetings of the Society for the Study of Social Problems, Washington, D.C., August 11, 1990).

68. Statements cited in ibid., 22.

69. The Working Seminar is housed in Marquette University's Institute for Family Studies. It is chaired by Michael Novak of the American Enterprise Institute, and includes Lawrence Mead, Charles Murray, and Glen C. Loury, among others. Ibid., 14–15. For a more extended discussion of their views, see the aptly titled Working Seminar on Family and American Welfare Policy, *The New Consensus on Family and Welfare: A Community of Self-Reliance* (Washington, D.C.: American Enterprise Institute for Public Policy Research, 1987).

70. Quoted in Naples, "Deconstructing Consensus," 13.

71. Ibid., 20.

72. "Aid to Families with Dependent Children: History of Provisions: Job Opportunities and Basic Skills Training," Social Security Administration, *Annual Statistical Supplement, 1994.*

73. Mimi Abramovitz, "Low-Income Women's Activism," *Off Our Backs,* November 1990, 15.

74. Department of Labor and Department of Health, Education, and Welfare, *The Comprehensive Employment and Training Act of 1973,* PL 93–203, sec. 2, reprinted in *Manpower Report of the President, 1974* (Washington D.C.: U.S. Government Printing Office, 1974), 193–242; and Jo Sanders, *Staying Poor: How the Job Training Partnership Act Fails Women* (Metuchen, N.J.: Scarecrow Press, 1988), 10.

75. In inflation-adjusted dollars, the $3.7 billion figure for 1987 was 30 percent of the FY 1980 CETA appropriation of $8.9 billion and 38 percent of the FY 1981 appropriation of $7.7 billion. Department of Labor, *Employment and Training Report of the Secretary of Labor, 1982,* (Washington, D.C.: U.S. Government Printing Office, 1982), 28; and Department of Labor, *Employment and Training Report of the Secretary of Labor, July 1986 through September 1987* (Washington D.C.: U.S. Government Printing Office, 1990), 6.

76. Sharon L. Harlan, "Women and Federal Job Training Policy," in Harlan and Steinberg, eds., *Job Training for Women,* 55.

77. U.S. Department of Labor, *Employment and Training Report of the Secretary of Labor, 1988,* 4–5.

78. Quoted in Sanders, *Staying Poor,* 18.

79. Harlan, "Women and Federal Job Training Policy," 66, in which she also cites Cynthia Marano, "Systemic Contradictions: A Practitioner's View of Public Employment and Training Policies for Low Income Women" (Wider Opportunities for Women, February 1987).

80. Quoted in Sanders, *Staying Poor,* 18.

81. Sar A. Levitan and Frank Gallo, *A Second Chance: Training for Jobs* (Kalamazoo, Mich.: The W. E. Upjohn Institute for Employment Research, 1988), 65.

82. Ibid., 69.

83. Ibid., 70.

84. CETA training programs in 1982 included the following: 11 percent in job search assistance; 12 percent in OJT; 29 percent in work experience; and 48 percent in CT. In contrast, the figures for JTPA in 1985 were as follows: 34 percent in job search assistance; 24 percent in OJT; 8 percent in work experience; and 34 percent in CT. Levitan and Gallo, *A Second Chance,* 67. More detailed descriptions of the program components can be found in Ibid., chap. 3; and Sanders, *Staying Poor,* chap. 2.

85. Quoted in Sanders, *Staying Poor,* 13.

86. Levitan and Gallo, *A Second Chance,* chap. 4.

87. Ibid., 69.

88. The performance standards for youths were initially set at the following: entered employment rate, 41 percent; positive termination rate, 82 percent; and cost per placement, $4,900. By 1987, the entered employment rate

had been increased slightly to 43 percent, the positive termination rate had been decreased to 75 percent, and the cost per placement remained the same. Ibid., 90, 97.

89. Levitan and Gallo, *A Second Chance,* 10.

90. The definition of "training costs" was somewhat fuzzy and included the following: outlays for equipment, classroom space, job-related counseling, most participant recruitment and eligibility determination, and half of the costs for work experience if it was of less than six months' duration and combined with another form of training. Furthermore, the extensive use of performance-based contracts, under which providers were paid only when enrollees obtained jobs, allowed all costs to be counted as training. Levitan and Gallo, *A Second Chance,* 63, 83–84.

91. Vikki Gregory, "JTPA and Women's Programs" (Washington, D.C.: Wider Opportunities for Women, 1984), 4.

92. Cited in Harlan, "Women and Federal Job Training Policy," 75.

93. Levitan and Gallo, *A Second Chance,* 86.

94. Some studies underestimate the extent of creaming, especially empirical simulation models that gauge differences from the result that would be expected if there were no creaming. For example, a study of the JTPA in Tennessee by Kathryn H. Anderson, Richard V. Burkhauser, and Jennie E. Raymond estimated a creaming rate of only 13 percent. However, this fails to account for creaming *within* populations, for example, choosing the most job-ready among AFDC recipients, a trend noted by the Department of Labor. Kathryn H. Anderson, Richard V. Burkhauser, and Jennie E. Raymond, "The Effect of Creaming on Placement Rates under the Job Training Partnership Act," *Industrial and Labor Relations Review* 46, no. 4 (July 1993): 613–624.

95. Gary Burtless, "The Effect of Reform on Employment, Earnings, and Income," in Phoebe H. Cottingham and David T. Ellwood, *Welfare Policy for the 1990s* (Cambridge, Mass.: Harvard University Press, 1989).

96. Quoted in Sanders, *Staying Poor,* 49.

97. Ibid., 112.

98. Ruth Friedman, Lin Fulcher, and Ronald Soloway, "The Job Training Partnership Act and its Impact on Young Women in New York City" (New York: Center for Public Advocacy Research, September 1985), 7; and Denise F. Polit, "Employment Services for Teen-Age Mothers," in Harlan and Steinberg, eds., *Job Training for Women.*

99. Department of Labor, *Employment and Training Report of the Secretary of Labor, July 1986–September 1987,* 32; and Levitan and Gallo, *A Second Chance,* 59.

100. Harlan, "Women and Federal Job Training Policy," 74.

101. Jill Miller, "Displaced Homemakers in the Employment and Training System," in Harlan and Steinberg, eds., *Job Training for Women,* 153.

102. Harlan, "Women and Federal Job Training Policy," 74.

103. Ibid., 64.

104. GAO, *Work and Welfare,* 75.

105. Levitan and Gallo, *A Second Chance,* 52.

106. Sanders, *Staying Poor,* 44.

107. Ibid., 42–47; and Lois Haignere and Ronnie J. Steinberg, "Nontraditional Training for Women: Effective Programs, Structural Barriers, and Political Hurdles," in Harlan and Steinberg, eds., *Job Training for Women,*

108. Katherine Solow with Gary Walker, "The Job Training Partnership Act Service to Women" (New York: Grinker, Walker and Associates), 20.

109. GAO, *Job Training Partnership Act: Information on Training, Placements, and Wages of Male and Female Participants* (Washington D.C.: U.S. Government Printing Office, September 1989).

110. Harlan, "Women and Federal Job Training Policy," 78.

111. Sanders, *Staying Poor,* 67.

112. Harlan, "Women and Federal Job Training Policy," 77–78.

113. This paucity of data was bemoaned by many researchers. Katherine Solow complained that "current data requirements, both state and federal, are so minimal that it is difficult to make any reasoned judgements about the impact of JTPA on women, and thus difficult for policy makers and managers to assess the program's cost efficiency, or need for change." Solow, "The Job Training Partnership Act," 27. See also Levitan and Gallo, *A Second Chance,* ix, 26, and 89; Sanders, *Staying Poor,* 90–91; and Harlan, "Women and Federal Job Training Policy," 67.

114. Sanders, *Staying Poor,* 17.

CHAPTER 7   *The War on Welfare*

1. "Novel Prescriptions for Aiding the Poor," *Business Week,* July 19, 1993, 86.

2. Charles Krauthammer, "Pull the Plug on Welfare to Solve Poverty," *Los Angeles Times,* November 21, 1993, M5.

3. Gross domestic product declined from the third quarter in 1990 through the first quarter in 1991, increased slightly in the second and third quarters of 1991, and fell slightly again in the fourth quarter. Council of Economic Advisors, *Economic Report of the President, 1994* (Washington, D.C.: Government Printing Office, 1994), table B-2: Gross domestic product in 1987 dollars, 1959–93.

4. Ibid., table B-41: Civilian unemployment rate by demographic characteristic, 1950–93.

5. Ibid., table B-42: Unemployment by duration and reason, 1950–93.

6. Ibid., table B-45: Hours and earnings in private nonagricultural industries, 1959–93; and table B-31: Median money income (in 1992 dollars) and poverty status of families and persons, by race, selected years, 1971–92.

7. Bureau of the Census, *Current Population Survey: Income, Poverty, and Valuation of Noncash Benefits: 1993* (Washington D.C.: Government Printing Office, March 1994), table C: Persons and families below poverty level, by detailed race: 1989–93.

8. "Jobs, Jobs, Jobs," *Business Week,* February 22, 1993, 68–74.

9. "Labor Dept. Plans for 'Re-Employment,'" *Los Angeles Times,* January 27, 1994, A18.

10. Robert Kuttner, "Talking Marriage and Thinking One-Night Stand," *Business Week,* October 18, 1993, 16.

11. "More Jobs—But They're Nothing to Get Worked Up About," *Business Week,* October 25, 1993, 29.

12. The statistics for inflation-adjusted income changes between 1980 and 1990 are given in chapter 6 of this book. The changes in after-tax inflation-adjusted family income between 1977, just before the tax breaks began, and 1992, is even more startling. While the after-tax income of the top 20 percent increased 34.2 percent, the top 5 percent saw a 63.4 percent rise, and the richest 1 percent experienced a 134.4 percent increase in their income. The fourth quintile (next to the highest) had a 8.2 percent rise in after-tax income, the middle quintile experienced a 2.3 percent increase, the second-lowest quintile saw their income fall 3.3 percent, and the bottom 20 percent saw their income fall 10.1 percent. This data is from the Congressional Budget Office. Center on Budget and Policy Priorities, "Selective Prosperity: Increasing Income Disparities Since 1977" (Washington, D.C.: Center on Budget and Policy Priorities, July 1991), 19. See also "The Rich are Richer—and America May be the Poorer," *Business Week,* November 18, 1991, 85–88.

13. This was slightly lower than in 1992, when average CEO pay was $3,842,247, 157 times as much as the average factory worker. "Executive Pay: The Party Ain't Over Yet," *Business Week,* April 26, 1993, 56–64; and "That Eye-Popping Executive Pay: Is Anybody Worth This Much?" *Business Week,* April 25, 1994, 52–58.

14. "CEO Pay: A Skyrocket that Could Backfire," *Business Week,* April 25, 1994, 146.

15. Although the rate of profit climbed to 7 percent, the rate of investment did not even regain its 1970s levels. For a clear and accessible analysis of the failure of right-wing economic policies, see Samuel Bowles, David M. Gordon, and Thomas E. Weisskopf, *After the Wasteland: A Democratic Economics for the Year 2000* (Armonk, N.Y.: M. E. Sharpe, 1990), part 3.

16. Council of Economic Advisors, *Economic Report of the President, 1994,* table B-31.

17. Ibid.

18. Ibid.

19. The only exception was black women who worked full-time, year-round; their median income increased a very slight 0.4 percent. Ibid.

20. Ibid., table B-38: Civilian labor force participation rate by demographic characteristic, 1954–93.

21. Ibid.

22. The poverty rate increasingly underestimates the extent of poverty in the U.S. Developed in the early 1960s, the initial measure began with a Department of Agriculture study of a minimum food diet, estimated to cost $1,000 a year, and multiplied it by three (since at that time the average family spent one-third of its income on food). Since then the poverty line has been adjusted annually for inflation. In the intervening years, however, other expenses, notably rent and utilities, have grown to consume a larger proportion of the average family's budget, leading some observers to claim that the poverty line should be

increased by at least 50 percent. If this were done, the 1994 poverty lines of $12,320 for a family of three and $14,800 for a family of four would rise to $18,480 for a family of three and $22,200 for a family of four. Figures for the percentage of people in poverty would increase dramatically—and the government might be more compelled to do something helpful.

23. Council of Economic Advisors, *Economic Report of the President, 1994,* table B-31.

24. Robert Greenstein, "Critics of welfare are ignoring the data," *Boston Globe,* January 26, 1994.

25. These trends are discussed in Teresa L. Amott and Julie A. Matthaei, *Race, Gender, and Work: A Multicultural History of Women in the United States* (Boston: South End Press, 1991), chap. 10.

26. Charles Murray, "The Coming White Underclass," *Wall Street Journal,* October 29, 1993.

27. Krauthammer, "Pull the Plug on Welfare." It's curious that the fusillade of complaints about illegitimacy omits the fact that sex is used in advertising to sell products from cars to beer to clothing. Given its ubiquitousness, it seems unrealistic to tell teens and others to "just say no."

28. House Committee on Ways and Means, *Overview of Entitlement Programs: 1994 Green Book,* table 22: Average monthly number of AFDC families and recipients, total benefit payments and administrative costs, and average payment per family and recipient, fiscal year 1993.

29. Casey McKeever, "Budget/Welfare Watchers Memorandum" (Sacramento: Western Center on Law and Poverty, March 23, 1994).

30. House Committee on Ways and Means, *Overview of Entitlement Programs: 1993 Green Book,* table 14: AFDC maximum benefit for a three-person family, by state for selected years.

31. Congressional Research Service, "Preliminary Materials from the Office of Financial Management for the [1994] *Green Book,*" Aid to Families with Dependent Children: Gross income limit, need standard, payment standard, and maximum benefit for a family of three.

32. House Committee on Ways and Means, *1993 Green Book,* table 22.

33. Simply to compensate for the rise in prices and maintain its purchasing power, the 1990 payment of $389 per month would have had to be increased to $430. Council of Economic Advisors, *Economic Report of the President, 1994,* table B-59: Consumer price indexes for major expenditure classes, 1950–93.

34. McKeever, "Budget/Welfare Watchers Memorandum," March 23, 1994. The "fair market rent" in California is calculated by the U.S. Department of Housing and Urban Development for the Los Angeles-Long Beach metropolitan area and is approximately equal to the amount throughout much of the rest of the state. It is defined as the amount "needed to rent privately owned, decent, safe and sanitary rental housing of a modest (nonluxury) nature with suitable amenities." McKeever, "Budgetwatchers Memorandum" (Sacramento, Calif.: Western Center on Law and Poverty, January 11, 1994).

35. McKeever, "Budget/Welfare Watchers Memorandum," March 23, 1994.

36. "Comparison of October 1992 AFDC Benefit Levels to FY '93 Fair

Market Rents (FMRs) for Two Bedroom Housing," *Family Matters* (Washington, D.C.: Center for Law and Social Policy, Spring 1994): 6; and House Committee on Ways and Means, *1993 Green Book,* table 12: Maximum AFDC benefits, by family size, January 1993.

37. McKeever, "Budgetwatchers Memorandum," January 11, 1994. Although Proposition 165, which contained the 10 to 15 percent AFDC payment cut, as well as many of the behavioral programs, was defeated in the November 1992 elections, Wilson continued to put forward these proposals.

38. Letter from Governor Pete Wilson to Donna Shalala, Secretary, U.S. Department of Heath and Human Services (August 25, 1994), Quoted in McKeever, "Budget and Welfare Watchers Memorandum" (Sacramento, Calif.: Western Center on Law and Poverty, September 8, 1994).

39. Isaac Shapiro, Steven D. Gold, Mark Sheft, Julie Strawn, Laura Summer, and Robert Greenstein, *The States and the Poor: How Budget Decisions in 1991 Affected Low Income People* (Washington, D.C.: Center on Budget and Policy Priorities, and Albany, N.Y.: Center for the Study of the States, 1991), 67–71.

40. "Foster Care Beats AFDC—Financially," *Family Matters* (Washington, D.C.: Center for Law and Social Policy, Winter 1994): 12–13.

41. "Why One Mother Might Turn to Foster Care," *Family Matters* (Winter 1994): 8.

42. "Cuts in General Assistance Programs Do Not Result in Sustained Employment but Do Contribute to Homelessness: Selected Background Material on Welfare Programs" (Washington, D.C.: Center on Budget and Policy Priorities, Center for Law and Social Policy, and Children's Defense Fund, February 21, 1992); and "Jobless, Penniless, Often Homeless: State General Assistance Cuts Leave Employables Struggling for Survival," *States Update* (Washington, D.C.: Center for Law and Social Policy, May 5, 1994): 25.

43. California Department of Social Services, Statistical Services Bureau, "Public Assistance Facts and Figures" (Sacramento, Calif.: Department of Social Services selected months).

44. Social Security Administration, *Social Security Bulletin Annual Statistical Supplement, 1994* (Washington, D.C.: U.S. Government Printing Office, 1994), table 9.G1: Average monthly number of recipients, total amount of cash payments, and average monthly payment, 1936–92; and "Welfare Reform Splits Democrats," *San Bernardino Sun,* January 27, 1994, A1, A4.

45. Congressional Research Service, Preliminary Materials from the Office of Financial Management for the *1994 Green Book,* AFDC Basic Payments, Families and Recipients, February 1994, and Unemployed Parent Payments, Families and Recipients, February 1994.

46. "HHS Approves 4 State Waivers," *States Update* (March 16, 1994): 12–16; and "Welfare Reforms Proposed by State Commissions," *States Update* (October 29, 1993): 3.

47. "House Republicans Introduce Welfare Reform Bill," *States Update* (December 23, 1993): 4; and "Nebraska and Oklahoma Commissions Posit Welfare System Changes: One Pulls Away any Safety Net, the Other Requires Workfare," *States Update* (November 8, 1993): 5–8.

48. Some of the states that applied for waivers to eliminate the hundred-hour rule included Arkansas, Connecticut, Iowa, Oklahoma, and Pennsylvania. "Welfare Reforms Proposed by State Commissions," *States Update* (October 29, 1993).

49. Panel on "Women and Welfare," *Priorities '95* (planning conference for the September 1995 UN Women's Conference in Beijing, Santa Monica, California, April 30, 1994).

50. Casey McKeever, "The Song Remains the Same: Reselling Proposition 165" (Sacramento, Calif.: Western Center on Law and Poverty, April 1993), 35.

51. Memo obtained from the San Bernardino County Department of Public Social Services, San Bernardino, California.

52. McKeever, "Budgetwatchers Memorandum," January 11, 1994), 3–4.

53. An exception in the popular media can be found in an editorial written by feminist economist Nancy Folbre and published in *Newsweek*. She applies the language of the welfare debate to describe the "spider's web of dependency" into which many of the men who ran the failed savings and loan institutions fell, as they depended on the government to bail them out. Nancy Folbre, "Those Welfare Bankers," *Newsweek*, October 16, 1989, 17.

54. "State Welfare Developments," *States Update* (August 10, 1993): 6; and Jodie Levin-Epstein and Mark Greenberg, *The Rush to Reform: 1992 State AFDC Legislative and Waiver Actions* (Washington, D.C.: Center for Law and Social Policy, November 1992), 10–15.

55. In addition, fear of violence keeps many students out of school. According to the National Education Association, each day approximately 160,000 students in the U.S. do not attend school because they fear bodily injury or intimidation by other students. "HHS: AFDC-UP Revised Policy Pulled," *States Update* (November 8, 1993): 17.

56. "Money Can't Buy Happiness . . . But It May Avoid Abuse," *Family Matters* (Winter 1994): 6–7. A University of Wisconsin study of the Learnfare program in Milwaukee found that more than 40 percent of sanctioned teenagers were already in the children's court system or were from families that had been identified for abuse or neglect. National Association of Social Workers, "Position Paper: Behavioral Welfare Initiatives" (Washington, D.C.: National Association of Social Workers, July 1992).

57. This point was made by Bev Littlejohn, San Bernardino County Department of Public Social Services, at a welfare policy teach-in held at California State University, San Bernardino, California, October 27, 1992.

58. Levin-Epstein and Greenberg, *The Rush to Reform*, 14.

59. National Association of Social Workers, "Position Paper."

60. Center for Law and Social Policy, "Teen Parent Residency Requirement," (September, 1993).

61. In *Poor Support*, David Ellwood, who was named one of the cochairs of the Clinton administration's committee to draft a welfare reform proposal, presents an extended discussion of the lack of correlation between AFDC payments and fertility rates. David Ellwood, *Poor Support: Poverty in the American Family* (New York: Basic Books, 1988), 57–61. See also Mark Greenberg, "Strik-

ing Out: House Republicans Offer a Troubling Vision for Welfare Reform" (Washington, D.C.: Center for Law and Social Policy, February 1994), 21–22.

62. Rank found a fertility rate of 45.8 per 1,000 for women on welfare compared to 75.3 percent for other women in the state and 71.1 percent for the nation as a whole. He concluded the "the financial and social situation that women on public assistance find themselves in is not conducive to desiring more children. Such women would appear to be motivated by cost/benefit considerations. But it is the costs that outweigh the benefits not vice versa." Mark R. Rank, "Fertility Among Women on Welfare: Incidence and Determinants," *American Sociological Review* 54 (April 1989): 296–304.

63. Social Security Administration, *Annual Statistical Supplement, 1994,* table 9.G1: Average monthly number of recipients, total amount of cash payments, and average monthly payment, 1936–92; and House Committee on Ways and Means, *1993 Green Book,* table 22.

64. Casey McKeever, "Easy Targets: A Critical Analysis of Proposition 165's Cuts to Needy Children and the Aged, Blind and Disabled" (Sacramento, Calif.: Western Center on Law and Poverty, September 1992), 19–25.

65. National Association of Social Workers, "Position Paper."

66. "Hispanic caucus and national organizations oppose cuts for legal immigrants," *States Update* (March 16, 1994): 5; and "CA immigrants study shows lower utilization of public assistance," *States Update* (August 10, 1993): 5–6.

67. McKeever, "Budgetwatchers Memorandum," March 23, 1994.

68. Mark Greenberg, "Welfare Reform on a Budget: What's Happening in JOBS" (Washington, D.C.: Center for Law and Social Policy, June 1992), 13–14.

69. "Pain for the Poor, A Play for the Middle Class," *Business Week,* April 13, 1992, 31–32.

70. Greenberg, "Welfare Reform on a Budget," 2.

71. Jan L. Hagen and Irene Lurie, *Implementing JOBS: Initial State Choices* (New York: The Nelson A. Rockefeller Institute of Government at the State University of New York, March 1992), 13.

72. "State Welfare Reform Finds Ongoing Success," *Los Angeles Times* April 20, 1993, A1, A21.

73. "Riverside Plan Puts Welfare Recipients on Job Track," *Los Angeles Times,* April 26, 1993, A1, A14, A15.

74. "State Welfare Reform Finds Ongoing Success."

75. The comparable figures for the control group are 22.9 percent employed and 62.7 percent receiving AFDC. McKeever, "Budgetwatchers Memorandum," May 28, 1993, 4.

76. James Riccio, Daniel Friedlander, and Stephen Friedlander, *GAIN: Benefits, Costs, and Three-Year Impacts of a Welfare-to-Work Program, Executive Summary* (New York: Manpower Demonstration Research Corporation, September 1994), 1.

77. Ibid., vi.

78. Interview with Portia Craven, San Bernardino, California, April 8, 1994.

79. Panel on "Women and Welfare," *Priorities '95* (planning conference

for the September 1995 UN Women's Conference in Beijing, Santa Monica, California, April 30, 1994).

80. Converting AFDC into a transitional program that allowed people to receive assistance for a limited amount of time was a central proposal advanced by Ellwood in *Poor Support.*

81. Mark Greenberg, *On, Wisconsin? The Case Against the "Work Not Welfare" Waiver* (Washington, D.C.: Center for Law and Social Policy, October 1993).

82. California Governor Wilson also picked up the banner for time limits, including a two-year limit in his 1994–1995 budget proposal. Thus, a family of three that currently receives $607 a month would have its payment reduced to $375 a month after an "able-bodied" adult received aid for a total of twenty-four months. Although it failed for the present, the proposal is still very much alive. McKeever, "Budgetwatchers Memorandum," January 11, 1994.

83. "Is Welfare a Way of Life?" *Family Matters* (August 1993): 2–5, 11.

84. James J. Kemple, Fred Doolittle, and John W. Wallace, *The National JTPA Study: Site Characteristics and Participation Patterns* (New York: Manpower Demonstration Research Corporation, March 1993), xxxiii–xxxvi.

85. "Changes to Job Training Act Fix Flaws, Target Needy," *Congressional Quarterly Weekly Report* 50, no. 33 (August 15, 1992): 2452.

86. For example, the administration proposed a Workforce Security Act in early 1994 to combine unemployment insurance with career counseling, as well as job training and placement. Elizabeth Shogren, "Labor Dept. Plans for 'Re-Employment,' " *Los Angeles Times,* January 27, 1994, A18.

87. Robert Reich, "An Antidote for Middle-Class Anxiety," *Los Angeles Times,* October 5, 1994, B7.

88. Shogren, "Labor Dept. Plans for 'Re-Employment.' "

89. Mickey Kaus, "The Work Ethic State," *The New Republic,* July 7, 1986, 22–33; and Mickey Kaus, *The End of Equality* (New York: Basic Books, 1992).

90. Kaus, *The End of Equality,* 127.

91. Ibid., 130.

92. Ibid., 134.

93. Martin Morse Wooster, "Bring Back the WPA? It Also Had a Seamy Side," *Wall Street Journal,* September 3, 1986.

94. Senate, 103rd Congress, first session, *The Community Works Progress Act of 1993 (S. 239): Executive Summary.*

95. Ibid., 2.

96. "The Entitlement Trap," *Newsweek,* December 13, 1993, 33–34.

97. David T. Ellwood, "Conclusion," in Phoebe H. Cottingham and David T. Ellwood, eds., *Welfare Policies for the 1990s* (Cambridge, Mass.: Harvard University Press, 1989), 269.

98. Materials from Working Group on Welfare Reform, Family Support, and Independence (Washington, D.C.: Working Group on Welfare Reform, Family Support, and Independence, 1994).

99. "Don't Back Off on Workfare," *Business Week,* March 7, 1994, 138.

100. Administration officials explained that this would probably lead to

cuts in the expansion of child care for the working poor, in demonstration projects (including child support enforcement), and failure to eliminate restrictions on AFDC eligibility for two-parent families; also, the work program would be gradually phased in, initially for younger recipients in order to "break the cycle of poverty for the younger generation." "Administration Fits Welfare Program to Funding," *States Update* (May 5, 1994): 1.

101. "The System Doesn't Work. This Might," *Business Week*, June 14, 1994, 61–62.

102. James Risen, "Overhaul of Welfare Will Drive Up Costs, Officials Say," *Los Angeles Times*, January 27, 1994, A14.

103. Quoted in Aaron Bernstein, "Why Clinton's Workfare Won't Work," *Business Week*, March 7, 1994, 92.

104. Ibid.

105. "The System Doesn't Work. This Might."

106. "Health Care: The Logjam May Loosen," *Business Week*, June 13, 1994, 38–39.

107. Deficit reduction is seen as important in order to maintain low long-term interest rates, which encourage borrowing for investment. This is easily undercut by the Federal Reserve Board, however, which has tended to raise the discount rate (the rate they charge member banks), leading to increases in all other interest rates, at the mere fear of inflation. Indeed, this describes FED policy from February through April, 1994. "Betting the House on Bonds," *Los Angeles Times*, April 24, 1994, D1.

108. It is instructive to compare Clinton's stimulus package to Carter's $31.2 billion proposal in 1977, $20.1 billion of which was passed by Congress. Given inflation and the erosion of the value of money during the intervening sixteen years, Clinton's proposal was only one-fifth as large as Carter's original figure and one-third the size of the eventual package passed by Congress.

109. A companion bill (S. 1795) was later introduced in the Senate. "House Republicans Introduce Welfare Reform Bill," *States Update* (December 23, 1993): 3–4.

110. Ibid.; Mark Greenberg, "Striking Out: House Republicans Offer a Troubling Vision for Welfare Reform" (Washington, D.C.: Center for Law and Social Policy, February 1994); "House Republicans Unveil Welfare Reform Package," *Youth Policy* 15, nos. 10 and 11 (Winter 1994): 14–18; and "Senate Republicans Welfare Reform Package," *Youth Policy* 15, nos. 10 and 11 (Winter 1994): 19.

111. Ibid.

112. "New Republican Bill Ends Welfare—A la Murray," *States Update* (May 5, 1994): 3–6.

113. "GOP Welfare Plan Proposes Severe Cuts in Spending," *Los Angeles Times*, February 10, 1995, A1, A20; "House Republicans Introduce the Personal Responsibility Act," *CLASP Update* (January 20, 1995): 1–4; and Mark Greenberg, "Contract with Disaster: The Impact on States of the Personal Responsibility Act," (Washington, D.C.: Center for Law and Social Policy, November 1994).

114. Cited in "Shalala vs. Archer: Differing Views on the Effects of the PRA," *CLASP Update* (January 20, 1995): 13.

115. "Coalition on Human Needs Welfare Reform Task Force Principles" (Washington, D.C.: Coalition on Human Needs, 1993).

116. "Coalition on Human Needs Welfare Reform Task Force," *Youth Policy* 15, nos. 10 and 11 (Winter 1994): 23–24.

117. "Representatives Woolsey and Regula Unveil Bipartisan Welfare Reform Plan," *States Update* (May 5, 1994): 2.

118. Ibid., 2–3.

119. "House Democrats Put Welfare Bills Into the Hopper," *States Update* (March 16, 1994): 6. Other Democratic measures, such as the Family Self-Sufficiency Act (H.R. 4767) introduced in July 1994 by Representative Robert Matsui (D-Calif.), also aim to move welfare recipients into the labor force but stress incentives, most importantly a more generous earnings disregard and more funding for child care, as well as excluding time limits. "Matsui Introduces Welfare Bill; CLASP Urges Endorsement," *CLASP Update* (July 20, 1994): 1–2.

120. "Coalition on Human Needs Welfare Reform Task Force Principles." See also National Association of Social Workers, "Real Reform: Recommendations On Welfare Policy" (Washington, D.C.: National Association of Social Workers, February 1994), 2.

121. Ellwood made these comments in response to a question posed by Nancy Fraser at a Washington, D.C. conference, "Women and Welfare Reform: Women's Poverty, Women's Opportunities, and Women's Welfare, convened in the summer 1994 by the Institute for Women's Policy Research. Question and answer session following David Ellwood, "Welfare Reform and the Clinton Administration," *Social Justice* 21, no. 1 (Spring 1994): 56–57.

CONCLUSION   *Replace Workfare with Fair Work*

1. The importance of the government paying for programs was stated by Juliet Schor in the session on "Economic Policy and the Ideology of Competitiveness" at the annual meeting of the American Economic Association, Boston, January 3–5, 1994.

2. See chapter 7, note 22.

3. "The Case for Incremental Change," *Family Matters* (August 1993): 6–7; Sheldon H. Danziger, Robert H. Haveman, and Robert D. Plotnick, "Antipoverty Policy: Effects on the Poor and the Nonpoor," in Sheldon H. Danziger and Daniel H. Weinberg, eds., *Fighting Poverty: What Works and What Doesn't* (Cambridge, Mass.: Harvard University Press, 1986), 75–76; and National Association of Social Workers, "Real Reform: Recommendations on Welfare Policy" (Washington, D.C.: National Association of Social Workers, February 1994), 8. The first article is an interview with Richard Nathan.

4. The Center on Budget and Policy Priorities has been a leader in advocating these policies. See, for example, Isaac Shapiro and Robert Greenstein, "Making Work Pay: The Unfinished Agenda" (Washington, D.C.: Center on Budget and Policy Priorities, 1993).

5. In order to bring a family of four to the revised poverty line in 1995, the minimum wage would be raised to approximately $9.50 per hour.

6. Roberta Spalter-Roth, Heidi L. Hartman, and Linda Andrews, "Combining Work and Welfare: An Alternative Anti-Poverty Strategy," (Washington, D.C.: Institute for Women's Policy Research, 1992).

7. "Alleged Refusal by Relief Clients to Accept Employment," *Monthly Report of the Federal Emergency Relief Administration* (June 1935), 1–8; "Summary Study of Alleged Job Refusals by Relief Persons," *Monthly Report of the Federal Emergency Relief Administration* (November 1935), 6–10.

8. Sar A. Levitan and Frank Gallo, *A Second Chance: Training for Jobs* (Kalamazoo, Mich.: The W. E. Upjohn Institute for Employment Research, 1988), 180.

9. Loic J. D. Wacquant and William Julius Wilson, "Poverty, Joblessness, and the Social Transformation of the Inner City," in Phoebe H. Cottingham and David T. Ellwood, eds., *Welfare Policy for the 1990s* (Cambridge, Mass.: Harvard University Press), 100.

10. National Association of Social Workers, "Real Reform," 2.

11. See Mimi Abramovitz and Fred Newdom, "The Truth about AFDC: Challenging Myths with Facts," *BCRS Reports* (Spring 1994). *BCRS Reports* is the newsletter of the Bertha Capen Reynolds Society for progressive social work.

Index

243

About the Author

Nancy E. Rose is a professor of economics and director of the women's studies program at California State University, San Bernardino. She has been involved in the women's movement and the welfare rights movement since the early 1970s. Her articles on women, welfare, and workfare have appeared in *Social Service Review*, *Feminist Studies*, *Journal of Progressive Human Services*, and *The Journal of Sociology and Social Welfare*.